day trips® from austin

Praise for previous editions:

"If you're looking for a one- or two-day getaway but you're not sure where to go, then Paris Permenter and John Bigley may have just the ticket for you."

—*Hill Country News*

"No matter how much you love living in the city, there's nothing more refreshing than leaving home for rest, relaxation, and a quick recharge. This book provides . . . detailed itineraries for residents and visitors looking for a rejuvenating getaway."

—*Advocate* (Victoria, Tex.)

"If the idea of traveling Texas this summer appeals to you, but you don't have a week or two to devote to wandering the farm-to-market roads searching for interesting Lone Star locales, there is a solution: day trips."

—*San Antonio Current*

"The value of any guidebook is its ease of use, and Day Trips is a very user-friendly guide. Day Trips has its share of golden nuggets. This guidebook is good for stashing in the car for those spontaneous Sunday drives or when planning a vacation."

—*Austin Chronicle*

help us keep this guide up to date

We would love to hear from you concerning your experiences with this guide and how you feel it could be improved and kept up to date. Please send your comments and suggestions to:

editorial@GlobePequot.com

Thanks for your input, and happy travels!

day trips® from austin

sixth edition

getaway ideas for the local traveler

paris permenter
and
john bigley

gpp®
travel

Guilford, Connecticut

All the information in this guidebook is subject to change. We recommend that you call ahead to obtain current information before traveling.

To buy books in quantity for corporate use or incentives, call **(800) 962-0973** or e-mail **premiums@GlobePequot.com**.

Editor: Kevin Sirois
Project Editor: Heather Santiago
Layout: Joanna Beyer
Text Design: Linda R. Loiewski
Maps: Trailhead Graphics, Inc. © Morris Book Publishing, LLC
Spot Photography: Brandon Seidel/Shutterstock

ISSN 1535-8232
ISBN 978-0-7627-6006-0

Printed in the United States of America
10 9 8 7 6 5 4 3 2 1

contents

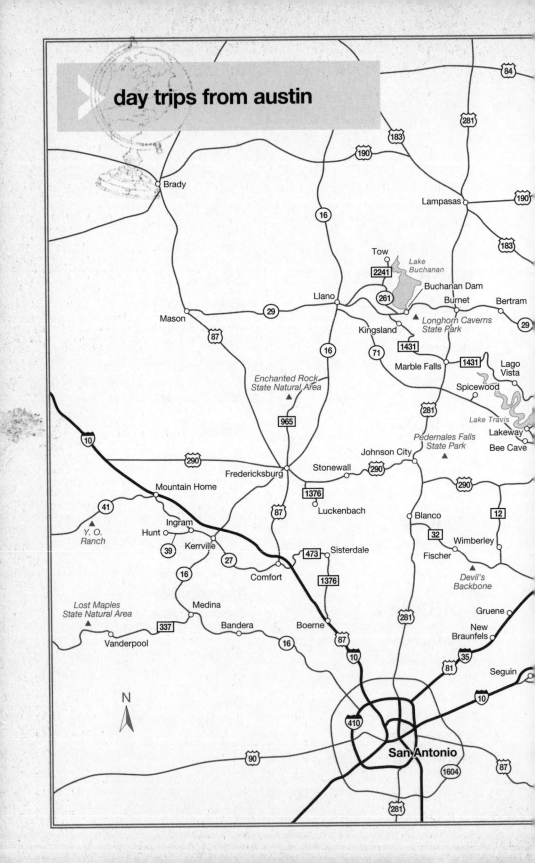

day trips from austin

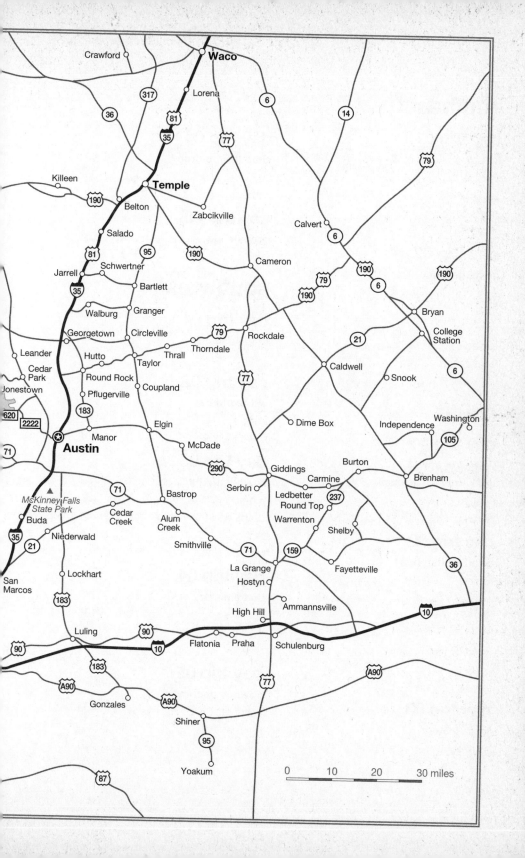

southeast

day trip 01

day trip 02

south

day trip 01

day trip 02

day trip 03

day trip 04

day trip 05

southwest

day trip 01

day trip 02

day trip 03

day trip 04

day trip 05

west

day trip 01

day trip 02

day trip 03

northwest

day trip 01

day trip 02

day trip 03

day trip 04

about the authors

John Bigley and **Paris Permenter** are a husband and wife team of travel writers. Longtime residents of Central Texas, they make their home in the Hill Country west of Austin, near Lake Travis.

John and Paris have authored 26 guidebooks including *Day Trips from San Antonio* and *Insiders' Guide to San Antonio.* Paris and John also publish www.Lovetripper.com, an online look at romantic destinations around the globe, www.TexasTripper.com, which focuses on travel across the Lone Star State, and www.DogTipper.com, filled with tips for dog lovers.

Both John and Paris are members of the prestigious Society of American Travel Writers. For more on the couple's writing and travels, see www.parisandjohn.com.

introduction

Most people have a mental image of Texas as miles of rugged, uncivilized land where the outlines of cattle and lonely windmills stretch above the horizon. But that's just one side of the Lone Star State, known as the "land of contrast." Texas also boasts high-tech cities, piney woods, sandy beaches, rolling hills, and fertile farmland—much of it within a two-hour drive of Austin.

The region covered in this book is as diverse as the more than thirty cultures who helped found the state. German, French, Mexican, Polish, and even Alsatian settlers brought their traditions to Texas in the 1800s. The influences of these pioneers are still apparent today in the varied festivals and ethnic foods that vacationers come here to enjoy.

The day trips within this book span terrain ranging from farmland to rocky hills. This difference in topography is the result of an ancient earthquake that created the Balcones Fault, which runs north to south. The fault line, slightly west of I-35, forms the dividing line between the eastern agricultural region and what is known as the Hill Country to the west.

Many of the attractions lie along the route taken by numerous Winter Texans who flock here during the cooler months. So, whether you're heading for the Rio Grande Valley, the coast, or the Mexican border, you'll find a wealth of useful tips and information in this guide. Be sure to check the sections marked "Especially for Winter Texans," which will help you identify special services, festivals, and parks aimed at making you feel right at home.

You'll find that Texans are friendly folk who wave on country roads and nod as they pass you on the sidewalk. Talk to local citizens as you wind through the back roads for even more travel tips and a firsthand look at the varied cultures that make up the pieces of your journey.

using this travel guide

hours of operation

In some cases, hours are omitted in the listings because they are subject to frequent changes. Instead, phone numbers and Web sites are provided as a resource for up-to-date information.

credit cards

In the interest of accuracy and because they are subject to change, attraction prices are given in general terms. Always remember to call ahead. You can assume all establishments listed accept major credit cards unless otherwise noted. If you have questions, contact the establishments for specifics.

pricing key

For Accommodations: Room prices are designated as $$$ (Expensive: more than $150 for a standard room); $$ (Moderate: $75–150); and $ (Inexpensive: less than $75).

For Restaurants: Per-person restaurant prices are designated as $$$ (Expensive: $20 and more per person); $$ (Moderate: $10–20); and $ (Inexpensive: $10 and less).

travel tips

carry a road map

Although we've included directions, it's best to carry a Texas road map as you travel. It's also advisable to carry a county map for a better look at farm-to-market (FM) roads and ranch roads (RR). To get brochures on Texas attractions and a free copy of the Texas State Travel Guide call (512) 936-0101 or visit www.traveltex.com. The guide is coded to a free Texas state map also provided by the highway department. These maps are also available from any of the tourist information centers located on routes into Texas and at the Texas State Capitol in Austin. The tourist information centers are open daily, except Thanksgiving, Christmas, and New Year's Day.

The expansiveness of Texas sets it apart from other states. Note the scale of the map. With 266,807 square miles of land, Texas is the second largest state in the country. One inch on the state road map spans 23 miles.

Driving varies with terrain: In the western Hill Country, towns are far apart and roads can be slow and winding. To the east, population is more dense, and day trips involve quiet, slow drives along farm-to-market and ranch roads.

For Texas travel questions, call (512) 936-0101 from anywhere in the United States or Canada.

be wary of weather conditions

As a general rule, the Austin region enjoys a very temperate climate. Winters are mild, with just about twenty-five freezing days annually. Snow is rare and, when it does occur, causes businesses and schools to close and roads to congest quickly.

The most pleasant seasons in the region are spring and fall. You'll find many Austin-area festivals are scheduled during these pleasant weekends, times when temperatures are in the 70–80°F range.

Austin receives less than 30 inches of rain annually, most of it arriving during the spring. Thunderstorms are common from April through September, especially during the late afternoon as temperatures rise. Tornados are most likely during May and June.

The biggest weather threat comes in the form of flash floods, especially in the Hill Country. The steep slopes, rocky terrain, and shallow topsoil of the region mean that even a few inches of rain can turn dry creek beds into roaring rivers capable of sweeping cars off the road. Drownings occur annually when drivers attempt to cross roadways covered with water.

avoid midday heat

In summer, Texas is hotter than a sizzling fajita. In this weather it's best to drive in the early-morning hours or after sunset. If you are traveling with children or pets, never leave them in a closed car; temperatures soar to oven-like heights in just minutes.

watch out for stray livestock

When driving through open-ranch cattle country on farm-to-market or ranch roads, be on the lookout for livestock and deer wandering across roads, especially near dusk. Deer can be a driving hazard even in populated regions.

highway designations

Federal highways are designated US. State routes use TX. Farm-to-market roads are defined as FM, and ranch roads are labeled RR. County roads (which are not on the Texas state map) are identified as CR.

where to get more information

Day Trips from Austin attempts to cover a variety of bases and interests, but those look-ing for additional material can contact the following agencies by phone, mail, or the Web. Regarding the latter, when checking out the various destinations, be aware that online reviews may be contradictory and conflicting. Everyone's experience can be different, and the Web allows for a forum for these diverse opinions. So call the place directly and be conscious of ratings such as AAA and the Better Business Bureau. Many of the areas have chain hotels and restaurants, which are generally not included in the listings in each chap-ter. Within each chapter we provide contact information for chambers of commerce and/or convention and visitor bureaus. Here are some additional general resources:

- **Office of the Governor, Economic Development and Tourism.** http://traveltex .com. This official Texas tourism Web site offers a free state map, narrated walking tours that you can download to your iPod, and the annual Texas Travel Guide.

- **Statewide Road Conditions.** (800) 452-9292; http://www.dot.state.tx.us/travel/road_ conditions.htm. Call or visit the Web site for up-to-date information on road conditions including construction, closures, flooding, or accidents which may impact your plans.

- **Texas Department of Transportation.** (512) 463-8586; www.txdot.gov/travel. Call to speak with a Texas travel counselor or to request regional literature. The Web site is a great resource for weather information, maps, travel safety tips and more.

- **Texas Travel Information Centers.** 112 East 11th St., Austin, TX 78701; (512) 463-8586 or (512) 475-3046; www.txdot.gov. This travel center, located at the Texas Capitol Visitors Center in Austin, is one of 12 official travel centers in Texas (and the only one within the scope of this book). Each offers maps, the Texas Travel Guide, brochures, and professional assistance on trip planning.

austin area overview

Welcome to Austin, the state capital and gateway to attractions in Central Texas. With Austin as your base, you'll have a chance to visit both rugged hills to the west and miles of scenic roads and interesting small towns to the east.

Austin is a high-tech city, with an economy based on computer-related industries and state government. The city of Austin takes in more than 760,000 residents, including a University of Texas population of more than 50,000 students and faculty from around the world. This gives Austin an international feel, with many ethnic restaurants and specialty grocery stores. Many people have relocated here, attracted by the clean industry and beautiful weather. Over the past decade Austin has burst its boundaries and now encompasses a sprawl of about 1.5 million residents in the metropolitan area.

New residents aren't the first to discover the beauty of Austin. When Mirabeau B. Lamar, the president-elect of the Texas Republic, set out to hunt buffalo in the fall of 1838, he returned home with a much greater catch than a prize buffalo: a home for the new capital city. Lamar fell in love with a tiny settlement surrounded by rolling hills and fed by cool springs. Within the coming year, the government arrived and construction on the Capitol building was begun. Austin was on its way to becoming a city.

Since those early days there's been no looking back. Today Austin is a city on the move. Hollywood has discovered this big city with a small-town atmosphere, and it's not uncommon these days to see film crews blocking off an oak-lined street. High-tech industries have also migrated to Austin, making this area Texas's answer to Silicon Valley.

But for all the changes that have occurred in this capital city, Austin is still very much a town with a past that the city is proud to preserve and show off to its visitors.

A visit to Austin should begin downtown, where the Colorado River slices through the heart of the city. Once an unpredictable waterway, the Colorado has now been tamed into a series of lakes, including two within the Austin city limits. The 22-mile-long Lake Austin begins at the foot of the Hill Country and flows through the western part of the city.

Lake Austin flows into Lady Bird Lake (named for former First Lady, the late Lady Bird Johnson). This narrow stretch of water, formerly known as Town Lake and recently renamed meanders for 5 miles through the center of downtown Austin. Several hotels overlook the beautifully planted greenbelts that line the lakeshore. In the late afternoon hours, locals grab their sneakers and head to the Zilker Park or the lake shores for a jog or leisurely walk. When the sun sets on summer days, attention turns to the lake's Congress Avenue bridge, the location of the country's largest urban colony of Mexican free-tailed bats. The bats make their exodus after sunset to feed on insects in the Hill Country.

Many of Austin's historical buildings are found downtown, and the granddaddy of them all is the State Capitol. Tours introduce you to this pink-granite building that holds the distinction of being the tallest state capitol in the United States.

The Governor's Mansion lies just south of the Capitol; following a 2008 fire, the mansion is under extensive renovation and is closed to the public.

Continuing south of the Capitol is the Driskill Hotel, Austin's most historic hotel. Since 1886 this property has been a stopover for dignitaries, heads of state, legislators, and vacationers from around the globe.

The Capitol, the Governor's Mansion, and the Driskill are all historical Austin landmarks, but they're just babes when compared with the French Legation, Austin's oldest existing home. Located in east Austin at 802 San Marcos, this is the only foreign legation in the country ever built outside of Washington, D.C. (Wondering why it was built in Austin? Don't forget: Texas was once a separate country—complete with its own foreign ambassadors!)

Austin's most famous museum is the Lyndon Baines Johnson Presidential Library, located on the University of Texas campus. Special exhibits illustrate the Vietnam conflict, the Civil Rights movement, and the advances in education that took place during these years. Visitors can also view extravagant gifts received from other countries, a limousine used by the president, and family memorabilia.

On the southern end of the University of Texas campus, you'll find Austin's newest museum, the Blanton Museum of Art. The largest university art museum in the country, the Blanton's collection includes more than 17,000 works and is recognized for its Old Masters paintings as well as modern and contemporary American and Latin American art. And off campus but within easy walking distance lies the Bob Bullock Texas State History Museum, which showcases the history of the Lone Star State from European exploration to recent times.

After a day of touring, Austin presents plenty of other entertainment options. The heart of Austin's nightlife is Sixth Street, a historic 7-block area with many nightclubs and

live-music capital of the world

Austin has earned its nickname thanks to the large number of live music venues scattered throughout the city. On any given night, about one hundred venues ranging from concert halls to alternative bars to honky-tonks move to the sound of live music. The city has drawn many well-known names who select Austin not just for performances but for their home. Today Austin is home to the Dixie Chicks, Shawn Colvin, Willie Nelson, Asleep at the Wheel, Don Walser, and others.

restaurants, as well as eclectic shops that are open during the day. And if you get hungry in the capital city, have no fear—Austin is home to more restaurants and bars per capita than any other city in the nation.

And if all that dining creates a need for a little activity, fun comes in many forms. In the warm months, Austin really lives up to its nickname, "The River City," since everyone takes to Lake Austin and nearby Lake Travis to enjoy swimming, scuba diving, skiing, and boating. Golfers find plenty of challenges in this area as well.

Austin spreads out into the suburban communities of Round Rock, Cedar Park, Oak Hill, and others. But beyond the reach of Austin's bedroom communities, you'll find a Texas that's largely unchanged. Bowling alleys still set pins by hand, businesses close on Friday nights during high school football season, and pickup trucks seem to outnumber every other form of transportation. Some of the best barbecue in the world comes from the small towns nestled in the Hill Country, a region so called because of its rugged terrain. The topographical change represents the 1,800-mile Balcones Fault, which has separated the western Hill Country from the flat eastern farmland ever since a 3.5-minute earthquake 30 million years ago.

This part of Texas gives you a chance to slow down, meet some local folks, and enjoy a good old-fashioned chicken-fried steak at the local diner.

For brochures, maps, and general questions on Austin area attractions, call (800) 926-ACVB, or write: Austin Convention and Visitors Bureau, 301 Congress Ave., Suite 200, Austin, TX 78701, or check out www.austintexas.org.

While you're downtown, stop by the Austin Visitors Center for information, tour tickets, and a chance to shop Austin's official gift shop. The center is located at 209 East Sixth St. and is open daily.

north

day trip 01

north

small-town texas:
pflugerville, round rock, georgetown, salado

Heading north of Austin on congested I-35, this day trip steps from one of the state's most populated cities to the quickly growing bedroom communities and suburbs then travels beyond commuter range to towns that still maintain the flavor of small-town Texas. Since the 1800s, this area has been primarily agricultural, settled by immigrant farmers from Sweden, Germany, and Czechoslovakia.

pflugerville

Heading north on I-35 you won't notice that you've left Austin and reached Pflugerville (pronounced "floo-gur-vil") unless you look for the signs. Technically about 15 miles north of the capital city, Pflugerville proper is located 4 miles east of I-35 on FM 1825 (look for I-35 exit 247).

Austin's urban sprawl has caught up to this place named for German immigrant Henry Pfluger. What began as a small town just after the Civil War became the fastest-growing community in Texas in the 1980s. Growth continues today but the community still holds onto its distinctive spirit in its historic downtown.

Continue east on FM 1825 past the subdivisions and strip centers to where FM 1825 becomes Pecan Street. Soon you'll see small-town Texas, especially if you turn north on Railroad Street and continue for 1 block to Main Street. Here you'll find the true "downtown" Pflugerville, with dining, shopping, and nightlife in historic buildings.

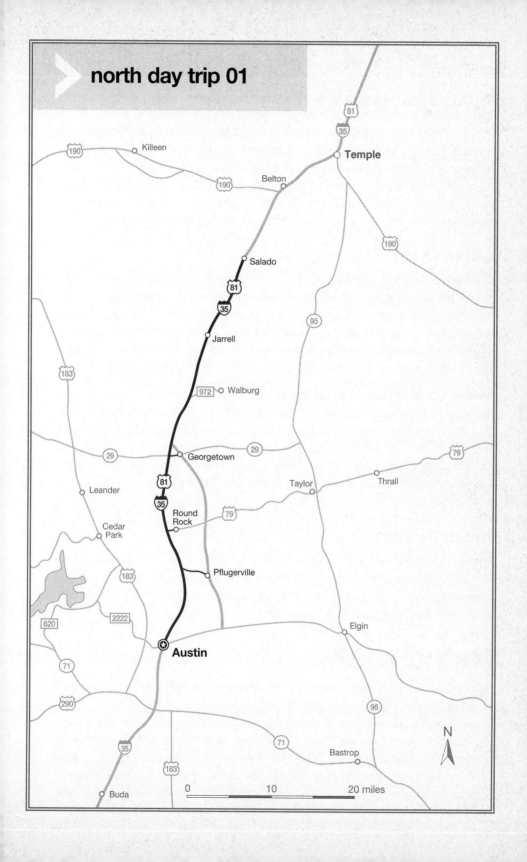

north day trip 01

Those historic buildings and the general Pflugerville setting have been the backdrop for many movies. Pflugerville's Chamber of Commerce (101 S. Third St., (512) 251-7799; www.pfchamber.com) is proud to point out its "PflugerWood" connection thanks to a role in movies, including *A Perfect World, Best Little Whorehouse in Texas, Courage Under Fire, The Newton Boys, Second Hand Lions,* and *What's Eating Gilbert Grape.*

During the third weekend in May, crowds flock to this bedroom community from the capital city for Pflugerville's annual Deutchen Pfest, complete with a parade, music, rides, food, and more.

where to eat

European-Bistro. 111 East Main St.; (512) 835-1919; www.european-bistro.com. Step back to the Old Country at this homey restaurant that specializes in Hungarian, German, Czech, and Russian dishes. Start with an appetizer of Armenian lamb dumplings or Russian pirogues, then move on to Hungarian-style roast duck, Wiener schnitzel—but be sure to save room for the strudel. Look for live music Fri, Sat, and Sun night and be sure to make reservations at that time. Open for lunch Fri through Sun, dinner Tues through Sun. $$.

Hanover's Draught Haus. 108 East Main St.; (512) 670-9617; www.hanoversaustin.com. Known for its live music (every Wed, Fri, and Sat night as well as an occasional Sun), its draught beer selection, and its large beer garden, you'll also find barbecue at this historic building. The structure dates to 1903, when it began as a saloon; later it was converted to a lumberyard and hardware store. Today the lively place is well known in the world of Austin live music. Families are welcome until 8 p.m., at which time only patrons age 21 and over are permitted. $.

where to shop

The Old Prague Market. 117 East Main St.; (512) 251-7330; www.oldpraguemarket.com. Next door to the European-Bistro, you'll find a slice of the Czech Republic. This gift shop specializes in Czech crystal, but you'll also find Czech dolls, polka music, and plenty of candles and stemware. Open Mon through Sat.

round rock

Now over 85,000 strong, this booming Austin community located north on I-35 is named for the circular rock formation that lies in the middle of Brushy Creek.

Round Rock was the scene of a Wild West shoot-out a century ago. Sam Bass was a well-known outlaw in these parts back then, a stagecoach and train robber who boasted that he'd never killed a man. Bass planned to make his first bank robbery in Round Rock, but things went awry when the Texas Rangers learned his scheme. They were waiting as Bass and his gang rode into town on July 19, 1878, and they gravely wounded him during a gun battle in the 100 block of East Main Street. Bass fled from town and died two days later.

This colorful figure was buried in the old Round Rock cemetery, situated on what's now known as Sam Bass Road. The grave is near an interesting slave cemetery, a reminder of the cotton industry and plantation system that once dominated this area.

Round Rock was also once a part of the stagecoach route that stretched from Brownsville, Texas, to Helena, Arkansas. Frontiersmen used the round rock to judge the depth of Brushy Creek before crossing. Today visitors still can see coach tracks in the Brushy Creek riverbed, just west of I-35.

Every July 4th Round Rock hosts Frontier Days, recalling its Wild West heritage with a reenactment of the Sam Bass shoot-out.

Today Round Rock is home to the Round Rock Express (512-255-BALL; www.round rockexpress.com), a AAA minor league baseball franchise. The city boasts an expansive sports facility off I-35 at US 79 near Old Settlers Park. The team comes to the community thanks to Texas baseball great Nolan Ryan.

where to go

Palm House Museum. 212 East Main St.; (800) 747-3479 or (512) 255-5805. Built in the 1860s, this historic home now contains a two-room museum and the local Chamber of Commerce. In the kitchen and parlor hang photos and artifacts from Round Rock's early days. Look for the silver bowl that had its lid blown off during the Sam Bass shoot-out. Open Mon through Fri 9 a.m. to 5 p.m. Admission is free.

where to shop

Round Rock Premium Outlets. 4401 North I-35; (512) 863-6688; www.premiumoutlets .com. Located between Round Rock and Georgetown on the east side of the interstate,

on the sam bass trail

Texas has more buried treasure than any other state, much of it tied to outlaw Sam Bass. The robber hid from the law in the town of Round Rock. Bass was in Round Rock making plans for a bank robbery, until a final shoot-out with the Texas Rangers on July 19, 1878. Before he died, however, many say that he hid much of the loot from his train, stagecoach, and bank robberies somewhere in the area.

The outlaw allegedly buried $30,000 in the community of McNeil. No treasure was ever recovered, and today there is little remaining of McNeil, located in the northern part of Travis County near Round Rock.

this outlet mall boasts 125 shops, mostly upscale brands such as Ann Taylor, Michael Kors, and Polo Ralph Lauren. Open daily.

georgetown

Georgetown is an elegant community of over 38,000 residents that rests on the border of farmland to the east and ranch land to the west. Located 10 miles north of Round Rock on I-35, this was once an active agricultural center. Today Georgetown is home to many Austin commuters and 1,300 students at Southwestern University, the oldest college in Texas.

Georgetown's first residents were the Tonkawa Indians, a resourceful group that drove buffalo off the bluffs of the San Gabriel River. Years later, the town of Georgetown was founded by a group of men that included George Washington Glasscock. After he donated the land for the town, it was named in his honor. Glasscock had come to Texas from the East after running a river barge business for a time in Illinois with Abraham Lincoln.

Georgetown became a cattle center after the Civil War and the starting point of many northern cattle drives. The community grew but remained a small town into the late 1900s. Austin's runaway growth during the 1980s eventually turned Georgetown into a bedroom community divided by I-35. To the west is "new" Georgetown, with many subdivisions, including nationally known Sun City, along Williams Drive on the way to Lake Georgetown. "Old" Georgetown sits east of the highway, and among its main attractions are the winding North and South San Gabriel Rivers, which join together in shady San Gabriel Park.

Georgetown was selected as one of five national winners of the Great American Main Street awards. To view the award-winning revitalization project, take exit 261 off I-35 and continue east to Austin Avenue. Turn left at the light for a look at the restored courthouse square. With its stately oaks and shady lawn, it is so typical of Texas that it's been used as a set for several movies and TV shows.

Georgetown has refined its recipe for community charisma as the city has grown and prospered. Serving as seat of the second-fastest-growing county in the nation, Georgetown continues to hang onto its cozy charm. Even with a growing population, it is proud to say that it's still the kind of place where folks can walk around the square and be welcomed by a smile and a friendly nod. Georgetown may have just found the secret ingredient: historic preservation.

North of the courthouse square, San Gabriel Park has served for centuries as a gathering site. Native Americans camped on the verdant grounds, pioneers met here, and early Georgetown residents congregated on the riverbanks for parades and meetings, including one event that featured speaker Sam Houston.

Today, park lovers enjoy shady picnics under the oak and pecan trees. Children romp on the playscape while anglers try their luck from the grassy riverbanks. Crystal-clear springs bubble up at three sites on the park grounds, and often you can watch these little "salt and pepper" springs spew up chilly water.

Upstream, the North San Gabriel River has been controlled to create Lake Georgetown, a 1,310-acre lake popular with anglers, boaters, water-skiers, and swimmers.

where to go

Georgetown Visitor Information Center. 101 West Seventh St., on the square; (800) 436-8696 or (512) 863-5598. Stop by for a copy of a Georgetown map, brochures on area attractions, and walking tour booklets. The center also sells many Georgetown items, from posters to T-shirts. Open Mon through Sat 9 a.m. to 5 p.m. and Sun 1 p.m. to 5 p.m.

Blue Hole. Austin Avenue at Second Street. West of the park at Blue Hole, where river waters reflect limestone cliffs, a revitalization has made this beautiful spot a place to be appreciated by residents and visitors once more. At Blue Hole, walkers and joggers journey along the wide paths that wind beside waters as green as fresh spring leaves. On quiet mornings anglers try their luck with just the sound of an occasional cardinal singing its friendly song in the distance. Free admission.

Inner Space Cavern. West off I-35 exit 259; (512) 931-CAVE; www.innerspace.com. Discovered during the construction of the interstate, this cave is a cool getaway for summer travelers and was once a hideaway for animals as well. A skull of a peccary (a pig-like hoofed mammal) estimated to be a million years old has been found here, along with bones of a giant sloth and a mammoth.

Enter the cavern on a cog railroad car, traveling down from the visitor center to the well-lit, easy-to-follow trail. Along the way, guides point out features of Inner Space, including large stalactite and stalagmite formations. Some of the larger formations of the cavern are "The Warriors," two stalagmites that have grown together, the "Flowing Stone of Time" in the Outer Cathedral, and "Ivory Falls," a beautiful flow of white stalactites. The cavern uses sound and light displays to create special effects, including the grand finale of the tour: a show at the "Lake of the Moon."

After reaching cave level aboard a small trolley, follow your guide for a tour of cave formations, a small lake, and evidence of those prehistoric visitors. Kids also enjoy the Inner Space Mining Company, where they can pan for gems and minerals. Open daily.

Lake Georgetown. FM 2338, 3.5 miles west of town; (512) 930-5253. Built on the north fork of the San Gabriel River, this lake spans 1,310 surface acres. Three public parks offer swimming, fishing, boating, camping, and hiking opportunities. Public facilities include **Jim Hogg Park** with overnight camping, electric and water hookups, and boat ramp; **Cedar Breaks Park** with picnic facilities and campsites with electric hookups; **Russell Park** for picnicking and camping; and **Tejas Park** for picnics and hikes among oak-shaded trails. Free admission. Fee for camping.

The 17-mile **Good Water Trail** follows the upper end of the lake. The trail was named in honor of the Tonkawa, a people who made the region near the San Gabriel River their home. Known for their flint arrowheads and tools, these Native Americans called this region *takatchue pouetsu* or "land of good water."

The trail is marked by mileposts as it snakes its way along the lake, passing through several historical points of interest. One such spot is Russell Crossing, later known as the **Second Bootys Crossing,** located near milepost one. In the late 1860s, Frank Russell resided at this crossing, and his rock house served as a postal substation. Mail was carried in saddlebags to the local residents.

Between mileposts two and three, hikers can see **Crockett Gardens,** a natural spring. A flour mill operated here in 1855, and a few decades later, the first strawberries in Williamson County were grown in truck gardens at this site. Today the remains of the springhouse and corrals can still be seen.

Besides man-made attractions, hikers are also surrounded by natural beauties. White-tailed deer, coyote, skunk, raccoon, ringtail, armadillo, and opossum thrive in this area. From Feb to Aug, the region is home to the endangered golden-cheeked warbler, a small bird that nests in older juniper trees.

San Gabriel Park. Off Austin Avenue; (512) 930-3595. This park, just south of the junction of the North and South San Gabriel Rivers, includes children's playscape, picnic sites, sunken gardens, a swimming pool, and walking trail. Open daily. Free admission.

Southwestern University. 1001 East University Ave.; (512) 863-6511; www.southwestern .edu. Southwestern holds the title of Texas's first institution of higher learning. Call for a guided tour. Open daily. Free admission.

The Williamson Museum. 716 South Austin Ave.; (512) 943-1670; www.williamsonmu seum.org. This local history museum is itself housed in a historic structure, the 1911 Farmers State Bank building. Today the Beaux Arts–style building contains exhibits that range

poppy fields

In late March, the fields and yards around Georgetown bloom with the vibrant color of red poppies. Georgetown holds the title of the "Red Poppy Capital of Texas," with both native and cultivated varieties growing throughout the town.

The poppies originate from seeds imported to the town by Henry Purl "Okra" Compton. During his service in World War I in Europe, he collected seeds and planted them around his mother's home upon his return.

Today the poppies brighten yards and highway right-of-ways from late Mar through May. Look for white signs indicating a "Poppy Zone" as you travel through town.

from cattle drives to Williamson County during wartime. Open Tues through Sat 10 a.m. to 6 p.m. Admission is free.

where to shop

Georgetown has more than a dozen antiques shops. For a free map of the shops listing hours and specialties, call (800) GEO-TOWN or (512) 930-3545, or stop by the visitor center on the square, where other brochures are also available.

Georgetown Antique Mall. 110 West Eighth St.; (512) 869-2088; www.georgetown antiquemall.com. This expansive shop features antiques from many dealers, ranging from collectibles to glassware to furniture. Open daily.

Rough and Ready Antiques. 602 Main St.; (512) 819-0463; www.roughandready antiques.com. This shop specializes in early Texas furniture as well as architectural details. Open daily.

The Windberg Art Gallery. 7100 N. I-35 at exit 268; (512) 819-9463 or (800) 252-9771; www.windberg.com. Georgetown is home to the renowned artist Dalhart Windberg. Known for his emotional portrayals of American landscapes and settings, the gallery offers both original art and handsome prints. Open Mon through Sat.

where to eat

Duke's BBQ Smokehouse. 408 West Morrow St., east of I-35 at exit 261A; (512) 930-2877; www.dukesbbq.com. Live music, outdoor and indoor dining, and a comfortable family atmosphere draw diners to Duke's—not to mention the tasty barbecue. Brisket, slow-cooked for fifteen hours over mesquite and oak, is tops here, but don't miss the sausage as well, prepared by Slovachek Sausage in Snook. Open 7 a.m. to 10 p.m. daily. $$.

The Monument Cafe. 500 South Austin Ave.; (512) 930-9586; www.themonumentcafe .com. Styled like an old-fashioned diner, this family restaurant serves up favorites ranging from chicken-fried steak to burgers. It is also a popular breakfast stop, serving excellent breakfast tacos as well as traditional fare. And, if you need to check e-mail during your day trip, the restaurant also has free Wi-Fi connectivity. Open Sun through Thurs 7 a.m. to 9 p.m. and Fri and Sat 7 a.m. to 10 p.m. $–$$.

Wildfire. 812 South Austin Ave.; (512) 869-FIRE; www.wildfiretexas.com. *Time* magazine said that this restaurant's blue cornmeal-encrusted catfish was reason enough to move to Georgetown. Southwestern-inspired cuisine, much of it prepared on an oak-burning grill, rules, although you'll also find dishes such as Jamaican jerk pork chops and New Zealand elk tenderloin. Open Mon through Sat 11 a.m. to 10 p.m. and Sun 10 a.m. to 9 p.m. $$$.

where to stay

Harper-Chesser Historic Inn. 1309 College St.; (512) 864-1887; www.harperchesserinn .com. One of Georgetown's oldest houses, listed in the National Registry of Historic Homes, today serves as a bed-and-breakfast inn. Four rooms, each with a private bath, await guests. The rooms feature hand-painted murals, antique furnishings, and cutwork linens. Traditional Southern breakfasts are served in the dining room, which is decorated with antique pine furnishings and features one of the inn's six fireplaces. The verandah overlooks the garden, a popular spot for weddings and parties. $$.

salado

Continuing north on I-35 to exit 283, you'll encounter Salado, a shopping stop for interstate travelers. Antiques stores, artists' galleries, and specialty shops fill the historic downtown buildings. Salado (pronounced "sa-LAY-dough") is a Spanish word meaning either "salty" or "amusing," although residents prefer the latter.

This community is located where Salado Creek flows beneath I-35. The site once was a stagecoach stop on the old Chisholm Trail and served the line that stretched from San Antonio to Little Rock, Arkansas.

Today the old rest stop has been converted to the modern Stagecoach Inn, located on the east side of I-35. Visitors' accommodations are found in a modern addition, and the original building, where Sam Houston once delivered an antisecession speech, has become an elegant restaurant.

The former stagecoach route, now called Main Street, is lined with historic structures housing antiques shops and specialty stores. In all, eighteen of these buildings are listed in the National Register of Historic Places, and twenty-three boast Texas historical markers.

where to go

Central Texas Area Museum. 423 South Main St., across from Stagecoach Inn; (254) 947-5232; www.ctam-salado.org. This museum traces the history of the Salado area and all of the Brazos Trail—the rich farming area near the Brazos River. Open Tues through Sat 10 a.m. to 5 p.m. Free admission, but donations are welcome.

Pace Park. Downtown, off Main Street; (254) 947-5040. This beautiful area, restored following a massive flood in 2009, is filled with tall oaks and is an excellent spot to bring a picnic lunch and wade in the creek. Don't miss the statue of Sirena, located in the middle of the creek. Local artist Troy Kelley created the statue cast in bronze of the legendary Indian maiden who was transformed into a mermaid by a magical fish. In the morning you can see fog rising from the chilly waters of the pure springs near the statue. Free admission.

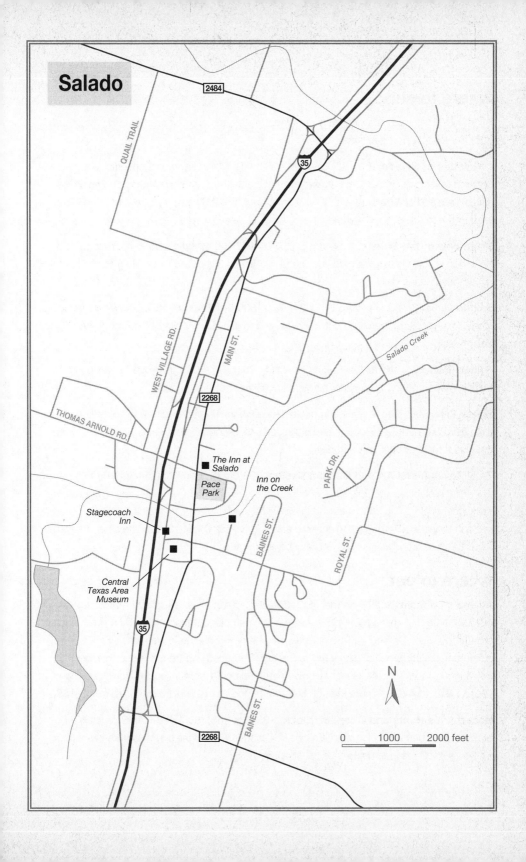

where to shop

Shopping is the main drawing card of Salado, and many stores are open daily. Most sell one-of-a-kind, handmade items.

Charlottes of Salado. 8 Rock Creek Dr.; (254) 947-0240; www.charlottesofsalado.com. Located one block east of Main Street, this rustic chateau-style shop features home accessories, gifts and colorful flora art. Open Mon through Sat 9:30 a.m. to 5:30 p.m., Sun 10:30 a.m. to 5 p.m.

Magnolias of the Square. 1 Salado Sq.; (254) 947-0323; www.magnoliasofsalado.com. This shop is actually a group of thirteen vendors offering a variety of specialty gifts and home accessories. Open daily.

Salado Haus. 209 South Main St.; (877) 947-1868 or (254) 947-1868; www.saladohaus .com. This gift store features Fenton art glass and other fine collectibles and home gifts. Open daily.

Salado Pottery. Next to the Stagecoach Inn; (254) 947-5935. Here you'll find beautiful Salado-made pottery, from water pitchers to bird feeders. Open daily.

Shady Villa. Main Street, across from Stagecoach Inn. This open-air mini-mall sells everything from unique kaleidoscopes and collectibles to Victorian jewelry and gifts from around the world. Most shops are open daily.

Truly Texan Metal Art and Custom Design. 408 South Main St.; (254) 947-8986; www .trulytexanmetalart.com. This store specializes in one-of-a-kind home accents with a true Texas touch. Here you'll find metal art in every shape and form, from tabletop cowboys atop bucking broncos to wall signs to shelving and end tables. The store also offers handcrafted rustic furniture, candles, jewelry, and etched glassware.

where to eat

Adelea's on Main. 302 North Main St.; (254) 947-0018; www.adeleas.com. Housed in a historic home that dates from 1925, this eatery is an elegant place to enjoy a quiet lunch or afternoon tea. Or, you can try out their raspberry margaritas in Hemingway's Bar. The restaurant is also open for dinner Thurs through Sun choosing from a menu that includes filet mignon, goat cheese lasagna, or parmesan-crusted honey mustard chicken. Open Wed 11 a.m. to 4 p.m., Thurs through Sat 11 a.m. to 9 p.m., Sun 1 a.m. to 4 p.m. $$–$$$.

Robertson's Hams and Choppin' Block. I-35, exit 285; (800) 458-HAMS or (817) 947-5562; www.robertsonshams.com. Enjoy a deli sandwich of sugar-cured ham, then shop for kitchen collectibles in the extensive gift shop. $.

Stagecoach Inn. I-35, east side; (254) 947-9400; www.stagecoachinn.com. The servers at this tiny restaurant come to your table and recite the day's offerings by heart. Entrees include chicken-fried steak, baked ham, whole catfish, roast prime rib of beef, and T-bone steak. Don't miss the hush puppies or banana fritters. Open daily for lunch and dinner. Reservations recommended. $$–$$$.

where to stay

For a list of Salado inns and bed-and-breakfasts, visit www.salado.com/lodging.cfm.

The Inn at Salado. North Main Street at Pace Park; (800) 724-0027 or (254) 947-0027; www.inn-at-salado.com. This lovely white bed-and-breakfast with eleven rooms and a cottage is located within walking distance of the main shopping district. Room rates include a full breakfast. $$–$$$.

Inn on the Creek. 602 Center Circle; (877) 947-5554 or (254) 947-5554; www.inncreek .com. This inn offers seven guest rooms in the manor house with 1892 Victorian elegance. Some rooms boast brass beds; all have private baths. Across the street, the Holland House offers five bedrooms (children in the manor house with special permission only), while the two-bedroom, two-bath Giles-Kindred House welcomes families. All guests receive a full breakfast. $$–$$$.

Stagecoach Inn. 401 Stagecoach Rd. off I-35, east side; (254) 947-5111; www.staystage coach.com. This throwback to Salado's early days started out as the Shady Villa Inn, an important rest stop on the Chisholm Trail. Today guests stay in a modern addition, and the original building, where Sam Houston once delivered an anti-secession speech, is now an elegant restaurant. Notable guests have included George Armstrong Custer, Robert E. Lee, and Jesse James. The inn also offers golf packages in conjunction with its sister property, Mill Creek Golf Club, home to three nine-hole courses designed by Robert Trent Jones Jr. $$.

day trip 02

north

>>> **military history:**
belton, killeen, temple

Beyond Georgetown and Salado (see North Day Trip 01 for attractions in those towns), I-35 continues its northward journey to two larger central Texas communities. If you're a military buff, take a short detour to Killeen, home of Fort Hood, the largest military base in the free world.

belton

Built on the Leon River and Nolan Creek, this community once named Nolanville was a place where merchants sold goods from wagons and tin cups of whiskey from barrels. Today Belton is a small town of over 15,000 residents, best known as home of the University of Mary-Hardin Baylor. The Baptist college began here over a century ago and was once the women's school for Waco's Baylor University. Visit www.beltonchamber.com for more information.

Two lakes, Stillhouse Hollow and the larger Belton Lake, lie outside the city limits. Both provide fishing, boating, camping, and a quiet retreat only a few minutes from busy I-35.

where to go

Bell County Museum. 201 North Main St.; (254) 933-5243; www.bellcountytx.com/Museum. This National Register property was first a Carnegie library. Today the Beaux Arts–style building and its newer addition house exhibits on Bell County's first century, 1850–1950. Special displays remember Miriam "Ma" Ferguson, Texas's first woman governor, as

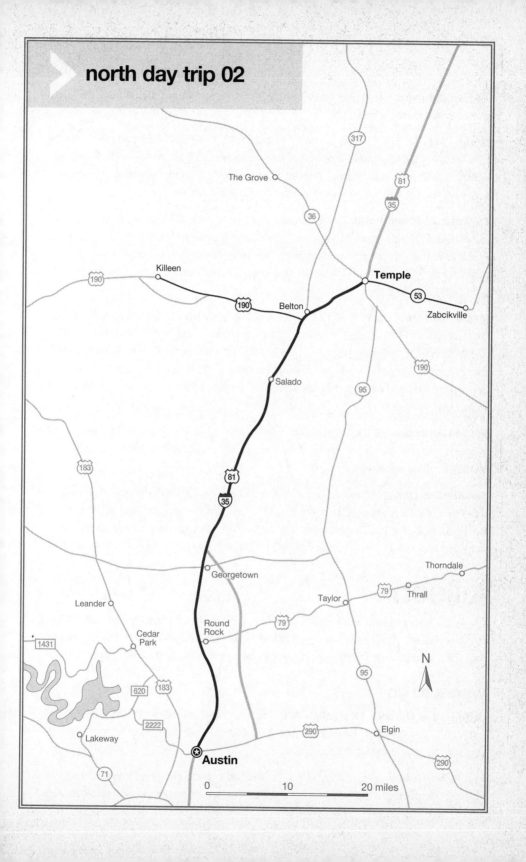

well as the history of Camp Hood, later to become Fort Hood. Open Tues through Sat noon to 5 p.m. Admission is free.

Belton Lake. TX 317, 5 miles northwest of Belton; (877) 444-6777 for camping reservations, (254) 939-2461; www.swf-wc.usace.army.mil/belton. Built on the Leon River, this winding 7,400-acre lake features thirteen public parks within its 110 miles of shoreline. Trailer sites, camping, nature trails, and boat ramps are available.

Cochran, Blair and Potts. 221 E. Central Ave.; (254) 939-3333. Something of a living museum, this store's claim as the oldest department store in Texas might well be true. Founded in 1869, it has remained owned by the same family for 140 years. It occupies an entire city block, and sells a wide variety of wares. Open Mon through Fri 8:30 a.m. to 5:30 p.m., Sat 9 a.m. to 5 p.m. Free admission.

Mother Neff State Park. 1680 TX 236; (254) 853-2389; www.tpwd.state.tx.us. From I-35 take exit 315 to FM 107 west to Moody, continue 6 miles west on FM 107, then take TX 236 for 2 miles to the park. Named for Isabella Neff, the mother of Governor Pat Neff, this park is nestled along the shady bottomland along the Leon River. A nice place for a quiet day of picnicking and walking, the park also offers periodic trailer rides to point out historical areas. Free admission.

Stillhouse Hollow. US 190, 4 miles southwest of Belton; (254) 939-2461. Six public parks surround this lake. You'll find the most facilities at Stillhouse Park, the first you'll come to on US 190. Free admission.

Summer Fun USA. 1410 Waco Rd.; (254) 939-0366; www.summerfunwaterpark.com. This 6.5-acre water theme park offers more than 900 feet of water slides to help you cool off in the Texas heat. Hop in an inner tube and enjoy the 750-foot Lazy River ride, or slide into the water from a 40-foot tower. There are picnic and concession areas as well. Open seasonally.

killeen

Military buffs should take a detour at this point in the journey and head west on US 190 to the city of Killeen. Twenty-five miles west of Belton, this small town is dwarfed by Fort Hood, one of the world's largest military posts and the largest training post on the globe.

where to go

Belton Lake Outdoor Recreation Area. Sparta Road northeast of Fort Hood; (254) 287-4907. This 890-acre park offers woodland hiking, equestrian trails, fishing, boating, paddleboating, and swimming. Open daily.

Fort Hood. US 190. www.hood.army.mil. Established in 1942, Fort Hood spans 339 square miles, encompassing more people and machines than any other post in the free world. The post is home to more than 42,000 soldiers. Access to the base is restricted, but the public is welcome at two museums: the First Cavalry and the Fourth Infantry Division Museums. Before traveling to the museums, you'll need to make your first stop at the **Marvin Leath Visitors Center,** (254) 287-9909; www.hood.army.mil/visitors.center.aspx; located at US 190 at the Main Gate. To obtain a driving permit for the base, you'll need to show identification and proof of driver's insurance. The Visitors Center issues permits from 10 a.m. to 2 p.m.

First Cavalry Division Museum. Building 2218, Headquarters Avenue; (254) 287-3626. Fort Hood is home to the First Cavalry Division Horse Detachment. Wearing authentic 19th-century uniforms, this group performs at exhibitions throughout Texas. The museum traces the history of this division from its days on the western frontier through its berm-busting attacks during Desert Storm. An outdoor area displays more than three dozen pieces of military equipment, including aircraft and tanks. Open Mon through Fri 9 a.m. to 4 p.m., Sat 10 a.m. to 4 p.m., and Sun noon to 4 p.m. Free admission.

Fourth Infantry Division Museum. Building 418, Battalion Avenue at Twenty-seventh Street; (254) 287-8811. Activated in response to the United States' declaration of war against Germany in 1917, the Fourth Infantry Division participated in four major campaigns during World War I. This museum allows the visitor to explore the history of the Fourth Infantry Division through a series of self-guided exhibits that use artifacts, texts, and photographs showing the soldiers in service through three wars. Open Mon through Fri 9 a.m. to 4 p.m., Sat 10 a.m. to 4 p.m., and Sun noon to 4 p.m. Free admission.

Mayborn Planetarium and Space Theater. On Central Texas College campus; (254) 526-1768; www.starsatnight.org. This facility, which opened in 2003, offers planetarium shows, laser light shows, and large format films. From US 190, take Clear Creek Road exit, cross over the highway, turn right at the first stoplight on University Drive. Proceed to the stop sign at the end of the road, and turn right onto Bell Tower Drive. Down the hill past Academic Drive, turn left into Planetarium Parking Lot J. Open for public shows on Fri and Sat afternoons and evenings.

temple

From Killeen and Fort Hood, return to I-35 and continue north to Temple. With more than 111,000 residents in the greater Temple area, this city is the medical center for Central Texas and an important industrial producer. Temple was established by the Gulf, Colorado, and Santa Fe Railroad and named for its chief construction engineer, B.B.M. Temple. Temple is also nicknamed "The Wildflower Capital of Texas." Visitors lucky enough to arrive in late March and April are greeted by a variety of native blooms.

zabcikville

It's a little too lively to be a true Texas ghost town, but the Czech community of Zabcikville, located 10 miles east of Temple on TX 53, is the next best thing. During its boomtown days in the 1940s, the population reached about eighty; today you'll find just a few dozen residents. There's still one good reason to make a detour to this town, though: **Green's Sausage House,** *(254) 985-2331. The only business in town packs in area diners eager to lunch on sausage burgers, hamburgers, and homemade kolaches. An adjacent meat market sells sausage, ham, turkey, bacon, and more.*

where to go

Miller Springs Nature Center. Off FM 2271 north of Lake Belton Spillway; (254) 939-2461; www.ci.temple.tx.us. Set on 260 scenic acres between the Leon River and soaring river bluffs and adjacent to Lake Belton, this natural area gives visitors the opportunity for fishing, hiking, picnicking, and rock climbing. It frequently hosts school groups as part of the Bell County Network for Educational Technology's "classrooms without walls" program. Open daily, dawn to dusk. Free admission.

Railroad and Heritage Museum. 315 West Avenue B; (254) 298-5172; www.rrhm.org. First housed in the former Moody depot, today this museum is located in a renovated Temple Santa Fe depot. Upstairs you'll find exhibits on the history of trains; outdoors check out the rolling stock. Open Tues through Sat 10 a.m. to 4 p.m.

where to eat

Clem Mikeska's Bar-B-Q Restaurant. 1217 South Fifty-seventh St.; (800) 344-4699 or (254) 778-5481; www.clembbq.com. A member of the legendary Mikeska family and often referred to as the "first family of Texas barbecue," Clem Mikeska has been serving up 'que since 1965. Clem and his family specialize in sirloin rather than brisket barbecue. You'll also find popular favorites like homemade sausage, cole slaw, potato salad, and banana pudding. Open daily 9 a.m. to 9 p.m. $.

Clem Mikeska's Grill. 1217 South Fifty-seventh St.; (800) 344-4699 or (254) 778-5481; www.clembbq.com. Located directly behind Clem Mikeska's Bar-B-Q Restaurant, this eatery specializes in Texas food, from chicken-fried steaks to fried catfish. An expansive salad bar rounds out the offerings. Open Mon through Thurs 11 a.m. to 9 p.m., Fri and Sat 11 a.m. to 10 p.m. $.

day trip 03

heart of texas:
lorena, waco

Waco is sometimes called the "Heart of Texas" for its central location in the Lone Star State. This day trip continues Day Trips 01 and 02, continuing north on I-35 through several small communities before reaching Waco, a city that has a large number of visitor attractions.

lorena

Located 80 miles north of Austin on I-35 at exit 322 (see North Day Trips 01 and 02 for attractions along this drive), the community of Lorena (254-857-4641; www.ci.lorena.tx.us/index.aspx) was formerly a railroad town. Named for the daughter of a local businessman, Lorena was a thriving town before the Depression. From the 1920s until the late 1960s, Lorena was especially quiet. In 1968 renovation began on several historic structures, and the town returned to life. Today the old part of the city (known as "Olde Town") is home to several antiques and specialty shops.

where to go

Library and Museum of the Lorena Women's Club. 101 Walter St. Since 2000 this small museum has celebrated the 100th Anniversary of the Lorena Women's Club. The museum contains household and agricultural items from Lorena's heyday. A collection of interest to historians and former residents, the museum is home to 6,000 donated books and local artifacts. Open the first and last Wed of each month.

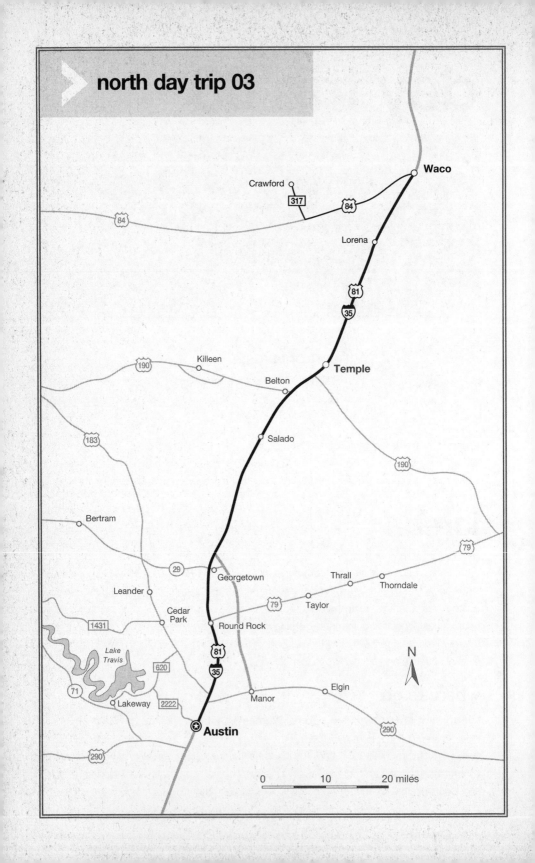

north day trip 03

where to shop

Center Street Antique Mall. 102 E Center St.; (254) 857-9656; www.centerstreetantique mall.net. This large antique mall offers wares from a multitude of vendors that sell furniture, clocks, toys, jewelry, pottery, lamps, quilts, glassware, and many other collectibles. Open Mon through Sat 10 a.m. to 6 p.m., Sun 1 p.m. to 6 p.m.

The Village Lamp Lighter. 103 East Center St.; (254) 857-4435; www.villagelamplighter .com. This shop, in business for over three decades, showcases lamps and lighting of all types. Open Mon through Sat.

where to eat

Raymond's Southern Kitchen. I-35 at exit 322; (254) 655-4196. This unassuming roadhouse serves up Texas favorites like chicken-fried steak, burgers, pork chops, and fried chicken. $–$$.

Texas Cheese House. 102 E. Center St.; (254) 655-4217; www.texascheesehouse.com. Owner chef Scott Simon is on a mission to prove that excellent cheese can be produced in Texas. His shop in downtown Lorena carries artisan cheese from several Texas cheese producers as well as goat and cow cheeses made in his own shop. The shop also serves appetizers, sandwiches on homemade bread, and soups all featuring—you guessed it—cheese. Open Mon through Sat 10 a.m. to 6 p.m., Sun 2 p.m. to 5 p.m. $.

waco

Continue north on I-35 to Waco, a city of more than 118,000 and named for the Hueco Indians who resided here before the days of recorded history. The Huecos were attracted to this rich, fertile land at the confluence of the Brazos and Bosque Rivers.

Although Spanish explorers named this site "Waco Village" in 1542, over 300 years elapsed before permanent settlement began. At that time, Waco was part of the Wild West, with cattle drives, cowboys, and so many gunslingers that stagecoach drivers called the town "Six-Shooter Junction." (Drivers routinely asked passengers to strap on their guns before the stagecoach reached the rowdy community!)

In the 1870s Waco became a center of trade with the completion of a 470-foot suspension bridge across the Brazos, the longest inland river in Texas. The bridge, which still stands, was designed by the same engineers who constructed New York City's Brooklyn Bridge years later.

Today Waco's Wild West heritage is tempered by a strong religious influence. The city is home to Baylor University, a Baptist liberal arts college of 15,000 students. The university has several excellent museums open to the public.

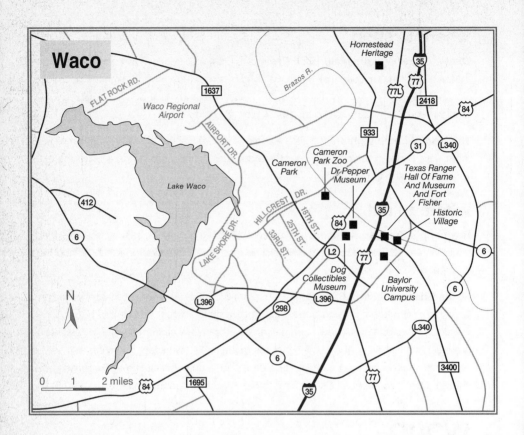

Some of the most scenic areas in Waco fall along the Brazos River. This waterway slices the city in half and provides miles of shoreline parks, shady walks, and a winding river walk, which begins at Fort Fisher Park and extends to Cameron Park.

where to go

City of Waco Tourist Information Center. Fort Fisher at exit 335B off I-35; (800) WACO-FUN. The visitor center provides helpful maps and brochures, and staff members give advice on Waco attractions, accommodations, and restaurants. Open daily. Free admission.

The Art Center Waco. 1300 College Dr. on McClellan Community College campus; (254) 752-4371; www.artcenterwaco.org. This exhibit hall and teaching center is located in the Mediterranean-style home of the late lumber magnate William Waldo Cameron. Exhibits focus on Texas artists in all media. Open Tues through Sat 10 a.m. to 5 p.m.; Sun 1 p.m. to 5 p.m. Free admission.

Baylor University. Exit 335B from I-35; (800) BAYLOR-U; www.baylor.edu. Chartered by the fledgling Republic of Texas in 1845, this Baptist-affiliated university is the oldest, continually operating university in the state. Now a nationally-ranked liberal arts institution, the Baylor campus fills 735 acres in downtown Waco. The university curriculum offers degrees in 151 areas of study, 6 master's programs and 30 doctoral programs. Major components of the university include the College of Arts & Sciences, the Hankamer School of Business, the School of Education, the School of Engineering & Computer Science, Graduate School, Honors College, Law School, School of Music, the Louise Herrington School of Nursing, George W. Truett Theological Seminary, and the School of Social Work.

Armstrong-Browning Library. 710 Speight St., Baylor University campus; (254) 710-3566; www.browninglibrary.org. The works of Elizabeth Barrett Browning and husband Robert Browning fill this two-story library. The building also boasts the world's largest collection of secular stained-glass windows, which illustrate the works of both writers (including Robert Browning's *The Pied Piper of Hamlin*). Take a guided tour to see the upstairs rooms furnished with the couple's belongings. Open Mon through Fri 9 a.m. to 5 p.m., Sat 9 a.m. to noon. Admission is free.

Mayborn Museum Complex. 1300 South University Parks Dr.; (254) 710-1110; www.maybornmuseum.com. This expansive museum complex includes exhibits on the region's natural and social history. Learn more about Waco with a visit to the Waco at the Crossroads of Texas Natural History Exhibits, which includes three walk-in dioramas of a limestone cave, Texas forest, and Waco mammoth experience. A popular area with children is the Discovery Center, where sixteen themed rooms offer hands-on learning in areas that range from vertebrates to TV weather to Native Americans. Beyond the museum walls the learning continues in fifteen wood-frame buildings found on the 13-acre Governor Bill and Vara Daniel Historic Village, a re-creation of a 19th-century cotton town. It includes a schoolhouse, a mercantile store, and, of course, a Wild West saloon. The buildings, once the property of the governor, were moved to this site from a plantation community in Liberty County and restored by Baylor University. Open Mon, Tues, Wed and Fri 10 a.m. to 5 p.m.; Thurs 10 a.m. to 8 p.m.; Sat 10 a.m. to 5 p.m.; Sun 1 p.m. to 5 p.m.

Cameron Park. Brazos River at Herring Avenue; (254) 750-8080. This 416-acre municipal park is one of the largest in the state and holds Miss Nellie's Pretty Place, a beautiful wildflower garden filled with Texas bluebonnets. Free admission.

Cameron Park Zoo. 1701 North Fourth St. in Cameron Park; (254) 750-8400; www.cameronparkzoo.com. This zoo features natural habitats and displays including the African savanna, Gibbon Island, Sumatran tigers, and Treetop Village. The newest exhibit area at the zoo is called the "Brazos River Country," which explores the Gulf to the Caprock regions through plant and animal life. Open Mon through Sat 9 a.m. to 5 p.m., Sun 11 a.m. to 5 p.m.

Dog Collectibles Museum. At exit 345 from I-35, 4 miles north of Waco; www.antiquibles .com. Located in Antiquibles Antique Mall, this unique museum features over 7,000 dog-related artifacts. The collection includes toys, paintings, advertising signs, walking canes, dolls, and hundreds of other items all with a dog motif. It's the world's largest museum of its kind. Open daily. Free admission.

Dr Pepper Museum and Free Enterprise Institute. 300 South Fifth St.; (254) 757-1025; www.drpeppermuseum.com. The famous Dr Pepper soft drink was invented by pharmacist Dr. Charles Alderton at the Old Corner Drug Store in Waco, which once stood at Fourth Street and Austin Avenue. Today the drugstore is gone, but the original bottling plant remains open as a museum. Interesting exhibits and films offer a look at some early promotional materials, as well as the manufacturing process of the unusual soft drink. (Also of note: the popular advertising slogan promoting Dr Pepper as an energy booster to be consumed at "10-2-and-4.") After a look through the museum, visit the re-creation of the Old Corner Drug Store fountain for an ice-cream soda or (what else?) a Dr Pepper. Open Mon through Sat 10 a.m. to 4:15 p.m., Sun noon to 4:15 p.m.

Fort Fisher Park. I-35, exit 335B; (800) WACO-FUN. This park was once the site of Fort Fisher, an outpost of the Texas Rangers built in 1837. The lawmen established a post here to protect the Brazos River crossing. Today the park contains the City of Waco Tourist Information Center and the Texas Ranger Hall of Fame and Museum. Free admission.

Historic Home Visits. Historic Waco Foundation, 810 Fourth St.; (254) 753-5166; www .historicwaco.org. Although a devastating tornado in 1953 destroyed many of Waco's historic structures, some still remain. On weekend afternoons the public can visit any of four historic homes as well as the McLennan County Courthouse, all in the downtown area. One of the most interesting stops is "East Terrace," an Italian villa on the east bank of the Brazos. Here guests once slept in unheated dormitories to discourage them from overstaying their welcome!

Homestead Heritage. Elm Mott; (254) 754-9600; www.homesteadheritage.com. From I-35, take exit 343 and turn west on FM 308, continue 3 miles to FM 933. Turn north on FM 933 and continue 1.5 miles to Halbert Lane. Turn left (west) onto Halbert Lane and continue for a half mile. This 510-acre Christian homesteading community is the site of a 200-year-old Dutch-style barn that showcases the crafts of the village's woodworkers as well as unique quilts, wrought iron, oil lamps, and more. You can take a walking tour of the village to see the potter's house, herb gardens, blacksmith's shop, and the restored 1760 gristmill. A deli serves all-natural sandwiches and ice cream. Open 10 a.m. to 6 p.m. Mon through Sat. Free admission.

Lake Waco. FM 1637, 2 miles northwest of the city on North Nineteenth Street; (254) 756-5359. This lake, part of the Bosque River, is a favorite with anglers and boaters. Several marinas and boat ramps offer access. Open daily.

Suspension Bridge and River Walk. University Parks Drive between Franklin and Washington Streets; (254) 750-8080. Spanning the 800-mile-long Brazos River, this restored suspension bridge was once the longest in the world. Built in 1870, it eliminated the time-consuming process of having to cart cattle across the water by ferry. Today the structure is used as a pedestrian bridge bearing the motto first across, still across, linking Indian Spring Park on the west bank and Martin Luther King Jr. Park on the east. On the west side, you'll find a walk to Fort Fisher Park in one direction and Herring Avenue Bridge in the other, 1.5 miles away. Open daily. Free admission.

Texas Ranger Hall of Fame and Museum. Fort Fisher, at exit 335B off I-35; (254) 750-8631; www.texasranger.org. If you're interested in the taming of Texas, budget a couple of hours for this large museum. Visitors here can see guns of every description used by the Rangers, who had the reputation of lone lawmen who always got their man. Dioramas in the hall of fame recount the early days of the Rangers, including their founding by Stephen F. Austin. A fifty-five-minute film shows several times daily. Open daily.

Texas Sports Hall of Fame. 1108 South University Parks Dr. and I-35 at exit 335B; (254) 756-1633; www.tshof.org. Waco's popular attraction is a tribute to the athletes of the Lone Star State. Sports memorabilia highlight more than 350 sports heroes, including an autographed baseball by former Texas Ranger Nolan Ryan, Earl Campbell's letter jacket, and one of Martina Navratilova's Wimbledon rackets, as well as displays featuring prominent Texas high school athletes. Open Mon through Sat 9 a.m. to 5 p.m., Sun noon to 5 p.m.

Waco Mammoth Site. 6220 Steinbeck Bend Rd. (exit 335C from I-35); (254) 750-7946; www.wacomammoth.com. Located northwest of Waco, this attraction features prehistoric Columbian Mammoth bones which were first discovered in 1978 and excavated by Baylor University archeologists. Now a public park, the 100-acre site includes a dig shelter reached via a suspended walkway for an overhead view and a scenic trailway with benches and rest areas. The park Welcome Center includes a gift shop and a ticket counter. Open Tues through Fri 11 a.m. to 5 p.m., Sat 9 a.m. to 5 p.m.

where to shop

Cameron Trading Company. 618 Austin Ave.; (254) 756-7662. This shop, which calls itself Waco's largest antiques mall, sells all types of items ranging from fine antiques to imports and flea-market finds. Open daily.

Craft Gallery Antique and Craft Mall. 7524 Bosque Blvd. in Bosque Square; (254) 751-0693. This shop is home to more than 225 vendors offering antiques, collectibles, candles, jewelry, garden accessories, stained glass, and more. Open daily.

The Market Place. 4700 Bosque Blvd. This shopping area, located just west of Waco Drive between Bosque Boulevard and Valley Mills Drive, is filled with unique specialty stores selling furniture, religious items, china, jewelry, lamps, silver, antiques, and fine art. Open daily.

Spice Home Furnishings and the Shops of River Square Center. 213 Mary Ave. in downtown Waco; (254) 757-1066; www.spicefurniture.com. This shop, housed in a restored warehouse, sells a variety of items ranging from antiques and collectibles to specialty furniture. Open daily.

where to eat

Elite Circle Grille. 2132 South Valley Mills Dr.; (254) 754-4941; www.elitecirclegrille.com. Longtime Texans know the Elite from its highway signs declaring it as the place where "the elite meet to eat." Dating to 1914, the Elite held the title as Waco's first restaurant with refrigeration and, later, the city's first eatery with air-conditioning. In 2003 the restaurant received a facelift that returned it to its early days. Menu items now range from baby back ribs to lemon rosemary chicken to Gulf shrimp, dishes special enough to make you feel, well, pretty darn elite. Open for lunch and dinner daily. $–$$.

Health Camp. 2601 Circle Rd.; (254) 752-2081. Perched right on the Waco traffic circle, this casual restaurant has been selling burgers, fries, malts, and shakes since 1949. Open daily for breakfast, lunch, and dinner. $.

Lake Brazos Steakhouse. 1620 North Lake Brazos Pkwy; (254) 755-7797; www.lake brazossteakhouse.com. This casual eatery serves up a Texas favorite—steak—as well as seafood, including many dishes from the Gulf. Open daily for lunch and dinner. $$.

the western white house

The tiny community of Crawford, with a population of under 700 residents, drew international attention with the 1999 arrival of two new residents: George W. and Laura Bush. The then governor purchased the 1,600-acre ranch, located 8 miles northeast of town on Prairie Chapel Road, and constructed a home that soon became host to world leaders.

Today Crawford remains a quiet town except when the former President is at the **Prairie Chapel Ranch,** which visitors can drive by. You'll know you're getting close when you see signs warning "no stopping, no standing, no parking." The ranch is located on the right side of the road heading north. To reach Crawford from Waco, take US 84 west, then turn right onto TX 317.

where to stay

The Cotton Palace. 1910 Austin Ave.; (877) 632-2312 or (254) 753-7294; www.thecotton palace.com. This Arts and Crafts–style 1910 home offers seven guest rooms, each with a private bath. Rates include a full breakfast with specialties such as lemon soufflé pancakes with blueberries or Cotton Palace cream-cheese bread. $$.

Judge Baylor House Bed & Breakfast. 908 Speight St.; (888) 522-9567 or (254) 756-0273; www.judgebaylorhouse.com. This 2-story inn offers 5 guest rooms, each with a private bath. The home is located adjacent to the Baylor University campus and is a favorite with visiting parents. Rates include a full breakfast. Through the years, the inn has hosted many well-known guests, including Henry Mancini and Burt Bacharach. $$.

northeast

day trip 01

northeast

farming heartland:
hutto, taylor, thrall

A magnet for immigrant farmers from Sweden and other Scandinavian countries in the 1800s, these fertile blackland prairies and small towns are rapidly evolving into bedroom communities for Austin commuters. Some of the agrarian spirit remains, however, and family farms coexist alongside housing developments and shopping malls.

hutto

Hutto, east of Austin, was once just another blackland farming community. For years the town was, well, pretty much just a wide spot in the road on US 79 between Round Rock and Taylor. Things changed, though, with both the booming of Austin's population and the construction of US 130. Today Hutto's population boom makes it one of the country's fastest growing communities.

Just a block off US 79, though, you'll find "old" Hutto, with historic buildings and small-town atmosphere. You also might spot something a little unusual for a small Texas town: hippo statues. More than 150 of them grace Hutto, ranging from a 14,000-pound hippo at the Hutto High School to smaller "yard hippos" in front of many businesses and private homes.

Why the hippos? According to local legend, a hippo escaped from a circus train near Hutto around 1915 and was recovered in a local creek. The residents seemed to fall in love with the idea of hippos and soon named their football team the Hutto Hippos (complete with the only hippo football mascot in Texas).

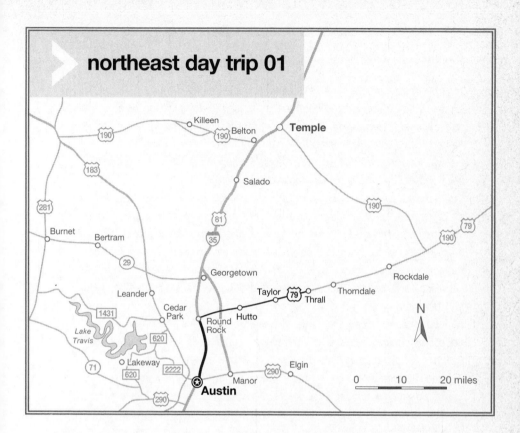

northeast day trip 01

where to go

Hutto Heritage Museum. 122 East St.; (512) 759-4400; www.hutto.org. Located in the Chamber of Commerce office, the museum traces local history through photos and documents. Don't miss the mural on the side of the building that recalls the famous hippo story. Open weekdays, 8 a.m. to 5 p.m. Free admission.

taylor

Taylor's claim to fame is its International Barbecue Cook-off in August and its controversial National Rattlesnake Sacking Championship and Roundup held every March. (See Festivals and Celebrations at the back of this book.)

Taylor was the hometown of former Texas governor Dan Moody as well as Bill Pickett, an African-American cowboy born in 1860. Pickett originated the practice of "bulldogging"—throwing a bull by twisting its head until it falls. The well-known cowboy also had a habit of biting a steer's upper lip, a trick called "biting the bull" that he practiced on the rodeo circuit.

smokin' in taylor

*Don't be alarmed during an August visit if you see smoke rising from the central-Texas town of Taylor, located northeast of Austin. That just means it's time again for the annual **International Barbecue Cookoff,** and contestants from around the Lone Star State are firing up their pits. With military-like precision, using recipes so carefully guarded it would make the Pentagon jealous, these cooks try their hand at preparing the best smoky delectables.*

In a state where you can hardly throw a sausage link without hitting a cook-off, Taylor's is one of the largest and also one of the most prestigious. It draws some of the state's best pitmasters. Although there are no cash prizes, up to one hundred teams show up every year to compete for twenty-seven cooking trophies plus prizes for showmanship. Besides the prestige of being able to claim the best brisket, poultry, lamb, goat, pork ribs, seafood, or wild game, the teams come for the pure enjoyment of the competition.

Using secret spices, the pitmasters season the meats and start the slow process of smoking over their chosen wood. Many cooks stay up through the night basting or "mopping" the meat with marinade to keep it from drying.

Judging takes place on Saturday afternoon, and once the judging is completed, the real fun begins. Cooks are encouraged, although they are not required, to provide the public with a sample of their craft. In the relaxed atmosphere after the judging, cooks also enjoy talking about the art of barbecueing, sometimes even sharing tips and secrets.

where to go

Moody Museum. 114 West Ninth St.; (512) 352-3463; www.moodymuseum.com/Welcome.html. Governor Dan Moody was born in this 1887 home, which today is filled with his furniture and personal belongings. He went to law school at the University of Texas, served in World War I, then returned to become governor at the age of thirty-three. The hometown hero was best known for prosecuting members of the Ku Klux Klan in Williamson County. Open Tues and Fri 8 a.m. to 5 p.m., Sun 2 to 5 p.m. and by appointment. Admission is free.

where to eat

Louie Mueller Barbecue. 206 West Second St.; (512) 352-6206; www.louiemuellerbarbecue.com. One of the most authentic barbecue joints in Texas, where diners eat off white butcher paper in a room decorated with free calendars and a corkboard filled with business cards (all imbued with enough smoke to give them the color of a grocery sack). But none of that matters. What matters is the barbecue: brisket, sausage, pork ribs, and steak. Mon through Sat 10 a.m. to 7:30 p.m. (or until sold out for the day). $–$$.

Rudy Mikeska's Bar-B-Q. 300 West Second St.; (800) 962-5706 or (512) 365-3722; www.mikeska.com. This popular restaurant tempts diners with sausage, lamb ribs, pork ribs, ham, and baby back ribs. In a state renowned for barbecue pit masters, the Mikeskas are the most famous. This restaurant has catered numerous governors' inaugurations and even served Prince Philip at a state event. Open for lunch and dinner, Thurs through Sat 11 a.m. to 7 p.m. $–$$.

Taylor Cafe. 101 North Main St.; (512) 352-8475. This local eatery has the atmosphere of a small-town diner—from its ceiling fans to its pool tables to the members of the local police force who often have lunch here. Barbecue is the house specialty. $.

thrall

When oil was discovered in 1915, more than 200 wells were drilled and Thrall's population skyrocketed. As the saying goes, what goes up must come down, and Thrall was back on its way down as soon as oil production diminished. Today it's once again a quiet spot on US 79, composed of a few blocks of homes that run parallel to the railroad.

the mikeska dynasty

In Texas, the Mikeska name is synonymous with barbecue, thanks to brothers Rudy, Maurice, Clem, Jerry, Mike, and Louis. Each man founded his own barbecue restaurant, spread throughout the state. This accomplishment made Texas Monthly *proclaim the brothers "The First Family of Texas Barbecue." Their restaurants were no chain of pits, however; each brother had his own preferences and his own way of preparing barbecue. "We're a very close family," explained CEO Tim Mikeska to us, "but we all do things a little different." Through the years, we've visited all the locations and found that each has unique menus and their own ways of preparing their specialties.*

The Taylor pit was the creation of Rudy Mikeska. During his lifetime, Rudy Mikeska was the dean of Texas pitmasters. If there was a political function to be held, whether it was a policemen's fundraiser or a governor's inauguration, Rudy Mikeska and his barbecue meats were there.

Rudy died in 1989, but he left a legacy of legendary barbecue that his children, Tim and Mopsie, continue.

where to go

Stiles Farm Foundation. US 79, east of Thrall; (512) 898-2214; www.agrilife-extadmin .tamu.edu/sff/stilebro.htm. This 3,200-acre farm is administered by Texas A&M University. Here new techniques are demonstrated to area farmers and ranchers. Visitors can take guided tours to see everything from hog raising to cotton growing. This is a great chance to have a look at an operating Texas farm and ranch. Call for appointment. Free admission.

day trip 02

northeast

texas two-steppin':
coupland, taylor, circleville, granger,
bartlett, new corn hill, walburg

This day trip encompasses many small farming communities that lie east of I-35. Much of this farmland, largely covered by cotton fields, was first settled by German, Czech, and Austrian immigrants in the mid- to late-1800s. Today it remains a quiet slice of central Texas, with the exception of the local dance halls that draw visitors from Austin and surrounding communities for evenings of live country music and dancing.

coupland

Located 8 miles north of Elgin on TX 95, this small community is home to about 600 families.

where to go

Huntington Sculpture Foundation. 212 North Broad St. at the corner of Hoxie Street; (512) 856-2334; www.huntingtonsculpture.org. With its miles of surrounding agricultural land, the last thing you might expect to see in tiny Coupland is a sculpture garden featuring an internationally known artist, but here it is. This garden and studio feature the work of Jim Huntington, whose installations are seen from Japan to Australia. Call for hours at the studio, although the large granite sculptures can be seen outdoors anytime.

The Old Coupland Inn and Dancehall. 101–103 Hoxie St.; (512) 856-2226; www.coupland dancehall.com. On weekends, tiny Coupland becomes a hot spot for major boot-scooting fun at this historic dancehall. Headliners from all over Texas and Nashville have performed

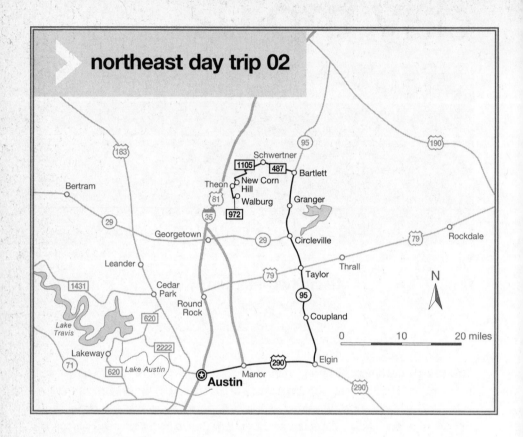

northeast day trip 02

here since 1910. If you're planning a late night of dancing, consider staying at the adjacent B&B located just above the dance hall; it's styled like a 1900s bordello. While it may not have ever served as a bordello, the property does have a rich history as a mercantile and even a newsletter publishing company. Open Thurs 8 p.m. to 11 p.m., Fri 8 p.m. to 12 a.m., Sat 8 p.m. to 1 a.m. Admission varies with performer.

where to eat

The Old Coupland Inn and Dancehall. 101–103 Hoxie St.; (512) 856-2226; www.coup landdancehall.com. Barbecue and steaks take center stage when it comes to dining at this historic dance hall. Start with a half rack of ribs or some stuffed jalapeños, then move on to the serious entrees: mesquite-trimmed sirloin steaks; catfish and shrimp; a mixed barbecue plate; or chicken-fried steak. Work off that big dinner with a twirl around the dance floor on Thurs, Fri and Sat nights, when country bands keep the evenings lively. Open for dinner Thurs, Fri, and Sat. $$.

taylor

Continue north on TX 95 to Taylor, the largest community on this tour. You'll find Taylor's attractions (and world-renowned barbecue) covered in Northeast Day Trip 01.

circleville

Continue north on TX 95 for approximately 5 miles to the community of Circleville. With a population that hovers around forty residents, Circleville has long been home to a cotton gin, evidence of the miles of cotton fields that surround this burg.

where to eat

Circleville Store & Grain. 600 South TX 95; (512) 352-6848. With its tin exterior, the Circleville Store doesn't look like much from the outside, but inside you'll find a classic Texas general store and small restaurant. Barbecue—in the form of brisket, ribs, and chicken—is the main draw Mon through Sat, while Wed through Sat you can order grilled items including burgers and, on some Fridays, catfish. Open for lunch and dinner Mon through Sat. $.

granger

Continue north on TX 95 to the agricultural community of Granger. Also the home of a cotton gin, Granger is also notable because of its brick Davilla Street, the community's main avenue. This street was paved with bricks in 1912, a feat that the Granger News said made Granger "the only city in the state of less than 5,000 inhabitants that has paved streets, or is paving them."

Today Granger still has far fewer than 5,000 residents and Davilla Street is still paved with red bricks. You'll find the town divided by railroad tracks with a few businesses both east and west of TX 95.

where to go

Granger Lake. (512) 859-2668; www.tpwd.state.tx.us. Located east of Granger, this 4,064-acre lake was created in 1980 on the San Gabriel River. Today the lake is a favorite with local anglers and boaters; you'll find four parks operated by the U.S. Army Corps of Engineers. Catfish and crappie are top catches in the lake, and lucky anglers also have the chance at white bass and largemouth bass. Parks are found on the north, west, and south sides of the lake.

> **Friendship Park.** North shore of the lake off FM 971. Includes a boat ramp and picnicking.

Taylor Park. South Shore of the lake off FM 1331. Offers picnicking, camping, and a boat ramp.

Willis Creek Park. CR 346. Offers picnicking, camping, and a boat ramp.

Wilson H. Fox Park. South shore of the lake off FM 1331. Offers picnicking, camping, fish-cleaning stations, and a boat ramp.

where to eat

Cotton Club and Steakhouse. 212 East Davilla St.; (512) 859-0700; www.cottonclub andsteakhouse.com. This Texas-size dance hall is open Fri, Sat, and Sun nights only, a time when couples from surrounding farmland—and surrounding cities—pack the dance floor for an evening of boot scootin'. There is a cover charge for the dance hall (unless it is rented out for a private function), but diners are welcome at the courtyard without cover. Diners find a traditional Texas menu: appetizers of jalapeño poppers; onion rings; queso and chips followed by favorites like chicken-fried steak, fried shrimp and catfish, steaks, and more. Open Fri 5 p.m. to 12 a.m., Sat 5 p.m. to 1 a.m., Sun 4 p.m. to 11 p.m. $$.

bartlett

From Granger follow TX 95 north for 5 miles to reach Bartlett. Once an agricultural boom-town with two weekly newspapers, today Bartlett's a quiet farm town, one so classic that it has appeared in several Hollywood movies, including *Stars Fell on Henrietta* and *The Newton Boys.*

where to shop

Bartlett Antique Mall. 137 East Clark St.; (254) 527-3251. This multivendor antiques mall includes everything from dolls and dishes to toys and trinkets.

where to eat

Bartlett Filling Station. 210 North Dalton St., (254) 527-3800. This eatery. located in the heart of Bartlett's tiny downtown, is a popular lunch and dinner stop for locals and visitors who are lured by menu selections all made "from scratch." Salads, burgers, and Texas specialties such as chicken-fried steak, catfish, and Czech sausage are featured, all served with a tempting array of side dishes such as Texas fried okra and baked mac and cheese. Open Sun, Mon and Thurs 11 a.m. to 9 p.m.; Fri and Sat 11 a.m. to 10 p.m. $$.

new corn hill

From Bartlett, turn west on FM 476 and continue for 5 miles to the intersection with FM 1105. At these crossroads, you'll find the hamlet of Schwertner. From there, head south on FM 1105, a pretty drive lined with rolling ranches and farms. Several miles before you reach New Corn Hill, you'll see the twin steeples of the historic Holy Trinity Catholic Church, built in 1913, one of few remaining structures in this town.

And where, you might ask, is Old Corn Hill? That community was consolidated with Jarrell (now on I-35). Some of its residents packed up and headed a few miles east to settle what's now called New Corn Hill.

where to go

Holy Trinity Catholic Church. 8626 FM 1105, (512) 863-3020.The twin neo-Gothic towers of Holy Trinity Church soar above the tiny town and surrounding farmland and can be seen from miles away. The church was established in 1889 to serve the nearby communities of Theon and Corn Hill and the present structure was built in 1913. The church still serves area residents and celebrates Mass on Sat and Sun. Free admission.

walburg

Continue south on FM 1105 to the German community of Walburg. First named Concordia, the town was later renamed by the local storekeeper after his hometown in Germany. It has always been small, although it represents many immigrant groups including Germans, Wendish, Czechs, Austrians, and Swiss.

the walburg boys

The Walburg Restaurant is owned by Ron Tippelt, who originally hails from Munich, Germany. Nearly two decades ago, Tippelt packed up his accordion and headed for Walburg, creating this restaurant with recipes from his homeland. Tippelt's contribution didn't end there, however; he also puts his musical talents to work in the biergarten. The accordionist and yodeler assembled The Walburg Boys, a band that plays Bavarian tunes that encourage patrons to take to the dance floor.

Tippelt is walking in the footsteps of another Munich immigrant: Hy Doering. In 1882, Doering settled in Walburg and built the Walburg Mercantile that today serves as the home of the popular restaurant.

where to eat

Dale's Essenhaus. 3900 FM 972; (512) 819-9175; www.dales-essenhaus.com. Less atmospheric than the larger Walburg Restaurant, Dale's is also known both for its menu and its live music. The restaurant is especially noted for its Dale's Walburger, a hamburger served with grilled onions, but fried catfish and chicken-fried steak are tops as well. Outside, the biergarten is open Fri and Sat night from Apr through Oct; food and drink are also served outside. Open Tues through Thurs 11 a.m. to 9 p.m., Fri and Sat 11 a.m. to 10 p.m. $–$$.

Walburg Restaurant. 3777 FM 972 at the intersection of FM 1105; (512) 863-8440; www .walburgrestaurant.com. This restaurant is housed in the 1882 Walburg Mercantile building and features authentic German food and music. Behind the restaurant, a converted cotton gin serves as a biergarten. The restaurant menu includes Wiener schnitzel, bratwurst, sauerbraten, and some Texas favorites like chicken-fried steak and catfish. The buffets are particularly popular and include a wide selection of the restaurant's top items. A more limited menu is served in the biergarten. The restaurant hosts several annual celebrations, including Maifest and Oktoberfest. Closed Mon and Tues. Open Wed and Thurs noon to 9 p.m., Fri and Sat noon to 10 p.m., Sun noon to 9 p.m. $–$$.

day trip 03

northeast

presidential corridor:
dime box, caldwell, snook,
bryan–college station

Between Austin and College Station lies the "Presidential Corridor," which links Austin's LBJ Library with Bryan–College Station's Bush Library.

Head east of Austin on US 290 through the towns of Elgin and McDade (see East Day Trip 01 for attractions along this route) before turning northeast on TX 21 through Caldwell and Bryan/College Station. For more on the Presidential Corridor (including a downloadable brochure), visit www.presidentialcorridor.org.

dime box

OK, there's not much in the town of Dime Box, but with a name like that, isn't it worth a quick detour? The burg is located just east of TX 21 on FM 141.

The town was originally named for its sawmill, but confusion with towns that had similar names led to its name change. The reason for the unusual moniker? Early residents could drop their mail—and a dime—in a box at the post office for delivery.

Actually Dime Box began up on TX 21, but when a rail line was built a few miles southeast of town, everyone up and moved. The original settlement became Old Dime Box and today's community is, well, New Dime Box.

The story of that namesake is recalled not only in the community's museum but in a transparent box perched alongside FM 141 that contains an oversize Liberty Head dime, a fun photo stop on your day trip.

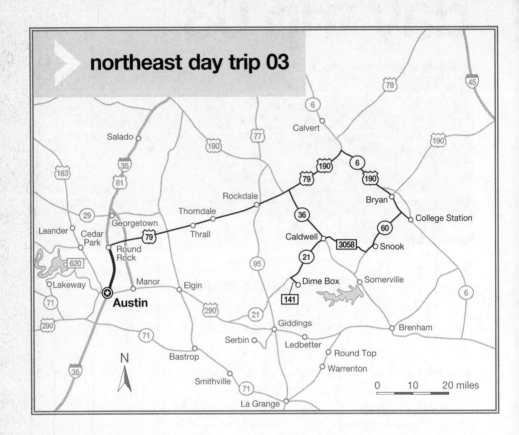

northeast day trip 03

Dime Box also got national attention in 1945, when it became the country's first community to have 100 percent participation in the new March of Dimes campaign. Dime Box's citizens filled a mailbox with their collected donations and sent the package—mailbox and all—to then President Franklin D. Roosevelt, who responded with a phone call to the city's postmaster and banker.

where to go

Dime Box Museum. Downtown on FM 141; (979) 884-0182. This small museum traces the history of this community that was settled by Czech, British, German and Polish immigrants. Exhibits include a pocket Communion Bible in Czech, a barber's chair and other farm and home memorabilia. Open Fri through Sun 1 to 4 p.m. Free admission.

caldwell

Nicknamed the "Kolache Capital of Texas" by the 71st Legislature, Caldwell is located just south of TX 21 on TX 36. This community is the capital of Burleson County (and it's confusing because there's a nearby county named Caldwell County—whose county seat is Lockhart.) You'll find a traditional Texas courthouse square downtown.

The biggest event in town takes place the second Saturday of September when Caldwell celebrates its annual Kolache Festival. The event was begun as a way to revive Czech traditions in the region. The kolache, the Czech wedding pastry that can be sweet or savory, is the focal point of the day, with everything from kolache baking contests to eating contests. Along with plenty of kolaches, the event includes Czech traditions such as stenciling, dances, egg decorating, cane weaving, and dulcimer playing.

where to go

Burleson County Czech Heritage Museum. 212 West Buck St., in Chamber of Commerce building. The longtime links between Caldwell and Prague are traced in this local history collection that includes a mural of the city of Prague, Czech costumes, and more. Open Sat 10 a.m. to 3 p.m.; other times by appointment. Free admission.

Burleson County Historical Museum. 100 West Buck St. (1st floor of the Burleson County Courthouse); (979) 567-7196. The focus of this museum is on early county settlement and history. The museum has a variety of resources and archives for research that may be used on-site. The Commission assists in research and can try to answer most questions. Open Fri from 2 p.m. to 4:30 p.m., or by appointment.

snook

From Caldwell, you can travel directly to Bryan on TX 21 or take a detour to the small community of Snook.

kolache country

A sweet reminder of the old country, anyone who tastes a freshly baked kolache can recognize that more than apricots, apples, or cottage cheese is wrapped inside the sugar-topped bread roll—the main ingredient of this pastry is a love for tradition. This wedding pastry was traditionally baked weeks before a local ceremony, then given as an invitation to the upcoming event.

Many Czechs immigrated to Texas in the mid-1800s in search of a more prosperous life, and today their descendants proudly pay homage to them each time they reach for a recipe for this tasty concoction

Like nearby Caldwell and many other neighboring communities, Snook was founded by Czech immigrants. First named Sebesta after a family of early settlers, the town's name was later changed to Snook to honor the postmaster, who arranged for the town to get its own post office.

The liveliest time to visit Snook is on the first Saturday in June, when it celebrates SnookFest, an event featuring a barbecue cookoff, antique farm equipment, and arts and crafts.

From Caldwell head east on FM 166 just over a mile to the intersection with FM 3058; turn right (southeast) on FM 3058 and continue until it dead-ends into FM 60. Then turn left and head north about 4 miles to Snook.

what to do

Slovacek Sausage Company. (800) 324-1361 or (979) 272-8625; www.slovacek.com. Slovacek has been cranking out tasty pork and beef sausage since 1957 in tiny Snook. The company has grown to become one of the premier sausage makers in the state. In addition to traditional beef and pork sausage, Slovacek now offers turkey sausage, hams, and hot jalapeño sausage. Most of their products can be purchased by phone and online.

where to eat

Czech-Tex BBQ, Steakhouse and Bakery. CR 269 in "downtown" Snook; (979) 272-8501; www.czech-tex.com. Texas favorites like chicken-fried steak, pit-cooked barbecue, and steaks share the menu with Czech dishes, including Czech-style sausage and Jaeger schnitzel, all served with homemade sauerkraut. Open Tues through Sat 11 a.m. to 2 p.m.; 5 p.m. to 9 p.m. $–$$.

Sodolak's Original Country Inn. 9711 FM 60; (979) 272-6002. Texas-size steaks, burgers, and chicken frieds fill the menu, but this restaurant's real claim to fame is its chicken-fried bacon. Featured on Texas Country Reporter, a television series, this dish features strips of raw bacon dipped in an egg batter, rolled in flour, then deep-fried to a golden crispiness that no doubt makes cardiologists cringe but keeps diners coming back for more. $–$$.

bryan–college station

From Snook, head northeast on FM 60 into College Station. Home of Texas A&M University, these adjoining communities are populated by 133,000 residents, and several attractions are of interest to travelers.

Bryan was chartered in 1855 in the area where early colonists led by Stephen F. Austin first settled. The agriculturally rich city still has an emphasis on farming thanks to Texas A&M University, the first public institution of higher learning in Texas. The college is well known for its agriculture, veterinary, and engineering programs, as well as its military Corps of Cadets.

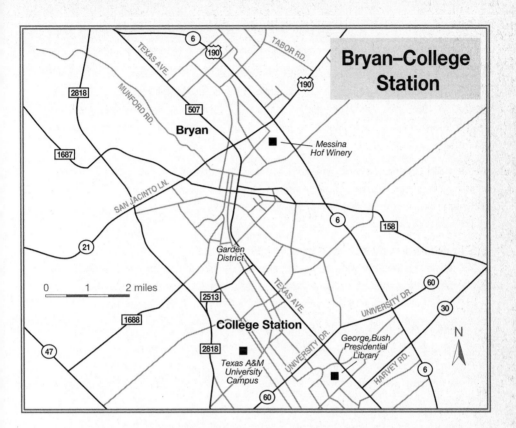

where to go

Benjamin Knox Gallery. 405 University Dr. East, College Station; (800) 299-5669 or (979) 696-5669; www.benjaminknox.com. This gallery features the work of Benjamin Knox, known locally as the "University Artist." Along with fine art, the gallery sells gift items. Open Tues through Sat 10 a.m. to 6 p.m.

Brazos Valley Museum of Natural History. 3232 Briarcrest Dr., Bryan; (979) 776-2195; www.bvmuseum.myriad.net. Bring the whole family to this collection of natural history with exhibits on life in the Brazos Valley more than 12,000 years ago. Open daily.

The Children's Museum of the Brazos Valley. 111 East 27th St., Bryan; (979) 779-KIDS; www.mymuseum.com. Teaching through hands-on exhibits, this museum gives kids the opportunity to do everything from shopping for groceries to creating a puppet show. Open Mon through Sat.

George Bush Presidential Library and Museum. 1000 West George Bush Dr., College Station; (979) 691-4000; www.bushlibrary.tamu.edu. The state's second presidential library contains exhibits on the first Bush presidency as well as research materials in the library center. Open daily.

Messina Hof Winery and Resort. 4545 Old Reliance Rd., Bryan; (979) 778-9463; www .messinahof.com. One of Texas's most celebrated wineries offers tours and tastings. Started in 1983, the winery includes 45 acres of vineyards and demonstrates the wine-making skills of the Messina, Italy, and Hof, Germany, regions. Public tours daily. Call for tour hours.

Texas A&M University. (979) 845-3211; www.tamu.edu. Several of the school's facilities here in College Station are of special interest to visitors, including the Floral Test Garden (Houston and Jersey Streets). Stroll among hundreds of varieties of flowers planted and studied by university students.

Appelt Aggieland Visitors Center. Rudder Tower in the Memorial Student Center Complex; (979) 845-5851; www.visit.tamu.edu. A good introduction to the A&M campus, the center offers tours, videos, and exhibits. Open Mon through Fri 8 a.m. to 5 p.m., Sat 9:30 a.m. to 3:30 p.m., Sun 1 p.m. to 4 p.m. Free admission.

Century Oak. In the central campus area near the Academic Building. One of the most beloved shrines on campus, this century-old live oak was among the first trees planted on campus. Over the years, generations of Aggies have gathered beneath its low hanging branches to celebrate engagements, weddings, and pose for photos. Free admission.

Sam Houston Sanders Corps of Cadets Center. (979) 862-2862; www.aggie corps.org/about-the-corps/sam-houston-sanders-corps-of-cadets-center.html. Learn more about the Corps of Cadets through College Station's displays that trace the graduates' service in World Wars I and II, Korea, Vietnam, the Gulf War, and more recent conflicts. Open Mon through Fri 8 a.m. to 5 p.m.

M. Benz Gallery of Floral Art. (979) 845-1699. Texas A&M University in the Horticultural and Forest Sciences Building on the west side of campus. This museum features everything related to floral art. Open weekdays. Free admission.

MSC Forsyth Center Galleries. 110 North Main St.; (979) 845-9251; www.forsyth .tamu.edu. This gallery features both touring exhibits and an extensive glass display. Open daily. Free admission.

J. Wayne Stark University Center Galleries. (979) 845-8501; www.stark.tamu .edu; Texas A&M University. Through 2012, the renovation of the Memorial Student Center has required the gallery to move from its normal location to a temporary site on the sixth floor of Evans Library, this gallery features Texas art and artists. Open Tues through Fri 10 a.m. to 6 p.m. Free admission.

Texas A&M Sports Museum. Bernard C. Richardson Zone at Kyle Field, Texas A&M campus; (979) 846-3024. The long tradition of Aggie sports is featured in this museum with exhibits that include not only all types of A&M sports, but also the Aggie band and interactive computers that display historical footage. Open Mon through Fri 9 a.m. to 5 p.m. and Sat afternoons during football games.

where to shop

The Garden District. 106–108 North Ave., Bryan. This unique shopping area is housed in a neo-antebellum home. Shops stock unique gift and specialty items including designer jewelry, candles, children's heirloom clothing, and collectibles. Open Mon through Sat.

The Texas Store. 1505 University Dr. East, Suite 120, College Station; (888) 693-2061 or (979) 691-2061; www.texasgiftitems.com. This shop features Texas goods from western hats to foods. Open daily.

where to eat

C&J Bar-B-Q Market. 4304 Harvey Rd., College Station; (979) 776-8969; www.cjbbq .com. This prize-winning restaurant has hundreds of loyal diners in the College Station area. Their specialties include beef, ribs, sausage, and chicken barbeque plates and sandwiches. Open Mon through Thurs 10:30 a.m. to 8:30 p.m., Fri and Sat 10:30 a.m. to 9 p.m., Sun 11 a.m. to 3 p.m. $$.

Cenare. 404 University Dr. East, College Station; (979) 696-7311; www.gotocenare.com. This restaurant features Italian cuisine ranging from veal marsala to homemade pastas. Open Mon through Thurs 11 a.m. to 2 p.m. and 5 p.m. to 9 p.m., Fri 11 a.m. to 2 p.m., Sat 5 p.m. to 9 p.m. $$–$$$.

Christopher's World Grille. 5001 Boonville Rd., Bryan; (979) 776-2181; www.christo phersworldgrille.com. Chef Christopher Lampo spent ten years wandering the globe before returning to his home region to restore a hundred-year-old ranch house and transform it into a fine dining destination. Mediterranean, South Pacific, and Louisiana touches grace the menu, which includes chile-cocoa rubbed ribeye on andouille sausage grits, Zihuatanejo snapper, and roasted halibut Provencale. Open for lunch and dinner daily; reservations encouraged. $$$.

where to stay

Hilton Hotel and Conference Center College Station. 801 University Dr. East, College Station; (979) 693-7500; www.hiltoncs.com. This hotel offers guests a pool, exercise facilities, restaurant, private balconies, and more. Located less than 2 miles from the Texas A&M campus. $$.

bonfire memorial

Throughout the state, the Texas Aggies had long been known for their pre-game bonfires, a tradition since 1909. On November 18, 1999, the tradition came to a halt when twelve students were killed by the collapse of the massive bonfire. To commemorate the fallen students and the longtime tradition, the university con-structed the Bonfire Memorial, a circular ring with doorways representing each of the lost students. The History Walk leading up to the memorial traces the tradi-tion's timeline, leading up to the 170-foot diameter circle representing the size of an actual Aggie bonfire. The memorial is located on the Polo Fields at the TAMU campus.

The Villa at Messina Hof Bed and Breakfast. 4545 Old Reliance Rd.; (979) 778-9463 ext. 222; www.messinahof.com. One of Texas's romantic bed-and-breakfast properties, guests enjoy an evening wine and cheese reception, European-style champagne breakfast and a winery tour. Featuring ten antiques-furnished guest rooms, it is a place where couples can enjoy an evening alone in the vineyards at this romantic hideaway. Book early for this popular getaway on weekends and holidays. $$$.

east

day trip 01

east

sausage country:
manor, elgin, mcdade, giddings, serbin

Driving from Austin's eastern side, you'll notice an abrupt change as the suburban environment melts away within a few miles and you find yourself in small-town Texas. The area is a major hotbed of barbecue culture centered around the town of Elgin, home of Elgin hot sausage.

manor

Manor was named for settler James Manor, who came to the state with Sam Houston. This community was a quiet suburb until Texas legalized pari-mutuel wagering. To reach Manor, drive east from Austin on US 290.

where to go

Manor Downs. 9211 Hill Lane; (512) 272-5581; www.manordowns.com. Just outside Manor, you'll find Manor Downs, Texas' oldest pari-mutuel horse racetrack, that holds quarter horse and thoroughbred races from late Feb through Mar and Apr; simulcast races are held daily except Tues. Call for race times.

elgin

Continue east from Manor on US 290 to Elgin. This city began as a railroad stop in 1872, named for the railroad commissioner. Often mispronounced (it rhymes with again), Elgin is

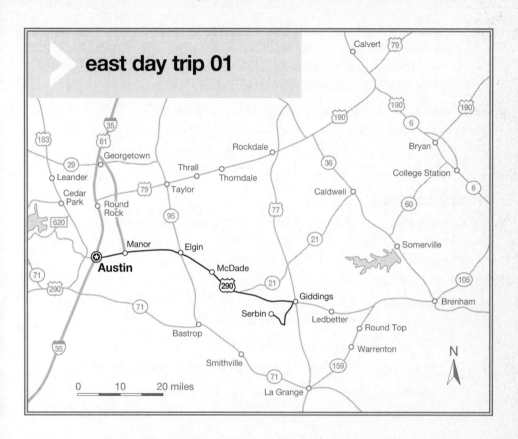

east day trip 01

known for two products: bricks and sausage. Red Elgin bricks are seen throughout Texas, and Elgin sausage is so prevalent that the city has been named by the Texas Legislature as the "Sausage Capital of Texas."

Much of the city lies along US 290, but its real history is found off the highway in its historic downtown. Named a Main Street City for its preservation efforts, the downtown is home to several renovated buildings that now house shops.

If some of those historic buildings look familiar, you might have seen them in the movies. Thanks to its proximity to Austin and its genuine small-town look, Elgin has appeared in many Hollywood productions, including *Texas Chainsaw Massacre, What's Eating Gilbert Grape, A Perfect World, Michael, Varsity Blues, Picnic, The Alamo,* and *Friday Night Lights.*

where to go

Historic Tour. Pick up a copy of the free historic tour brochure at the Chamber of Commerce office (512-285-4515) at 114 Central Ave. Or download a walking-tour brochure by visiting www.elgintx.com (see "Tourism Info"). This self-guided tour takes travelers past historic points such as the 1903 Union Depot, now home to the Elgin Depot Museum with information on the town's railroad history; the 1906 Nofsinger House, a Victorian home that now serves as Elgin City Hall; and past "ghost signs" that once advertised businesses such as Owl Cigars. 22 sites on the tour are within walking distance and others such as original home of Southside Market, built in 1882, are further afield.

Union Depot Museum. Depot Square at Main Street; (512) 285-2000; www.elgintx.com. Operated by the Elgin Historical Association, this former depot now houses displays on the town's early days and includes a photo collection and archives. Open Tues through Sun, 2 p.m. to 5 p.m.

where to shop

Elgin Antique Mall. 195 US 290; (512) 281-5655. This multi-dealer mall is filled with all things antique and collectible, from furniture to dolls to housewares. The merchandise changes continually, brought to the mall by more than fifty dealers. Open daily 10 a.m. to 6 p.m.

Meyer's Elgin Sausage. 188 US 290; (512) 281-5546. Stop here to buy a gift box or a freezer full of Elgin's most famous product: sausage.

hot guts

Yes, it's true; Elgin sausage is sometimes (make that often) referred to as Elgin Hot Guts. No, it's not an appetizing moniker. Nonetheless, this spicy sausage is the standard against which other Texas sausages are judged.

We both grew up cutting our teeth on the hot links, a staple at Sunday dinners, picnics, and any special event throughout the state. The best-known of Elgin's smokin' stops is the Southside Market (1212 US 290 West), probably one of the most recognized names in Texas barbecue lore. In business since 1882, the market is known for its sausage. The mainstay in many barbecue restaurants around the state, the Southside's product is what many people have in mind when they order sausage. Spicy but not hot, the concoction is all beef.

For generations, Southside was located in a smoky den that spoke volumes about the history of barbecue. Sadly, the business outgrew its old home and now sits in a red tin building with a concrete floor—less atmospheric but now one of the largest barbecue restaurants in the state. The building may have changed, but the product remains the same. It's one we pick up fresh whenever we pass through Elgin; the smoky scent serves as a fragrant billboard long before you reach the Southside building.

where to eat

City Cafe. 19 North Main St.; (512) 281-3663. Stop by for the buffet lunch at this downtown diner that serves up traditional small-town cookin' at its best. $.

Meyer's Elgin Sausage. 188 US 290; (512) 281-5546 or (800) MRS-OINK; www.cuetopia texas.com. Since 1949 this sausage has been a regional favorite. The restaurant includes plenty of sausage as well as smoked turkey, ribs, and more. You can also purchase gift boxes of Meyer's sausage to go. Open Mon through Thurs 10 a.m. to 8 p.m., Fri and Sat 10 a.m. to 9 p.m., Sun 10 a.m. to 7 p.m. $.

Southside Market and B-B-Q. 1212 US 290 West; (877) 285-3407 or (512) 285-3407; www.southsidemarket.com. This casual barbecue eatery has been the source of Elgin sausage since 1882. Although the market has moved from its original downtown location, the dining room is still filled with Formica tables, the smell of smoke, and happy customers. Open Mon through Thurs 8 a.m. to 8 p.m., Fri and Sat 8 a.m. to 10 p.m., Sun 9 a.m. to 7 p.m. $.

mcdade

About 8 miles outside of Elgin lies the small community of McDade. The town has always depended heavily on farming and ranching. The town is especially noted for its watermelon crop, but its claim to fame was its role in the TV miniseries *True Women.* An annual watermelon festival is a big draw to the area.

where to go

Annual Watermelon Festival at the McDade Fairgrounds. 143 Bastrop St.; (512) 273-0018. The festival includes prizes for the largest watermelon and best watermelon seed spitting, as well as for bingo and horseshoe and washer pitching competitions. Other activities include a grand parade through downtown McDade, a car show, live music, and food vendors. Festivities conclude with a barbecue dinner and the crowning of the Watermelon Queen. Held the second Saturday in July.

giddings

From McDade, continue east on US 290 to Giddings. This town began as a railroad community in the 1870s. At that time, most of the residents of Giddings were Wendish immigrants (Germans of Slavic descent); these founders later moved to the community of Serbin. Today Giddings remains a quiet railroad town, although oil production has taken over as the major economic activity.

where to go

Fireman's Park. 2 miles west of Giddings on US 290. This park includes an RV park, picnic grounds, ball field, adjacent rodeo grounds, and even an antique carousel. The carousel, restored by local citizens, was left in Giddings during the Depression by a traveling carnival as a debt payment. Today it is run only during city events. Open daily. Free admission.

Lee County Museum. Grimes and Industry Streets. This small museum contains numerous local history displays. It is located in the former house of a pioneer doctor. Open Tues and Fri afternoons 2 to 5 p.m. No phone.

where to shop

Lee County Coop General Store. US 290 West; (979) 542-3188; www.leecountygeneral store.com. Owned locally by a farmer's coop, this is a true general store selling everything from livestock feed to gifts and clothing. It's also the scene of a farmer's market Wed and Sat. The store is open Mon through Fri 7:30 a.m. to 6 p.m. and Sat 7:30 a.m. to 4 p.m.

serbin

Turn south on US 77, then south again on FM 448, continuing for 5 miles. At the intersection with FM 2239, turn right and continue 2 miles to the hamlet of Serbin.

This town was settled by the Wendish, who came to Texas in the 1850s and brought with them the Gothic architecture of their homeland. From 1865 to 1890 this was a thriving town, boasting dry goods, jewelry, music stores, a drug store, three doctors, and two dentists. When Serbin was bypassed by the railroad, it quickly declined.

where to go

St. Paul Lutheran Church. Off FM 2239 on CR 211; (979) 366-9650. This historic church, a smaller version of the elaborate German cathedrals of the 18th and 19th centuries, was built in 1859 of native sandstone. To replicate marble, the parishioners skillfully painted the plaster walls using turkey-feather brushes creating a faux-stone effect. This church once had an unusual seating arrangement: Men sat in the balcony and women and children took the pews on the floor. Open daily. Free admission.

Texas Wendish Heritage Museum. Off FM 2239 on CR 211, near St. Paul Lutheran Church adjacent to the Wendish Cemetery; (979) 366-2441; www.texaswendish.com. You'll find antique furniture and household items as well as photos of the early days in this local history museum. Open Tues through Sun 1 p.m. to 5 p.m. Under fourteen free.

day trip 02

east

birthplace of texas:
ledbetter, carmine, burton, brenham,
independence, washington-on-the-brazos

This day trip is an extension of East Day Trip 01, for travelers looking for a longer getaway. This trip is filled with early Texas history including the location of the first Texas capital in Washington-on-the Brazos. Begin by taking US 290 East from Austin beyond Elgin and Giddings, following a route nicknamed the Presidential Corridor.

ledbetter

From Giddings, drive east on US 290 for 9 miles to the tiny community of Ledbetter. Once the first town in the county to boast a railroad, its importance declined when nearby La Grange became a freight center.

where to go

Stuermer Store. South side of US 290; (979) 249-3066. This metal building has served as a general store since 1870. At one time, the current owner's grandfather ran a saloon next door. Now the businesses are joined, creating a general store, museum, and soda shop all in one. A working museum exhibits the tools of the early grocery, from cheese cutters to coffee grinders. Today the wildest drink in the saloon is an old-fashioned malt. You can order up some local Blue Bell ice cream or fresh sandwiches at the fountain and listen to free tunes on a jukebox packed with oldies. Open Mon through Sat. Free admission.

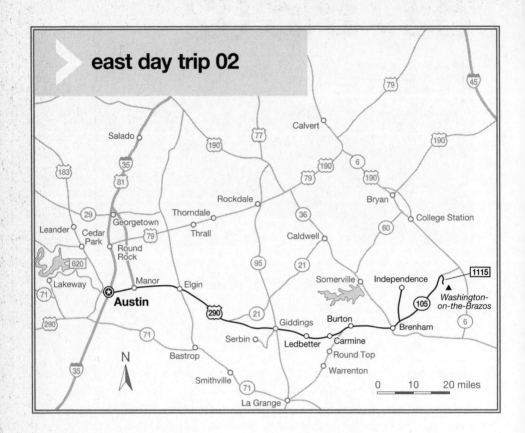

carmine

Continue east on US 290 to the community of Carmine, covered in Southeast Day Trip 02 and best known for its participation in the Round Top area's Antiques Week sales.

burton

Follow US 290 to the tiny agricultural community of Burton, located just off US 290 on FM 390. With a population of slightly more than 300, this town has a surprising number of shops and businesses, many open only on weekends.

Take some time to walk around the historic buildings and drop in to the Burton Cafe. Here you can make arrangements for a guide to take you on a tour of the restored cotton gin, railroad depot, and old caboose.

where to go

Burton Cotton Gin and Museum. 307 North Main St., across from the Burton Cafe; (979) 289-3378; www.cottonginmuseum.org. Stop in the Burton Cafe to arrange a forty-five-minute tour of this restored gin, a Texas Historic Landmark. You'll see the engine room, the mechanical floor, the ginning floor, and an old cobbler shop where harnesses were made for the horses that pulled the cotton wagons. Tours can be conducted in German. The site also includes the historic Wehring Shoe and Leather Shop, the Wehring House, and the Cotton Warehouse. Open Tues through Sat 10 a.m. to 4 p.m.

brenham

Return to US 290 and continue east to Brenham. In this state, Brenham is synonymous with Blue Bell ice cream, one of the biggest independent ice cream manufacturers in the country, selling more than 25 million half-gallon containers a year. It's as Texan as bluebonnets and two-stepping, and expatriates have been known to carry back picnic freezers full of Brenham's product.

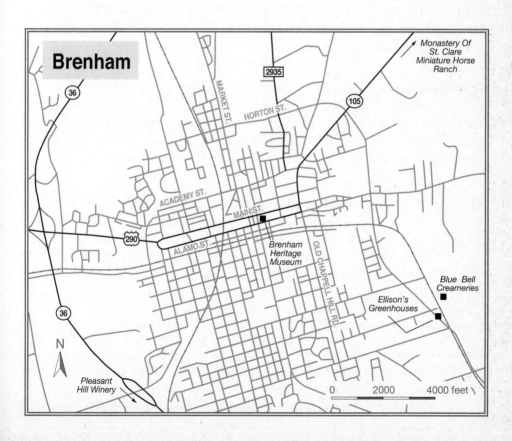

Brenham has a host of other less-fattening attractions as well, including a historic downtown that's filled with antiques and specialty shops, and residential streets that show-case splendid antebellum and Victorian homes.

A free visitors' guide of historic sites is available from the Washington County Chamber of Commerce, 314 South Austin St. in Brenham; (888) BRENHAM or (979) 836-3695.

where to go

Blue Bell Creameries. Loop 577 off US 290 West; (800) 327-8135 or (979) 830-2197; www.bluebell.com. Blue Bell has been making ice cream since 1911, when it packaged its product in wooden tubs and delivered it by horse-drawn wagon. The "tasting room" here is an antique soda shop where visitors can choose from among twenty-five flavors. After a free dish of your personal favorite, you can have a look around the Country Store, which sells everything from strawberry-scented pencils to piggy banks in the shape of the company's early delivery trucks. Note that cameras are not permitted on tours. Open daily. Tours conducted Mon through Fri; call for times.

Brenham Heritage Museum. Main and Market Streets; (979) 830-8445; www.brenham heritagemuseum.org. This museum, housed in a historic post office building, features the history of Brenham and Washington County through permanent and rotating displays. Next to the museum a Silsby steam fire engine from the late 1800s is on display. Open Wed 1 p.m. to 4 p.m., Thurs through Sat 10 a.m. to 4 p.m. Free admission.

Ellison's Greenhouses. 2107 Stone St., south of Blue Bell Creameries on Loop 577; (979) 836-6011; www.ellisonsgreenhouses.com. Ellison's produces African violets, Easter lilies, mums, tulips, and many other decorative flowers. Every year it grows 250,000 poinsettia cuttings and 80,000 finished poinsettias, some of which find their way to the State Capitol and Governor's Mansion. Open Mon through Sat 8 a.m. to 6 p.m., Sat and Sun 10 a.m. to 5 p.m. Fee for guided tours.

Monastery of St. Clare Miniature Horse Ranch. TX 105, 9 miles northeast of Brenham; (979) 836-9652; www.monasteryminiaturehorses.com. This monastery is occupied by a group of Catholic nuns who raise and sell miniature horses to support themselves. The tiny horses, some less than 34 inches tall, bring in anywhere from $3,000 to $30,000. On self-guided tours visitors see the barn and grooming facilities (with miniature carriages and harnesses) and the Mini Mansion where the horses are reared. The Art Barn brims with thousands of ceramics made by the nuns, including tiny reproductions of the horses. Open Tues through Sat 1:30 to 4 p.m.

Pleasant Hill Winery. 1441 Salem Rd., just south of US 290 and TX 36 intersection; (979) 830-VINE; www.pleasanthillwinery.com. Travel just a few hundred yards west and a hillside vineyard will appear. Free tours and tastings are offered inside the carefully reconstructed old barn at the top of the hill. Enjoy the spectacular view of the vineyard below. Spend some time studying the corkscrew collection and winery artifacts, or just enjoy the warmth and beauty of the barn's interior. The tour will take you through the path of the grape as it makes its transformation from vine to wine. Gift shop with Texas wines and souvenirs for sale. Open Sat 11 a.m. to 6 p.m. and Sun noon to 5 p.m. Groups may request other tour times by appointment.

where to stay

The Brenham area is home to more than thirty bed-and-breakfasts, many located in historic homes or on local farms. The city also has several motels. For more information on accommodations, call (979) 836-3695; write Brenham–Washington County Convention and Visitor Bureau, 314 South Austin St., Brenham, TX 77833; or visit www.brenhamtexas.com.

Ant Street Inn. 107 West Commerce St.; (800) 481-1951; www.antstreetinn.com. Located in the Ant Street Historic District, this historic structure includes fifteen guest rooms. The on-site rooms each include individual climate control, wireless high-speed Internet service, polished hardwood floors, and antique furnishings. $$–$$$.

The Inn at Nueces Canyon Ranch. 9501 US 290 West; (800) 925-5058 or (979) 289-5600; www.nuecescanyon.com. This expansive equestrian center offers group activities on a working ranch. Guests can watch cutting horses at work, enjoy a hayride, and relax with a barbecue dinner. The center also hosts cutting-horse shows most weekends. Accommodations are available as well. Advance reservations are required for all tours and activities. $$.

James Walker Homestead. Old Chappell Hill Rd., a few miles east of Brenham; (979) 836-6717. This structure was built in 1826 as the home of James Walker, one of the first 300 colonists who came to Texas with Stephen F. Austin. Today the original log construction is still visible inside the home, which is furnished with Texas antiques. The bed-and-breakfast does not allow children, and no smoking is permitted in the house. Lodging includes one bedroom with sleeper bed for extra guests. $$$.

independence

From Brenham, head east on TX 105 then turn north on FM 50 to reach the community of Independence. This historic town, founded in 1835, served as the original home to Baylor University; Sam Houston and his family also resided here. Today the town works hard to preserve its historic roots with many projects sponsored by the nonprofit Independence Preservation Trust. If you'd like to leave your car and tour Independence by bicycle, you'll also find a self-guided bike tour at www.independencetx.com that travels along rural roads to many of the community's historic sites as well as scenic views of the Brazos River Valley.

The Antique Rose Emporium. 10,000 FM 50 (head northeast from Brenham on TX 105, then turn north on FM 50 and continue for 9 miles); (800) 441-0002 or (979) 836-5548;

www.antiqueroseemporium.com. This display garden showcases the many products of the emporium, and a nursery specializing in historic types of roses. You'll find varieties that once graced early Texas homes such as "Adam," considered the first of the tea roses and dating to 1838, and the even older "Archduke Charles," whose flowers change colors in the heat of the Texas sun. The display gardens include historic structures, cottage gardens, herb gardens, and more. Open Mon through Sat 9 a.m. to 6 p.m. and Sun 11 a.m. to 5:30 p.m.

John P. Coles Home Tours, Independence. (979) 830-0230; www.independencetx .com. Guided tours of the area's earliest homes (built during the days of independence) are available on weekends during spring months and by appointment at other times. The tours include a look at early dogtrot cabins, a 1900 one-room schoolhouse, and more. Tours on some March and April weekends or by appointment.

Texas Baptist Historical Center-Museum. (979) 836-5117. 12 miles north of Brenham at the intersection of FM 50 and FM 390 in Independence. This Baptist church, once attended by Sam Houston, is one of the state's oldest Baptist churches as well as the birthplace of Baylor University. Open Tues through Sat 9 a.m. to 4 p.m. Free admission.

washington-on-the-brazos

To reach this community, also known as Washington, take TX 105 northeast of Brenham for 14 miles, then turn right on FM 912.

The town dates to the days of a ferry landing on the Brazos River that operated at the site from 1822. Washington has become best known, however, as the birthplace of Texas. On a cold March day in 1836, founders gathered here and signed the Texas Declaration of Independence, establishing the state as a sovereign nation.

From 1842 to 1845, Washington served as the capital of the republic, also gradually becoming a commerce center on the busy Brazos. When the seat of government was moved to Austin, the town hung on, kept alive by its position on the river. Eventually, though, in the 1850s, Washington was bypassed by the railroads, and the community dwindled to a tiny dot on the map.

One of the hidden treasures of the Texas parks system is the Washington-on-the-Brazos State Historical Park. Today the park includes a visitor center and interpretive trails that introduce visitors to the importance of this site where the early Texans declared an independent and sovereign nation.

Near the center, the Star of the Republic Museum, built in the shape of a star, highlights the history of the Republic of Texas with exhibits and special collections. Exhibits cover all aspects of commerce during the nineteenth century, including displays on the general store, blacksmithing, steamboats, and carpentry.

The park's interpretive trail winds from Independence Hall—a replica of the original building where the signing of the Texas Declaration of Independence took place—to the historic Washington town site. To reach Washington-on-the-Brazos State Historical Park from Brenham, take TX 105 northeast of the city for 14 miles, then turn right on FM 912 to reach the park. The facility is open daily from 8 a.m. to sundown.

where to go

Washington-on-the-Brazos State Historical Park. Between Brenham and Navsota off TX 105 on FM 105; (936) 878-2214; www.birthplaceoftexas.com. Located on the banks of the Brazos, this quiet park is shaded by acres of walnut and pecan trees. This is a day-use park, with picnic tables along the river. Free admission to the park; admission for specific sites. Combination tickets for multiple sites at the park are available at any site or at the Visitor Center. Its main sections include the following points of interest:

Visitor's Center. (936) 878-2214. Features interactive exhibits highlighting the historic attractions located within the park. Also includes the Washington Emporium gift shop. Tickets to the park's main attractions can be purchased here. Open daily 9:30 a.m. to 5 p.m.

Barrington Living History Farm. (936) 878-2214. This was once the home of Anson Jones, the fourth and last president of the Republic of Texas. A self-guided tour of the site includes a two-story home that has been relocated, an orchard, a demonstration garden, a carriage shed, a corn crib, a kitchen, and more. Open daily 10 a.m. to 5 p.m.

Independence Hall. (936) 878-2214. The original building where the signing of the Texas Declaration of Independence took place did not survive the 19th century. In 1901 a group of citizens erected a monument at the site. The simple frame building reconstructed here holds long, mismatched tables and unadorned chairs. Fifty-minute guided tours are available; call to confirm tour times. Open daily (check the Visitor's Center for tour times and prices).

Star of the Republic Museum. (936) 878-2461; www.starmuseum.org. Built in the shape of the Lone Star State, this museum covers the republic period. Visitors can start with a twenty-minute film narrated by Bill Moyers for an overview of the period. Upstairs, exhibits cover all aspects of commerce during the 19th century, including displays on the general store, steamboats, blacksmithing, and carpentry. Open daily 10 a.m. to 5 p.m.

southeast

day trip 01

southeast

lost pines:
bastrop, cedar creek, smithville,
la grange

One of Texas's natural anomalies, the Lost Pines forest is the westernmost stand of loblolly pines in America. Scientists believe that these trees were once part of the forests of East Texas, but climatic changes over the last 10,000 years account for the farmland now separating the Lost Pines from their cousins to the east.

bastrop

To reach Bastrop, take TX 71 southeast from Austin. Unlike the juniper-dotted hills to the west or the rolling farmland to the east, the Bastrop area is surrounded by a pine forest called Lost Pines. Bastrop holds the honor as one of the oldest settlements in the state, built in 1829 along the Camino Real, a road also known as the King's Highway and the Old San Antonio Road. This was the western edge of the "Little Colony" established by Stephen F. Austin. Settlers came by the wagonload from around the country to claim a share of this fertile land and to establish homes in this dangerous territory. Even as houses were being built, Indian raids continued in this area for many years.

Bastrop is a popular day trip for Austinites looking for a chance to shop and savor some quiet country life in a historic setting. Outdoor-lovers can enjoy two nearby state parks as well as the Colorado River, which winds through the heart of downtown. Canoe rentals and guided trips along the river are available.

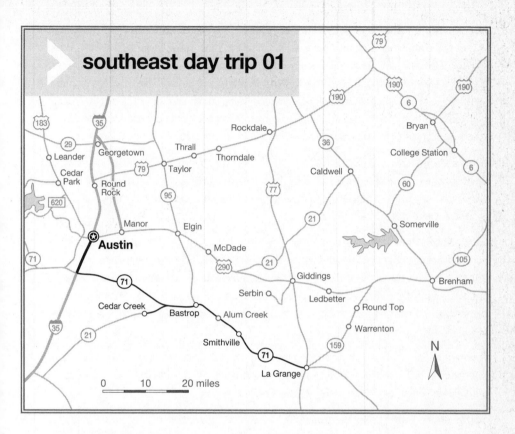

southeast day trip 01

where to go

Bastrop "Old Town" Visitor Center. 1016 Main St.; (512) 303-0904; www.visitbastrop .org. Located in the old lobby of the 1889 First National Bank building, this official visitor center has information on Bastrop attractions, accommodations, and events. Open daily.

Bastrop County Historical Society Museum. 702 Main St.; (512) 303-0057. This 1850 frame cabin contains Indian relics and pioneer exhibits. Open Mon through Fri 1 p.m. to 5 p.m., Sat 10 a.m. to 2 p.m.

Bastrop Opera House. 711 Spring St.; (512) 321-6283; www.bastropoperahouse.com. Built in 1889, this building was once the entertainment center of town. After a major renovation in 1978, it's again the cultural center of Bastrop, the site for live theater ranging from mysteries to vaudeville.

Bastrop State Park. TX 21, 1.5 miles east of Bastrop; (512) 321-2101 or (512) 389-8900; www.tpwd.state.tx.us. Beautiful piney woods are the main draw at this 3,500-acre park, the fourth-busiest state park in Texas. Facilities include an eighteen-hole golf course, campsites, and a ten-acre fishing lake. The 1930s-built stone and cedar cabins are very popular, so book well in advance. They feature fireplaces, bathrooms, and kitchen facilities. Guided bus tours every other Saturday during summer months introduce visitors to the park's unique ecology and to an endangered resident, the Houston toad.

Lock's Drug. 1003 Main St.; (512) 321-2422. This drugstore features an antique mirrored fountain where you can belly up for a thick, creamy malt. Built-in cabinets are still labeled with the names of their original contents, and old apothecary tools are displayed in the front windows. Open daily except Sun.

North Shore Park. Lake Bastrop. (800) 776-5272; www.lcra.org. 3 miles east of Bastrop and 40 miles east of Austin. From Austin, take TX 71 east to Bastrop and travel north on TX 95. After 2 miles, turn right on FM 1441. Travel approximately 4 miles and the park entrance is on the right. Day travelers and overnight campers can use the park. Facilities include campsites, RV sites, group pavilions, a two-lane boat ramp, a fishing pier, playgrounds, trails, and more. Open daily.

Riverwalk. Enjoy this nature walk along the banks of the Colorado River. Opened in 1998, the half-mile trail features a variety of trees, native plants, and wildflowers. It is accessible from either Fisherman's Park or Ferry Park. Free admission.

South Shore Park, Lake Bastrop. (800) 776-5272; www.lcra.org. Take TX 71 east to Bastrop and travel north on TX 95. After traveling about 1.5 miles, take TX 21 east and travel about 3 miles to South Shore Road (CR 352). Turn left on South Shore Road. Park entrance is on the right. This popular Lower Colorado River Authority (LCRA) park includes restrooms, showers, a group facility, hike/bike trails, picnic facilities, and a boat ramp. Open daily.

where to shop

Park your car and enjoy an afternoon of browsing through the many antiques and specialty stores along Main Street.

Apothecary's Hall. 805 Main St.; (512) 321-3022. Shop in this downtown store for antiques ranging from collectibles to furniture.

where to eat

Maxine's on Main. 905 Main St.; (512) 303-0919; www.maxinesonmain.com. Open for breakfast, lunch and dinner, Maxine's has become a beloved fixture in downtown Bastrop. The restaurant is known for its griddle cakes, burgers, chili, and homemade pie. Live music is featured every Friday evening. Open Mon through Thurs 7 a.m. to 2 p.m., Fri 7 a.m. to 9 p.m., Sat 7 a.m. to 9 p.m., Sun 7 a.m. to 2 p.m. $–$$.

where to stay

Bastrop State Park. TX 21, 1.5 miles east of Bastrop; (512) 321-2101 or (512) 389-8900; www.tpwd.state.tx.us. These picturesque stone and cedar cabins were built in the 1930s by the Civilian Conservation Corps from native materials. They feature rustic fireplaces, bathrooms, and kitchen facilities. Note: due to their popularity, cabins should be booked well in advance.

cedar creek

Originally a small town located 11 miles west of Bastrop, the Cedar Creek area has spread north, reaching TX 71. The town was first settled in the 1830s as a farming community tucked between piney woods and blackland prairies. Cedar Creek's early population peaked at around 600 in the late 1800s when it became a shipping terminal for cotton and other agriculture. Although some petroleum deposits were discovered in the early 1900s, the town gradually declined until recent times when suburban development from Bastrop began to rapidly populate the Cedar Creek area.

where to go

Central Texas Museum of Automotive History. South on FM 304 to FM 535; left 1 mile to Rosanky; (512) 237-2635; www.ctmah.org. This private museum is dedicated to the collection and preservation of old cars and accessories. The vehicles on display include a 1935 Rolls-Royce Phantom, a La France fire engine, and a 1922 Franklin. Open Apr 1 to Sept 30: Wed through Sat: 10 a.m. to 5 p.m.; Oct 1 to Mar 31: Fri and Sat 10 a.m. to 5 p.m., Sun 1:30 p.m. to 5 p.m.

The Dinosaur Park. 893 Union Chapel Rd.; (512) 321-6262; www.thedinopark.com. This attraction features—you guessed it—life-sized dinosaur replicas in an outdoor setting that kids will enjoy. Other activities include a fossil-dig, playground, picnic area, and a Dinosaur Store. Open Sat and Sun 10 a.m. to 4 p.m.

McKinney Roughs Nature Park. (512) 303-5073; www.lcra.org. 8 miles west of Bastrop at 1884 TX 71. A favorite with both hikers and equestrians, this 1,100-acre park preserves several ecosystems as well as an extensive riverbank. Open Mon through Sat 8 a.m. to 5 p.m., Sun noon to 5 p.m.

where to stay

Hyatt Regency Lost Pines Resort and Spa. 575 Hyatt Lost Pines Rd.; (13 miles east of Austin-Bergstrom International Airport on TX 71); (512) 308-1234; www.lostpines.hyatt .com. Opened in 2006, this luxury resort offers 491 guest rooms and a distinctive central Texas atmosphere. The hotel spans over 400 acres and offers an equestrian center, an Arthur Hills–designed golf course, rafting on the Colorado River, supervised children's programs, a full-service spa, and more. $$$.

where to shop

Berdoll Pecan Candy and Gift Company. 2626 TX 71 West; (800) 518-3870; www .berdollpecanfarm.com. For nearly 30 years this unique shop on TX 71 has sold all things pecan, from the nuts themselves (grown in their own pecan orchards located nearby) to pies, candies, and a myriad of other items. If you happen by when they are closed, never fear, a vending machine on the front porch sells several of their items, including pecan pies! Open daily 9 a.m. to 5:30 p.m. in fall and winter, 9 a.m. to 7 p.m. in spring and summer.

smithville

Continue east from Bastrop on TX 71 to Smithville, a small town built alongside the railroad tracks at the edge of the piney woods and home of Buescher State Park. Smithville was once a riverboat ferry stop on the Colorado. In the 1880s, the railroad replaced the ferries as the main mode of transportation, and tracks were laid across town. Today the railroad still plays an important part in Smithville's economy.

Smithville was the backdrop for the Sandra Bullock movie *Hope Floats.* Many local citizens had small parts in the film.

where to go

Buescher State Park. 3 miles north of town, via TX 71 and FM 2104, or access from Park Road 1; (512) 237-2241; www.tpwd.state.tx.us. Buescher (pronounced "BISH-er") neighbors Bastrop State Park, but the two boast different environments. Oaks dominate this park, along with a few pines. The park is especially popular for its 30-acre lake. Visitors can enjoy ample campsites and screened shelters, as well as a playground and picnic area.

Railroad Museum and Depot. 100 West First St.; (512) 237-2313. Built beside the tracks, this park has two cabooses and a depot relocated here from West Point, a community east of town. The Chamber of Commerce office is housed adjacent to the depot as well. Open Mon through Sat 10 a.m. to 5 p.m. Free admission.

Rocky Hill Ranch Mountain Bike Resort. FM 153, 2 miles northeast of Buescher State Park; (512) 718-8822; www.rockyhillranch.net. Beginner, intermediate, advanced, and expert trails tempt mountain bikers with more than 1,200 acres that include gentle slopes and challenging grades as well as stream crossings. More than 25 miles of trails are available for use by helmeted bicycle riders. The ranch includes a casual restaurant with horseshoes, shuffleboard, and beach volleyball; campsites are available along small creeks and spring-fed water holes.

Smithville Heritage House Museum. 602 Main St.; (512) 237-4545. This 1908 home contains the Smithville archives and a museum of local memorabilia. Open Tuesday mornings. Free admission.

Vernon L. Richards Riverbend Park. TX 71 where it crosses the Colorado River, just north of Smithville; (800) 776-5272 or (512) 237-2343 for campsite reservations; www.lcra .org. The park entrance is located off the highway shoulder on the westbound side of the highway. This LCRA park includes restrooms, a group facility, hike/bike trails, kids' playground, picnic facilities, and a boat ramp. Open daily for day use and camping.

where to shop

Izadora's Antiques & Vintage. 116 Main St.; (512) 237-2600. Izadora's has a unique specialty: vintage garden items, as well as other unusual items from days gone by. Open Thurs through Mon 11 a.m. to 5 p.m.

la grange

Just 4 miles southeast of Smithville on the left side of TX 71 is a scenic overlook, an excellent place to pull over for a picnic. From here you can gaze at the miles of rolling hills and farmland that attracted many German and Czech immigrants a century ago.

Continue on TX 71 to the somewhat infamous community of La Grange. For generations this was a quiet town in the center of a farming region. In the 1970s, however, La Grange caught the attention of the public with the unveiling of the Chicken Ranch, a brothel that became the subject of the Broadway musical and movie *The Best Little Whorehouse in Texas*. The Chicken Ranch is gone now, but La Grange still has other sights to see.

where to go

Fayette Heritage Museum and Archives. 855 South Jefferson St.; (979) 968-6418. Housed with the public library, this museum contains displays on the area's rich history. Open Tues through Sat; call for hours. Free admission.

Lukas Bakery. 135 N. Main St.; (979) 968-3052. Since 1947, this landmark bakery has been turning out fragrant delights like bread, kolaches, pigs in the blanket and ana bars. Open Mon through Sat 5 a.m. to 1 p.m.

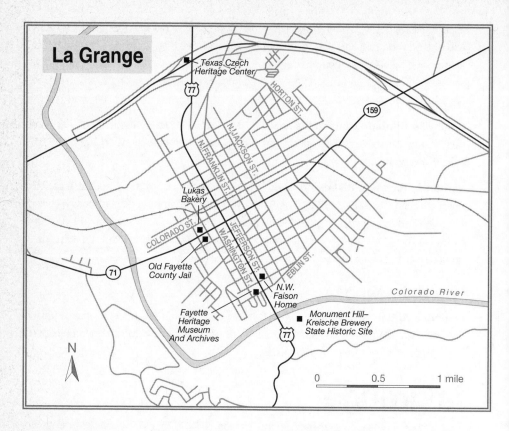

La Grange

Texas Czech Heritage Center

77

159

HORTON ST.

N. JACKSON ST.

N. FRANKLIN ST.

Lukas Bakery

COLORADO ST.

JEFFERSON ST.

WASHINGTON ST.

EBLIN ST.

71

Old Fayette County Jail

N.W. Faison Home

Colorado River

Fayette Heritage Museum And Archives

Monument Hill– Kreische Brewery State Historic Site

77

N

0   0.5   1 mile

Monument Hill–Kreische Brewery State Historic Site. US 77, 1 mile south of La Grange; (979) 968-5658; www.tpwd.state.tx.us. Located on a 200-foot bluff high above town, this site is home to two combined parks.

The Kreische Brewery State Historic Site recalls a far more cheerful time in Texas history. Heinreich Kreische, who immigrated here from Germany, purchased the hilltop and the adjoining land in 1849, including the burial ground of those Texas heroes, for his brewery site. Before closing the brewery in 1884, Kreische became the third-largest beer producer in the state. Open daily 8 a.m. to 5 p.m. One admission covers both adjacent sites.

Monument Hill Historical Park is the burial site for the Texans who died in the Dawson Massacre and the Mier Expedition, two historic Mexican conflicts that occurred in 1842, six years after the Texas Revolution. The Dawson Massacre took place near San Antonio when La Grange citizen Nicholas Dawson gathered Texans to halt continual Mexican attacks. Dawson's men were met by hundreds of Mexican troops, and thirty-five Texans were killed.

The Mexican village of Mier was attacked in a retaliatory move, resulting in the capture of Texas soldiers and citizens by Mexico's General Santa Anna, who ordered every tenth man to be killed. The Texans were blindfolded and forced to draw beans: 159 of them white and 17 black. Men who drew white beans were imprisoned; those who drew black ones were executed.

Muster Oak. Northeast corner of Courthouse Square. Beneath this historic oak tree, Captain Dawson gathered 53 troops to join the Texas-Mexican Revolution in 1842.

N. W. Faison Home. 822 South Jefferson St.; (979) 968-5756; www.faisonhouse.org. N. W. Faison was a survivor of both the Dawson Massacre and the Mier Expedition. The Faison family resided in this home for more than twenty years, and today it contains the family's furniture as well as exhibits from the Mexican War. Open by appointment.

Oak Thicket Park. (979) 249-3504; www.lcra.org. From La Grange travel east on TX 159 for about 7 miles. Turn right at the sign for Fayette County Lake. This 65-acre park offers plenty of family-oriented activities: a playground, fishing piers, and a good swimming area on Lake Fayette. Camping is available, as well as eight cabins.

Old Fayette County Jail and Visitors Center. 171 South Main St.; (800) 524-7264; www .lagrangetourism.com/History/History-Jailhouse.html. Now the home of the La Grange Area Chamber of Commerce, this historic building once housed the Fayette County Jail, serving in that role for a century. Open weekdays 8 a.m. to 5 p.m. Free admission.

Park Prairie Park. (979) 249-3504; www.lcra.org. From La Grange travel 10 miles east on TX 159 to the park entrance. Located on 2,000-acre Lake Fayette, Park Prairie is another favorite with families, thanks to volleyball courts, plenty of picnic space, tent camping, and even some pelicans and gulls along the shores of the lake. Hikers can walk to Oak Thicket Park on a 3-mile trail. Other facilities include restrooms, showers, a group facility, and a boat ramp.

Texas Czech Heritage and Cultural Center. 250 West Fairgrounds Rd.; (888) 785-4500 or (979) 968-9399; www.lagrangetourism.com/History/History-Texas-Czech.html. Located near the fairgrounds, this home, with its original hardwood floors, now contains displays about the region's Czech history. Exhibits are in English and Czech. Plans are under way for the construction of the Texas Polka Music Museum at the site as well, to include costumes and memorabilia about the Czech, Polish, and German musicians who entertained in the region. Open weekdays 10 a.m. to 4 p.m. and on weekends by appointment.

White Rock Park. (979) 968-5805; www.lcra.org. On the east bank of the Colorado River, just south of La Grange. From La Grange, take US 77 (Jefferson Street) south to Elbin Road, and continue about three-quarters of a mile to Mode Lane (CR 134). Take a right on Mode Lane and travel about a quarter mile to this park that was developed by the LCRA but is

the chicken ranch

La Grange drew international attention in 1973 when the story of what many believe was the country's oldest continuously run brothel was exposed by consumer affairs reporter Marvin Zindler from KTRK-TV in Houston. The report would inspire a Broadway musical and movie as well as lot of curiosity about the site, which was located on eleven acres outside of La Grange. The house, which was added on to many times as the number of women increased, was nicknamed the Chicken Ranch during the Great Depression. When customers grew more scarce, the proprietor, a woman known as Miss Jessie, began allowing men to pay in chickens. Soon the ranch was overrun with both poultry and eggs, both of which they sold locally.

As economic times improved, the ranch returned to a cash basis. Ownership changed in 1952 to Edna Milton, a madam who become one of La Grange's largest philanthropists.

When the Chicken Ranch closed, the building was moved to Dallas and, for a while, became a chicken restaurant.

operated by the City of La Grange. Park entrance is on the right. This day-use park includes restrooms, hike/bike trails, picnic facilities, and a canoe launch.

where to eat

Prause Meat Market. 253 West Travis St.; (US 77) on Courthouse Square; (979) 968-3259. The front of this meat market sells fresh cuts, but it's behind that counter where business is smoking—literally. The barbecue side of this business is hot; so hot, in fact, that when the high demand means they run out of barbecue (and they often do early in the day), these folks just close up shop. Get there early for a chance at some sausage or brisket; you'll be served on butcher paper and can take it into the back room to eat on long tables. Open for lunch Mon through Sat. $.

Weikel's Bakery. 2247 West TX 71; (979) 968-9413; www.weikels.com. The Czech pastry specialties for which this region is known make up many of the offerings at this highway-side bakery. Kolaches and pigs-in-a-blanket are top items; kolaches come in a range of flavors, from pineapple to poppy seed to prune. The bakery may not look like much from the outside (well, actually, it looks like a gas station) but it was named one of America's top ten bakeries by foodies Jane and Michael Stern in *Epicurious*, and for good reason. Open Mon through Thurs 5 a.m. to 9 p.m., Fri through Sun 5 a.m. to 10 p.m. $.

day trip 02

southeast

petite getaway:
carmine, round top, winedale,
shelby, fayetteville, warrenton

This day trip can be reached from Southeast Day Trip 01 via La Grange or East Day Trips 01 and 02, which take you through Elgin and Giddings, turning south in Carmine.

While these towns may be petite in terms of population, they pack a wallop when it comes to drawing vacationers, especially during "Antiques Week," traditionally scheduled for the first full weekend in April (although this can vary with the timing of Easter) and October. During Antiques Week, dozens of antiques shows dot the countryside, featuring thousands of vendors and tens of thousands of shoppers from across the country.

If you think you might want to expand your day trip into a multiday shop-a-thon, book accommodations months in advance. Lodging can be very hard to come by for these prime weekends. You'll find a lodging request form on the Round Top Area Chamber Web site; www.roundtop.org; they'll send your lodging request to member accommodations to check for availability.

carmine

Located on busy US 290, tiny Carmine is easy to miss during most of the year, but during Antiques Week in the spring and fall, it becomes the first shopping stop for many Austin travelers.

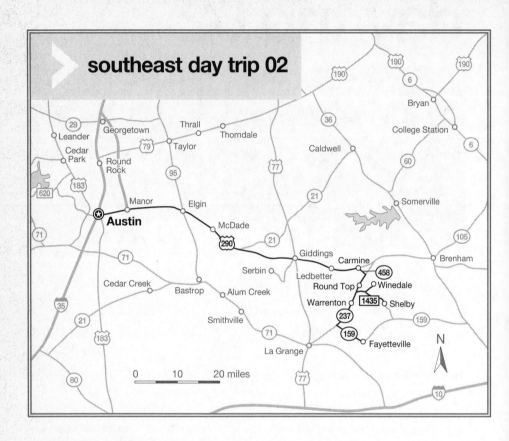

southeast day trip 02

where to shop

La Bahia Antiques Show. TX 237, north of where Spur 458 intersects with the highway; www.labahiaantiques.com. This antiques show takes place in an historic community center in April and October. Free admission.

County Line Antique Show. Intersection of Spur 458 and TX 237. www.countylineantique show.com. This antiques show takes place in several historic buildings that are themselves part of the fun. Shop in a former gas station, an old sausage company, and even an air-conditioned building as well as open-air tents during the twice-annual event.

The Original Round Top Antiques Fair at the Carmine Dance Hall. 2 blocks north of US 290 at highway crossover sign; www.roundtopantiquestexas.com. One of five venues offered by this very popular company, one ticket offers admission to all five sites. Many consider this market, held at an authentic old-time dancehall, one of the best.

round top

From Carmine, take Spur 458 south to TX 237, turning south of TX 237 to continue to Round Top. Officially founded in 1835 by settlers from Stephen F. Austin's second colony, this town is filled with restored homes, log cabins, and country stores.

Round Top is also home to a world-class music facility. The International Festival Institute, located just outside of town, offers performances by visiting symphony orchestras under the summer stars.

"Downtown" Round Top consists of several blocks flanking the old courthouse. Today the county seat is located in nearby La Grange, but the lawn of the Round Top courthouse is still faithfully maintained by the DYD (Do Your Duty) Women's Club, as it has been since the 1930s.

where to go

Henkel Square Museum Village. TX 237, on the town square; (979) 249-3014; www .texaspioneerarts.org. This is one of the finest restorations of pioneer buildings in the state. This collection of forty historic homes and businesses, dating from 1824 to 1915, was assembled from around Fayette County. The apothecary shop now serves as a visitor center, where tours of the schoolhouse-church, log house, and the Henkel house originate. Open Thurs through Sun noon to 5 p.m.

Round Top Family Library. West Mill Street; (979) 249-2700; www.ilovetoread.org. Serving as a traditional lending library for the residents of Round Top, this facility is also the home of the Bybee Texas Heritage Collection, focusing on Texas history, furniture, decorative arts, and architecture as well as oral histories of the pioneers who settled this region. The library is housed in the 1925 Hope Lutheran Church, a Gothic structure moved to Round Top from Milam County. Open Tues through Fri 1:30 p.m. to 5:30 p.m., Sat and Sun 1 p.m. to 4 p.m.

Round Top Festival Institute. 246 Jaster Rd. off TX 237, 5 blocks north of Henkel Square; (979) 249-3129; www.festivalhill.org. This music and theater center was founded by noted pianist James Dick. During the school year, the Institute presents monthly concerts. In the summer, the center hosts students from around the world who entertain guests with musical performances. The center is housed in historic buildings, including an 1870 farmhouse and a former school for African Americans.

The focal point of this site is the concert hall, a limestone structure fitted with 1,000 seats. In its grandiose scale and its dedication to craftsmanship, the concert hall rises from its rural surroundings like a grand cathedral. Work continues on the concert hall and the rest of the site.

Even if you don't have the opportunity to attend a concert here, call to schedule a tour. Your look at the Institute can include the David Guion Museum Room, housing a collection of belongings and music of this Texas composer, and the Oxehufwud Room, a collection of Swedish decorative arts that recall the life of a Swedish noble family whose final member retired in La Grange. Bring a picnic lunch and enjoy the one-hundred-acre grounds, which are planted with thousands of trees and include walking trails and a stonework bridge, constructed to resemble a Roman footbridge.

where to shop

Antiques Fairs. Round Top holds antiques fairs like no place else in the state. These events draw collectors from across the country for staggered antiques shows that range over a one-week period (deemed "Antiques Week") in both the spring and fall, with limited shows in June as well.

Emma Lee Turney's Round Top Folk Art Fair and Creative Market. 1235 TX 237, north of Round Top (across from the Festival Institute); (281) 493-5501 www .roundtopfolkartfair.com. Held in an air-conditioned show barn, this four-day event features artisans that range from tinsmiths to woodcarvers. It is coordinated by Emma Lee Turney, one of the state's best-known names when it comes to antiques shows (and a driving force behind the success of tiny Round Top).

Marburger Farm Antique Show. TX 237 between Round Top and Warrenton; (800) 999-2148; www.roundtop-marburger.com. This sale, which has been featured in top magazines such as *Country Living,* offers indoor and outside stalls spanning ten large tents and twelve historic buildings. The 27 acres of parking gives you an idea of how popular this show is, which offers, for a higher fee, an early bird sales day.

The Original Round Top Antiques Fairs. At the Big Red Barn on TX 237; (512) 237-4747; roundtopantiquesfair.com. These megafairs draw antiques lovers from around the state to more than 300 booths. The four-day shows are scheduled for the first full weekend in April (depending on when Easter falls) and October and a two-day show in June.

Texas Rose Show. 2075 South State TX 237; (256) 390-5337; www.texasroseshow .com. Collectibles, not flowers, are the hallmark of this show held in Mar and Oct. Vendors display their wares over 5 acres and within a 36,000-square-foot building. Free admission (and free parking).

Round Top General Store. TX 237; (979) 249-3600. Since 1848 this general store has been serving the community in many ways. Besides its role as general store and hardware store, it has operated as a barbershop, funeral home, and hotel. Today it offers an impressive array of gift items and antiques, and a confectionery up front serves fudge (try the jalapeño!) prepared in the store.

where to eat

Klump's Restaurant. On the square; (979) 249-5696. Klump's started out as a grocery store, serving barbecue on the weekends. Folks started asking for that 'que, though, and the Klump family decided to start a restaurant. Open for breakfast and lunch Mon through Sat, dinner Wed through Sat. $.

Royers Round Top Cafe. On the square; (979) 249-3611 (for mail order); www.royers roundtopcafe.com. You wouldn't expect to find shrimp scampi, fresh fettuccine, or pasta with fresh marinara sauce at a small-town diner, but here it is. This lively joint serves up some of the best cooking in central Texas in a fun atmosphere that's popular with locals and visitors alike. It's all topped off with homemade pies that include butterscotch tollhouse, buttermilk, and that Texas favorite, pecan. Royers operates a mail-order and wholesale sauce business, featuring pepper sauce, citrus vinegar, mint vinegar, and marinades. Open Thurs through Sat 11 a.m. to 9 p.m.; Sun 11 a.m. to 3 p.m. $–$$.

winedale

If you're continuing on a collectibles hunt during Antiques Week, skip Winedale and continue on to Shelby. Otherwise, make time to detour to historic Winedale.

To reach the tiny burg of Winedale, head east of Round Top on FM 1457, then north on FM 2714. This town does not appear on the official Texas State Map, but it's definitely on the map as far as many Shakespeare buffs go, thanks to the University of Texas productions here.

Winedale started out in 1870 as a German community named Truebsal. Eventually the community relocated slightly and, thanks to a grape crop from area farmers, got a post office with the official name of Winedale. Today the area is best known as the home of the Winedale Historical Center, part of the University of Texas's Center for American History. Winedale's preservation dates back to the early 1960s, when conservationist Miss Ima Hogg worked to preserve the old Samuel Lewis homestead here, later donating it to the university.

where to go

Things are pretty quiet in Winedale for most of the year, except during the Shakespeare at Winedale events.

Winedale Historical Center. 4 miles east of Round Top via FM 1457, then north on FM 2714; (979) 278-3530; www.cah.utexas.edu. Although Shakespeare at Winedale is a limited activity, the center is a year-around attraction. The 215-acre complex is home to a collection of eight historic structures, a research center, a nature trail, and a picnic area. Weekend tours take visitors through homes furnished with period antiques and details such as stenciled ceilings that recall the area's German heritage. Open Mon through Fri 9 a.m. to 5 p.m.

Shakespeare at Winedale. 4 miles east of Round Top via FM 1457, then north on FM 2714; (512) 471-4993 or (512) 471-4726; www.shakespeare-winedale.org. Operated by the University of Texas at Austin, this center hosts annual Shakespeare productions that draw visitors from across the state. Students from assorted disciplines have come to Winedale every summer since 1970 to perform the works of the Bard in an old hay barn that has been refitted as an Elizabethan-style theater. For fifteen to eighteen hours a day, the students make costumes, prepare lighting, and rehearse. Public performances are held Thurs through Sun evenings in late July and early Aug as well as the last Fri and Sat in Apr. Reservations for the performances are highly recommended.

shelby

To reach Shelby, head 6.1 miles east from Round Top on FM 1457. If you've made the Winedale detour, return to FM 1457 by retracing your steps on FM 2714, then turn east on FM 1457.

The small community of Shelby is old by Texas standards, first getting a post office in the 1840s. The post office closed in the early 20th century, but Shelby still brings many visitors during Antiques Week, thanks to several shows held in this burg.

where to shop

Shelby Antique Show. Harmonie Hall, FM 389, half mile past intersection of FM 389 and FM 1457; (979) 836-7474 or (979) 836-5778. This show isn't as large as the ones you'll find in Round Top, but many shoppers like the smaller crowds at this country show held in a historic (but air-conditioned) dance hall.

fayetteville

This scenic little community dates back to Texas's early days. It was settled by three families from Stephen F. Austin's Old Three Hundred, the first colony settlers who received land grants. They were soon followed by Czech, German, and other immigrants who through the years named and renamed the community. Its most interesting moniker? Lick Skillet. The name came from the days when free meals were distributed and those who arrived too late were told to "lick the skillet."

Today the town recalls that heritage with an October Lick Skillet Festival. The town also participates in Antiques Week (although you'll find antiques shops open year-round). Downtown, don't miss the 1880 precinct courthouse, built to help residents avoid the journey to the county courthouse in La Grange. The precinct courthouse also has a chiming clock, donated by the women's Do Your Duty Club, making Fayetteville the world's smallest town with a clock of that type.

Things are generally very quiet in Fayetteville, with limited hours at some shops and restaurants. During Antiques Week in the spring and fall, however, look for extended hours (and larger crowds).

where to go

Fayetteville Area Museum. 217 North Washington St., just off TX 159; (979) 378-2378. Housed in a historic building, this museum traces the history of Fayetteville. Don't miss the displays on the Baca (pronounced Batcha) Band, a Czech family band that started in the late 1800s and became one of Texas's top musical acts. Open Fri and Sun 2 p.m. to 4 p.m. and Sat 10 a.m. to noon.

where to eat

Joe's Place. 120 North Live Oak St.; (979) 378-9035. A fixture on Fayetteville's square, Joe's serves Texas favorites like chicken-fried steak, barbecue, steaks, and seafood. Its century-old shotgun-style interior is packed at lunch time with locals who show up for the daily specials. Open daily 11 a.m. to 9 p.m. $–$$.

Keiler's Restaurant & Lodge. 107 West Fayette St. (on the square); (979) 378-2578. You don't need an address for Keiler's; just look for the two-story wooden building that resembles a western saloon, and you're there. This restaurant serves traditional Texas fare, from burgers to chicken-fried steaks. Open Wed and Thurs 8 a.m. to 9 p.m., Fri and Sat 8 a.m. to 9:30 p.m. $.

Orsak's Café. On the square; (979) 378-2719. Country food is the order of the day at this Fayetteville favorite. Catfish is tops, as are chicken-fried steak and burgers, but save room for the ice cream. Open daily for breakfast, lunch, and dinner. Open Sun through Thurs 8 a.m. to 9:30 p.m. Fri and Sat 8 a.m. to 10 p.m. $.

warrenton

From Fayetteville head west on FM 1291 to Warrenton, best known as the home of the smallest Catholic church in the world.

where to go

St. Martin's Church. Billed as the world's smallest Catholic church, St. Martin's, located on the west side of TX 237 north of town, is a simple white frame building. Inside the Lilliputian house of worship, plain wooden benches serve as pews before an ornate altar. Step inside for a look; visitors are welcome.

Sterling McCall's Cadillac Museum. 4212 TX 237; (979) 249-5089; www.sterlingmccall museum.org. Car buffs enjoy this museum, which traces the evolution of the Cadillac automobile. Open Sat and Sun 10 a.m. to 4 p.m.

where to shop

Like nearby Round Top, Warrenton is home to several antiques shows in both the spring and fall. Many of the Warrenton booths open days before the Round Top booths.

Cole's Antique Show. TX 237 at intersection with FM 954; (281) 485-2277; www.coles fleamarket.net. This antiques show spills out of a massive, air-conditioned building into tented booths with ten acres of parking.

The Zapp Hall Antique Show. TX 237; (713) 683-8029; www.zapphall.com. With a motto of "Come for the antiques, stay for the atmosphere," this market is known not only for its fine antiques but also for its other activities, including free live music, a beer garden, and even an annex of Round Top's famous Royer's Round Top Cafe. The whole event takes place in a historic dance hall.

To head back to Austin from Warrenton, continue west on FM 1291; the road continues through the agricultural community of Walhalla before turning north and continuing to Ledbetter. At Ledbetter, you'll intersect with US 290; turn west and continue to Austin.

You can also choose to head south to La Grange on TX 237, continuing as it becomes TX 159. This will take you through the community of Oldenburg, then to La Grange, where you can join Southeast Day Trip 01 and return home via La Grange, Smithville, Cedar Creek and Bastrop.

south

day trip 01

south

barbecue trail:
mckinney falls state park, lockhart,
luling

Fragrant smoke from famous Texas barbecue restaurants pervades the region along US 183 south from Austin. Barbecue enthusiasts from all over the world converge on Lockhart and Luling to sample the smoky delights.

mckinney falls state park

McKinney Falls State Park. (512) 243-1643; www.tpwd.state.tx.us. 13 miles southeast of downtown Austin off US 183, take McKinney Falls Parkway south. A favorite with those looking for a quick getaway from the city, this park includes plenty of chances to view the area's wildlife, including white-tailed deer, raccoons, squirrels, and armadillos. Campers can choose from several types of sites as well as screened shelters.

lockhart

Lockhart is a conglomeration of the stuff of Texas legends: Indian battles, cattle drives, cotton, and oil. This small town, located 23 miles south of Austin on US 183, contains a state park and lots of history.

The biggest event in Lockhart's past was the Battle of Plum Creek in 1840. More than 600 Comanches raided the community of Linnville and were on their way home when they passed through this area. A group of settlers joined forces with the Tonkawa Indians

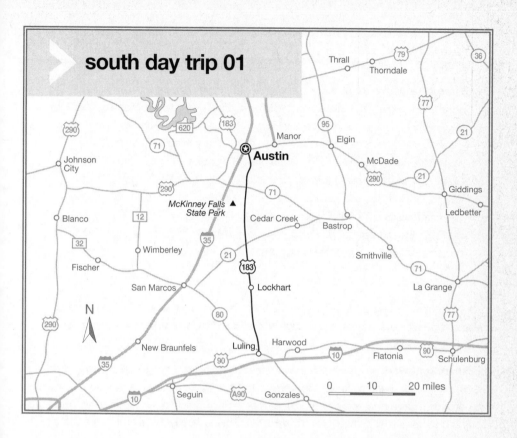

> **south day trip 01**

Thrall
Thorndale
79
36
77
290
620
183
95
21
Manor
Elgin
71
Austin
McDade
Johnson
City
290
21
McKinney Falls ▲
State Park
290
71
Giddings
Blanco
12
Cedar Creek
Ledbetter
Bastrop
32
35
Wimberley
21
Smithville
Fischer
183
Lockhart
71
La Grange
San Marcos
80
77
N
290
Harwood
New Braunfels
Luling
10
Flatonia
35
90
90
Schulenburg
0   10   20 miles
10
Seguin
A90
Gonzales

to attack the Comanches, driving them further west and ending the Indian attacks in the region. This battle is reenacted every May at the Chisholm Trail Roundup.

Lockhart is also well known as the home of Mebane cotton. Developed by A. D. Mebane, this strain is resistant to the boll weevil, an insect that can demolish not only whole fields but also entire economies.

where to go

Caldwell County Museum. 315 East Market St.; no phone. You can't miss this old building—just look for the five-story red brick castle. Built in 1908 as the county jail, this imposing structure was designed with Norman-style castellations, giving it almost a fairy tale look. Today the building, which houses items detailing the settlement and history of the region, is operated by the Caldwell County Historical Commission and is open to the public on Sat and Sun from 1 p.m. to 5 p.m.

Dr. Eugene Clark Library. 217 South Main St.; (512) 398-3223; www.lockhart-tx.org/web98/history/dreugeneclarklibrary.asp. Built in 1889, this is the oldest continuously

> ## lockhart meets hollywood
>
> *While its reputation as the barbecue capital of Texas has made Lockhart legendary among foodies, its historical architecture and small-town charm has secured this Hill Country community a place in Hollywood history. The Muldoon Blue sandstone facade of the Caldwell County Courthouse played a starring role alongside Johnny Depp in a scene from the 1993 drama* What's Eating Gilbert Grape, *and the 19th-century structure also appears in the cult comedy favorite* Waiting for Guffman. *Locals lined the bleachers at the high school football field in 1998 for the sci-fi flick* The Faculty, *and residents shop in the same aisles of the Wal-Mart that actress Natalie Portman wandered in 2000 when she filmed the screen adaptation of the best-selling novel* Where the Heart Is.

operating library in Texas. Modeled after the Villa Rotunda in Vicenza, Italy, it has stained-glass windows, ornate fixtures, and a stage where President William Taft once spoke. Open daily. Free admission.

Lockhart State Park. (512) 398-3479; www.tpwd.state.tx.us. 1 mile south of Lockhart on US 183 to FM 20, head southwest for 2 miles to Park Road, continue 1 mile south. This 263-acre park has a nine-hole golf course, fishing on Plum Creek, picnic areas, a swimming pool, and campsites for both tents and trailers. Many of the facilities were built by the Civilian Conservation Corps in the 1930s. Open daily.

where to shop

Manny Gammage's Texas Hatters. 911 South Commerce St; (512) 312-0036; www.texashatters.com. Formerly in Buda, this store's founder, the late Manny Gammage, was "Texas's Hatmaker to the Stars." His hats topped the heads of Roy Rogers, Willie Nelson, Ronald Reagan, Burt Reynolds, and many other celebrities whose pictures decorate the shop walls. Besides the obligatory cowboy hats, this store also sells hand-blocked high rollers, Panamas, and derbies. Open Tues through Sat.

where to eat

Black's Barbecue. 215 North Main St.; (512) 398-2712; www.buyblacksbbq.com. This cafeteria-style restaurant is reputedly the oldest barbecue joint in Texas under the same continuous family ownership. Beef brisket is the specialty of the house, along with sausage, ribs, chicken, and ham. There's also a fully stocked salad bar. Open Sun through Thurs 10 a.m. to 8 p.m., Fri and Sat 10 a.m. to 8:30 p.m. $–$$.

Kreuz Market. 619 North Colorado St.; (512) 398-2361; www.kreuzmarket.com. For generations, Kreuz (pronounced "Krites") Market was the stuff of legend. The menu at this meat-lover's paradise features brisket, beef shoulder clod, spicy sausage, pork loin, prime rib, and pork ribs, all served on butcher paper and without a drop of barbecue sauce. Open Mon through Sat 10:30 a.m. to 8 p.m. $.

Smitty's Market. 208 South Commerce St.; (512) 398-9344; www.smittysmarket.com. Since 1900 this store was part of Kreuz Market, the no-frills barbecue joint and Texas legend. "Smitty" Schmidt bought the restaurant from its original owner in 1948 and devised the huge pit system for barbecuing. The smokehouse was run first by Schmidt, then by his two sons until 1999, when the family divided the business: Sister Nina Schmidt Sells took the building and brother Rick took the name, moving it to a newer building that houses Kreuz Market. Today the original brick building is home to Smitty's Market, which still operates much as the original did. The specials include brisket, pork chops and sausage with ribs on the weekends. Side dishes are also sold here, including potato salad, coleslaw, and beans. Open weekdays 7 a.m. to 6 p.m., Sat 7 a.m. to 6:30 p.m., and Sun 9 a.m. to 3 p.m. $.

luling

Continue south on US 183 for 17 miles to the oil town of Luling. Oil was discovered here in 1922, and fields pumping this "black gold" can still be seen throughout the Luling area. Even before that time the town had a reputation as the toughest town in Texas, frequented by gunfighters like John Wesley Hardin and Ben Thompson. Luling was also a cattle center and one end of a railroad line to Chihuahua, Mexico.

When oil was discovered, the economy of the town shifted to this profitable industry. Today 184 wells pump within the city limits. As part of a beautification effort, the Chamber of Commerce commissioned an artist to transform several of the pump jacks into moving sculptures in the shapes of cartoon characters. There's even a Santa Claus and a butterfly to brighten up the streets.

where to go

Central Texas Oil Patch Museum & Luling Chamber of Commerce Visitors' Center. 421 Davis St.; (830) 875-2444. Luling's oil businesses, starting with Rafael Rios No. 1 (an oil field 12 miles long and 2 miles wide), are explored in this museum. Open Mon through Fri 9 a.m. to 4 p.m., Sat 10 a.m. to 4 p.m. Free admission.

Luling Zedler Mill Paddling Trail. 5 miles west of Luling where US 90 crosses the San Marcos River; www.tpwd.state.tx.us/fishboat/boat/paddlingtrails/inland/luling. In the 1870s both a gristmill and cotton mill were built at this site to harness the power of the San Marcos

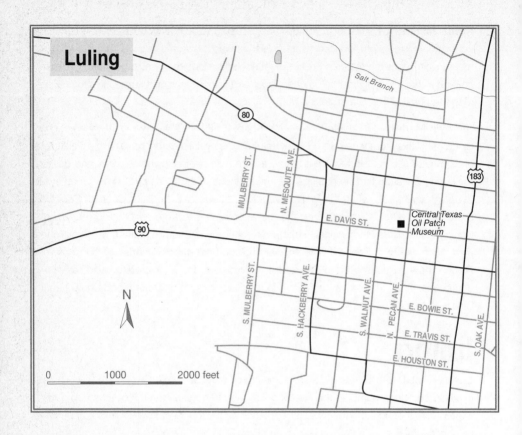

River. The cotton gin was destroyed by flash flood, then rebuilt, only to become an electric plant. This site became part of Texas's first paddling trail, operated by Texas Parks and Wildlife. You'll put into the river 6 miles upstream, then come out at Zedler Mill, located within city limits. (There's a dam beyond the mill, so be careful not to go beyond the mill.) Check the Web site for information on local canoe rentals, shuttles, and even Global Positioning Satellite coordinates along the river.

Palmetto State Park. (830) 672-3266; www.tpwd.state.tx.us. Six miles southeast of town on US 183, then southwest on Park Road for 2 miles, along the banks of the San Marcos River. Palmetto State Park is a topographical anomaly amidst gently rolling farm and ranch land. According to scientists, the river shifted course thousands of years ago, leaving a huge deposit of silt. This sediment absorbed rain- and ground-water, nurturing a marshy swamp estimated to be more than 18,000 years old. Now part of the state park, the swamp is filled with palmettos as well as moss-draped trees, 4-foot-tall irises, and many bird species. Nature trails wind through the area.

The park has full hookups and tent sites. There's also picnicking, but bring along mosquito repellent during the warmer months. Open daily.

where to eat

Luling City Market. 633 Davis St.; (877) LCM-BBQ1 or (830) 875-9019; www.lulingcity market.com. This is small-town barbecue the way it ought to be: served up in a no-frills meat market, with ambience replaced by local atmosphere. The Luling City Market turns out smoked brisket, sausage, and ribs. $.

day trip 02

south

painted churches:
flatonia, praha, schulenburg, dubina,
ammannsville, hostyn, high hill

This day trip continues the journey of South Day Trip 01 on US 90, traveling east of Luling
to the small German and Czech communities where the largest building in town is often a
historic church. These are called collectively the Painted Churches of Texas, known for their
elaborately painted interiors and faux details such as marbleized columns, all reminders of
the homelands left behind.

The churches on this tour are open occasionally, but, if you drive by, it's worth a stop to
see if you might be able to take a peek at the beautiful interiors. The Schulenburg Chamber
of Commerce offers guided group tours with prior arrangement and also offers maps to the
locations. You'll also find more details about these churches on the PBS documentary *The
Painted Churches of Texas* and its accompanying Web site, www.klru.org/paintedchurches.

flatonia

Return to US 90 and continue east to the small town of Flatonia. This community was
settled by English, German, Bohemian, and Czech immigrants, many of whom came to the
United States in the 1850s and 1860s to avoid Austro-Hungarian oppression.

Flatonia also hosts market days once per quarter, featuring local merchants and artisans. Markets are held in March, June, September and a special Christmas market in early
December. Visit the Chamber of Commerce Web site at http://flatoniachamber.com.

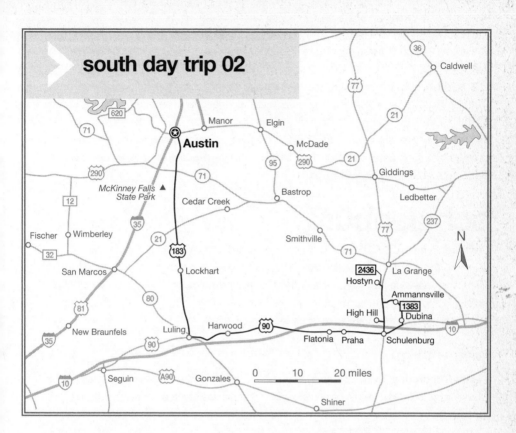

south day trip 02

Caldwell
36
77
21
Manor
Elgin
71
620
★ **Austin**
McDade
95 290 21
Giddings
290
71
Ledbetter
McKinney Falls ▲
State Park
12
Cedar Creek
Bastrop
237
35
Fischer ○ Wimberley
21
Smithville
77
N
32
San Marcos
Lockhart
2436 La Grange
Hostyn
Ammannsville
80
1383
High Hill
Dubina
81
Harwood
Luling
90
10
New Braunfels
Flatonia Praha
Schulenburg
35
90
Seguin
A90 Gonzales
0   10   20 miles
10
Shiner

where to go

E. A. Arnim Archives and Museum. 101 East Main St.; (361) 865-3920. This local history museum contains exhibits on Flatonia's early days and its settlement by many cultural groups. Open Mon through Thurs 8:30 a.m. to 4:30 p.m. and Fri 8:30 a.m. to noon. Free admission.

praha

Three miles east of Flatonia on US 90 is Praha (the Czech spelling for "Prague"). Named for its European counterpart, Praha holds a predominantly Czech population, descendants of immigrants who came here in 1855.

where to go

Assumption of the Blessed Virgin Mary Church. Located 2 miles east of US 90 on FM 1295. No phone. The main structure in Praha is the Assumption of the Blessed Virgin Mary

Church, often called St. Mary's. Built in 1895, it is one of a half dozen painted churches in the area. Although few examples remain today, they were not unusual in the nineteenth century.

St. Mary's has a beautifully painted vaulted ceiling, the work of Swiss-born artist Gottfried Flury. Never retouched, the 1895 murals on the tongue-and-groove ceiling depict golden angels high over a pastoral setting. This Praha church, as well as ones in High Hill and Ammannsville, are listed in the National Register of Historic Places. The churches are open Mon through Sat 8 a.m. to 5 p.m., although it is not guaranteed that the doors will be unlocked at all times. Free admission.

schulenburg

Continue east on US 90 to the agricultural community of Schulenburg (meaning "school town" in German). The Carnation milk company's first plant was built in Schulenburg in 1929, and even today dairy products generate a major source of income for the area. Schulenburg is known as the "home of the painted churches," although the elaborately painted structures are actually located in nearby small communities.

where to go

Painted Churches Tour. With two- or three-week notice, the Schulenburg Chamber of Commerce (866-504-5294) provides guides for tour groups of ten or more. The guided tour includes many of the churches found in this chapter: Praha's Assumption of the Blessed Virgin Mary Church, Dubina's Saints Cyril and Methodius Catholic Church, Ammannsville's St. John the Baptist Catholic Church, and High Hill's Nativity of the Blessed Virgin Mary Church. You can always enjoy a self-guided tour; maps of the church locations are available at the Schulenburg chamber office at 618 Main St.

where to eat

Oakridge Smokehouse Restaurant. I-10 and US 77; (800) 548-6325; www.oakridge smokehouse.com. Hungry travelers between San Antonio and Houston know all about Oakridge Smokehouse. In business for nearly half a century, this family-owned company churns out barbecue and sausage to please travelers and mail-order customers. The comfortable restaurant is popular with families, not just for its extensive menu, but also for its large gift shop up front. $–$$.

dubina

From Schulenburg, head northeast on US 90 to the intersection with FM 1383. Turn north on 1383 and continue just over 2 miles to the community of Dubina.

Nicknamed the "Mother Czechs in Texas," Dubina holds the title as the first Czech settlement in the Lone Star State. Even its name—derived from the term for an oak grove—harkens back to its Czech roots.

where to go

Saints Cyril and Methodius Catholic Church. FM 1383; no phone. Built in 1909, this church is home to spectacular murals. Covered over during a 1952 remodel, the paintings were uncovered in 1981 and renovated by a local parishioner. The murals depict winged angels and elaborate stenciling. Mass is held here on Sat at 4 p.m. and Sun at 10:15 a.m.

ammannsville

From Dubina, continue north on FM 1383, turning west as FM 1383 intersects with FM 1965 and continues as FM 1383. Ammannsville was settled by both German and Czech immigrants in the 1870s, growing by 1900 to include multiple stores, blacksmiths, a physician, and two gins. Eventually the population of this agricultural community dwindled, though, and today only about forty or so residents call Ammannsville home.

where to go

St. John the Baptist Catholic Church. 7745 Mensik Rd.; (979) 743-3117. Built in 1918, this painted church has stained-glass windows illustrating the Czech history of the parish. Mass is held at this church on Sat at 5 p.m. (in odd months), Sun at 9:30 a.m. (in even months), and Fri at 5 p.m.

hostyn

From Ammannsville, continue west on FM 1383 to the intersection with US 77, turning north to the intersection of FM 2436. Turn left on FM 2436 and continue 1 mile to the community of Hostyn.

It's easy to see why this town was first named Bluff; the town overlooks the Colorado River. Settled by Germans in the 1830s and joined by Czech settlers twenty years later, the name was later changed to Hostyn after a Moravian city.

where to go

Hostyn Grotto. FM 2436. This grotto, a replica of France's Grotto of Lourdes, was constructed in 1925 in thanks for the end of the 1924–1925 drought. The grotto is located at the Holy Rosary Catholic Church; the grounds are also home to an adjoining cemetery. The cemetery is of interest not only for its Czech tombstones but also for the graves of a father and son buried side by side—although they fought on opposing sides during the Civil War. Open during daylight hours.

high hill

From Hostyn, return to US 77 and head south just over 5 miles to the intersection with FM 956. Turn right and head west on FM 956 for slightly more than a mile to the intersection with FM 2672. Turn left and drive south for 2.7 miles to the community of High Hill.

This town was once a thriving community on a stagecoach line but, when bypassed by the railroad in 1874, the population began dwindling—but not before the construction of the Nativity of Mary, Blessed Virgin church, also known as St. Mary's.

where to go

Nativity of the Blessed Virgin Mary Church. 2833 FM 2672; (979) 561-8455 or (979) 743-3117. Also called St. Mary Church, this structure was built in 1906 and painted six years later. The Gothic-style red brick building designed by Texas architect Leo Dielmann is noted for its wooden columns painted to resemble marble, stained-glass windows, and religious statuary. The church also has a history of a European-style seating arrangement, with women on the left and men on the right. Mass is held Sat at 6:30 p.m. and Mon at 6 a.m.

day trip 03

south

texas history:
gonzales, shiner, yoakum

This history-filled day trip offers a look at a historic battleground, one of Texas's most popular breweries, and one of the world's biggest leather producers.

To begin this trip, head south on US 183 through Lockhart and Luling (see South Day Trip 01 for information on attractions in those cities).

gonzales

Continue south on US 183 for 13 miles to Gonzales, one of Texas's most historic cities. This is the "Come and Take It" town where the Texas Revolution began in 1835.

Plagued by constant Indian attacks, Gonzales's citizens received a small brass cannon for protection sent by the Mexican government in 1831. Four years later, when relations between Texas and Mexico soured, more than 150 Mexican soldiers staged a battle to retrieve the weapon. The soldiers were faced with eighteen Gonzaleans, who stalled the army while other citizens rolled out the small fieldpiece and prepared for action. Meanwhile, other townsfolk sewed the first battle flag of Texas, which pictured a cannon beneath the words "Come and Take It," a motto by which Gonzales is still known. The Texans fired a shot and the Mexican troops retreated. Although the confrontation was brief, it set off the Texas Revolution.

The site of this historic first conflict is marked by a monument located 7 miles southwest of Gonzales on TX 97. The first shots were fired a half mile north of the present monument.

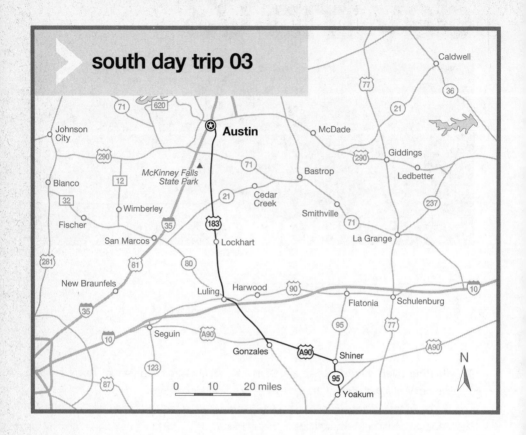

where to go

Chamber of Commerce. 414 St. Lawrence St.; (830) 672-6532. Located in the Old Jail Museum, this office has brochures on local attractions and events. Open weekdays.

Gonzales Pioneer Village Living History Center. 2122 Joseph St., a half mile north of town on US 183; (830) 672-2157. This center takes visitors back to Gonzales's frontier days. The village is composed of log cabins, a cypress-constructed house, a grand Victorian house, a smokehouse, a blacksmith shop, and a church. The village also stages reenactments, including the "Come and Take It" celebration in Oct. Open 10 a.m. to 2 p.m. Tues through Sat; group tours by appointment.

Memorial Museum. 414 Smith St., between St. Lawrence and St. Louis Streets; (830) 672-6350. This museum is dedicated to the history of Gonzales. Exhibits on the town's early days include the "Come and Take It" cannon. Open Tues through Sat (closed at lunch hour) and Sun afternoon. Free admission.

Old Jail Museum. 414 St. Lawrence St. (830) 672-6532. This unusual museum is housed in the old Gonzales jail, built in 1887 and used until 1975. Downstairs you can tour the room where female prisoners and mentally ill persons once were incarcerated together. Exhibits include jail weapons created from spoons and bedsprings.

The walls of the second floor are chiseled with graffiti of past residents. The large room is rimmed with iron cells, all overlooking a reproduction of the old gallows that carried off its last hanging in 1921. According to legend, this prisoner continually watched the clocks on the adjacent courthouse, counting the hours he had left to live. He swore that he was innocent and said that if he were hanged, the clocks would never keep accurate time again. Although the four clock faces have been changed since then, none of them has ever kept the same time again.

The museum, located in the Chamber of Commerce building, is open daily (afternoons on Sun). Free admission.

shiner

Take US 90A east of Gonzales for 18 miles to the tiny town of Shiner, best known as the home of Shiner Beer. If you make the trip during the week, stop by the Spoetzl Brewery for a free tour and a sample of the hometown product.

where to go

City Hall. US 90A, downtown; (361) 594-4180. This 2-story building houses the fire department, police department, and city offices. Enter on the left side for city brochures and a free map.

Cigar Factory and Green Cabin Museums. 817 North Ave. E (Hwy 90-A); (361) 594-4180. Two historic buildings grace Shiner's downtown. The Louis Ehlers Cigar Factory opened in 1895 and their products once enjoyed widespread popularity in the area. The Green Cabin Museum preserves the home of prominent local businessman William Green, Jr. The cabin was built in 1853. The Shiner Chamber of Commerce office is next door.

Edwin Wolters Memorial Museum. 306 South Ave. I off TX 95 South; (361) 594-3774. This museum is filled with home implements, weapons, fossils, and even a country store representing the community's early days. Open weekdays and the second and fourth Sunday afternoons of the month. Free admission.

The Gaslight Theatre. 207 East Seventh St.; (361) 594-2079. Shiner's Gaslight Theatre's graceful facade has been a downtown landmark since 1985 and was the town's social center for many years. Now restored and modernized, it hosts amateur stage productions several times a year.

Spoetzl Brewery. 603 Brewery St., off TX 95 North; (361) 594-3852; www.shiner.com. This tiny but historic brewery was founded in 1909 by Kosmos Spoetzl, a Bavarian brew-master. Here several Shiner beers are produced in one of the smallest commercial brew kettles in the country and the oldest independent brewery in Texas. Across the street a museum and gift shop overflow with Shiner memorabilia, antiques, and photos of Spoetzl's early days. Brewery tours are conducted on weekdays at 11 a.m. and 1:30 p.m., with additional tours at 10 a.m. and 2:30 p.m. in the summer. Hospitality room open following tour. Free admission.

Welhausen Park. 901 North Ave. E (Hwy 90-A); (361) 594-3362. This park occupies a full city block just west of downtown. Beneath its large shade trees you'll see an old-time bandstand, children's playscape and several granite markers each commemorating historic events in the city's past. Its a good spot for a picnic. Free admission.

where to stay

The Old Kasper House. 219 Ave. C; (361) 594-4336; www.oldkasperhouse.com. This bed-and-breakfast is located in the former home of a cotton ginner and his wife from east-ern Europe who was best known as a relative of Gregor Mendel, discoverer of genetic infor-mation (remember those Mendel pea models in Biology I?). Today the two-story house is a great small-town getaway, offering seven rooms with private baths and a cottage. Behind the bed-and-breakfast there's an RV park with eight full-service hookups. $–$$.

yoakum

From Shiner, drive south on TX 95 for 8 miles to US 77A. Turn right and continue for 2 miles. Yoakum was the starting point of many cattle drives along the Chisholm Trail, and in 1887 it became the junction for the San Antonio and Aransas Pass Railroad. When the railroad came to town, meat-packing houses followed. In 1919 the first tannery opened, producing leather knee pads for cotton pickers. Soon other leather businesses arrived, and eventually Yoakum earned its title as "the Leather Capital of the World."

Today nine manufacturing firms with sixteen locations produce belts, saddles, bull-whips, gun slings, and wallets. Although the companies do not sell directly from their factories, the Leather Capital Store operates as a showroom and factory outlet for many Yoakum manufacturers. Tours of the leather companies are offered during the annual Land of Leather Days festival on the last weekend in Feb.

where to go

Yoakum Heritage Museum. 312 Simpson St.; (361) 293-7022. This two-story museum is filled with Yoakum memorabilia, from railroad paraphernalia to household items. The most

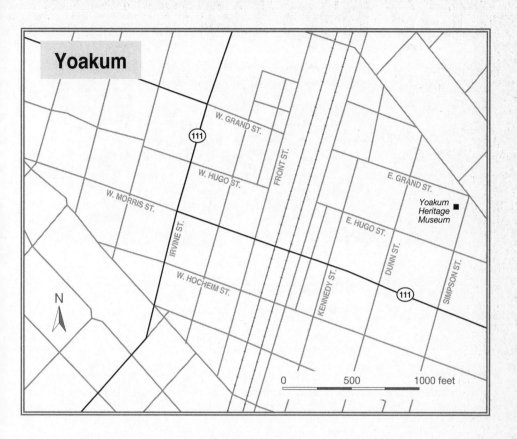

interesting exhibit area is the Leather Room, with its displays on the leather factories. Open Tues, Thurs, Fri, and Sun afternoons. Free admission.

Return home from Yoakum by retracing your steps or by heading north on TX 95 to Flatonia. From here, go west on either I-10 or US 90.

day trip 04

south

shop 'til you drop:
buda, san marcos

Bring your credit card on this day trip as it leads to some of Texas's finest outlet shopping destinations. Ever-expanding outlet malls featuring world-famous labels line I-35 as you head south to Buda and San Marcos.

buda

Head south from Austin on I-35 to the small town of Buda, located on Loop 4 to the west of the highway. This sleepy railroad town is a busy spot on weekends, when shoppers come to hunt antiques.

Buda is one of the most mispronounced communities in Texas (and with names like Gruene, Leakey, and Boerne around, that's saying a lot). To sound like a local, just say, "b-YOU-da." The name has caused more than one visitor to come here expecting an Old-World Hungarian settlement. Though possibly a reference to Budapest, it's more likely of Spanish origin. According to legend, several widows cooked in the local hotel restaurant that was popular with employees of the International–Great Northern Railroad. The Spanish word for "widow" is viuda. Since the "v" is pronounced as a "b" in Spanish, Buda may be a phonetic spelling for viuda.

Buda is still a railroad town, with double tracks running parallel to Main Street.

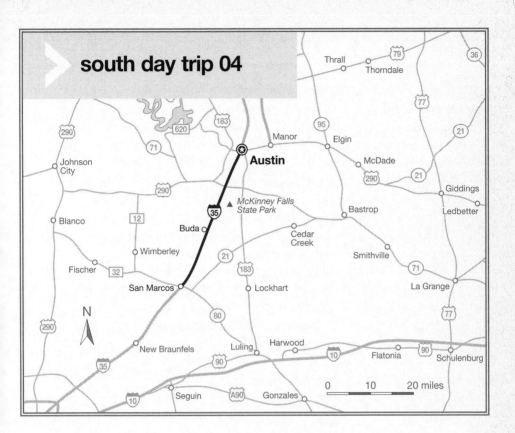

south day trip 04

where to shop

Many Buda stores are closed Mon through Wed, although some are open by appointment. Most shops are located in a 2-block stretch of Main Street.

Cabela's Buda. 15570 I-35; (512) 295-1100; www.cabelas.com. This Texas-size outdoor store is an attraction for everyone. The 185,000-square-foot store features a large fresh-water aquarium as well as a large "mountain" exhibit dotted with trophy animals of all types. The store also has an indoor archery range, dog kennels, a restaurant, live bait, and RV parking. Open daily.

san marcos

Head south on I-35 to San Marcos, the home of Texas State University, two Texas-size outlet malls, and the crystal-clear San Marcos River.

Like the neighboring community of New Braunfels, San Marcos is best known for its pure spring waters. The San Marcos River, used by humans for more than 13,000 years,

alice's restaurant

There's not a lot in Niederwald these days. Come to think of it, there never has been a lot in Niederwald. Founded by German pioneers and named "Brushwood" for the mesquite that dots the area, the town was a stop on the old Austin–San Antonio road. Now it's still a stop on today's Austin–San Antonio road, I-35.

But there's one good reason to make a day trip detour to Niederwald: **Alice's Restaurant.** *This eatery, housed in a frame house and accompanied by a small biergarten, combines good food and good music in one entree, with a healthy side serving of Austin funkiness. The menu ranges from pork chops to shrimp skewers, but the live music is just as much of a draw. Austin talent, including many singer-songwriters, headline here three nights a week.*

To reach Alice's Restaurant, in Buda turn east off I-35 on FM 2001 (exit 220) and continue 9 miles to the intersection with TX 21. Alice's is just a quarter mile east of the intersection on TX 21 at 14100 Camino Real. (If you'd prefer to take this detour from San Marcos, continue on this day trip and then head east on TX 21 in San Marcos for 14 miles.) For a schedule of performers, call (512) 376-2782 or see www.alicesrestauranttx.com. Alice's is open Thurs 10 a.m. to 10 p.m., Fri and Sat 10 a.m. to midnight, and Sun 11 a.m. to 3 p.m.

flows through town, providing the city with beautiful swimming and snorkeling spots and a family education park.

Permanent settlement of the area began in 1845. Today San Marcos is a popular tourist town. On the third weekend of every month, the downtown courthouse lawn is used for Market Days. Shop for arts and crafts, antiques, and specialty food and gift items at this old-fashioned outdoor market.

When the city of San Marcos looked around for a slogan, it decided to choose one that naturally fits the riverside city. "San Marcos, A Texas Natural" is more than a nickname: It's a description of the attractions that draw visitors to this city of just more than 46,000 permanent residents. One of the best-known attractions is Aquarena Center, which features the ecological and archaeological riches of the region. Nearby, another park offers a look at San Marcos's natural attractions both above and below the ground. Scientists believe Wonder Cave was created during a violent earthquake thirty million years ago.

There's no better way to see San Marcos during warm weather than from the river. Across from Texas State University, the Lions Club (512-396-LION; www.tubesanmarcos .com) rents inner tubes from May through Sept so that you can float down the San Marcos

Loop. The floating excursion, in 72°F water, takes about an hour and a half. Snorkeling is popular here as well, and you might see a freshwater prawn (which can reach 12 inches in length), the rare San Marcos salamander, or one of fifty-two kinds of fish.

Of course, not all of San Marcos's attractions are natural. Downtown, shops are encouraged to feature Texas-made items. While you're downtown, you'll notice the city's fresh face, thanks to more than $16 million in renovations in the last decade, transforming it into a shopping and dining area.

The Texas theme even carries into the only downtown bed-and-breakfast. The Crystal River Inn offers accommodations in rooms named for Texas rivers. It also offers popular murder mystery weekends where costumed guests work to solve a mystery using clues based on actual events in San Marcos history.

where to go

Tourist Information Center. 617 I-35 on the northwest side of town at exit 204B (C. M. Allen Parkway); (888) 200-5620 or (512) 393-5930; www.toursanmarcos.com. Traveling from the north, take exit 204B. From the south, take exit 205. Stop here for brochures on area attractions and accommodations, as well as free maps. Open daily. Free admission.

Aquarena Center. 921 Aquarena Springs Dr.; (512) 245-7570; www.aquarena.txstate .edu. Take Aquarena Springs exit from I-35 and follow signs west of the highway. This resort dates to 1928, when A. B. Rogers purchased 125 acres at the headwaters of the San Marcos to create a grand hotel. He added glass-bottom boats to cruise Spring Lake, which is fed by more than 200 springs that produce 150 million gallons of water daily. This 98-percent-pure water is home to many fish (including white albino catfish) and various types of plant life. Today visitors can still enjoy a cruise in the glass-bottom boats and will see the site of an underwater archaeological dig that unearthed the remains of Clovis Man, one of the hunter-gatherers who lived along the river more than 13,000 years ago.

Formerly a family amusement park, Aquarena Center now focuses on ecotourism, with exhibits and activities aimed at introducing visitors of all ages to the natural history and attractions of this region. This family park features glass-bottom boat rides, an endangered species exhibit, the San Xavier Spanish Mission, and plenty of educational fun.

Open daily, although hours change seasonally. Free admission. (Fee for glass-bottom boats).

The Calaboose Museum of African American History. 200 West Martin Luther King Dr.; (512) 353-0124. Housed in the 1873 building that served as Hays County's first jail, this museum preserves the history of the African Americans of San Marcos. Along with an extensive collection of books and artifacts, the museum also schedules frequent educational programs and public events. Open Sat afternoon and by appointment. Donation.

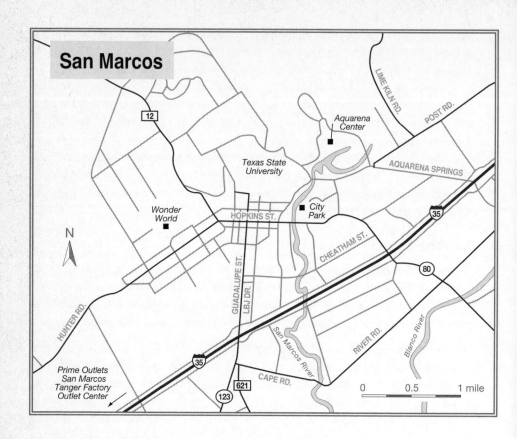

Centex Wing Museum. 1841 Airport Dr.; (512) 396-1943. Operated by the Central Texas Wing of the Commemorative Air Force, the museum is housed in a vintage wooden hangar at the San Marcos Municipal Airport. This collection contains World War II artifacts and several historic aircraft. A unique display is a replica of the CAF Japanese "Kate," built for the movie *Tora! Tora! Tora!* Open Mon, Wed, Fri, and Sat 9 a.m. to 4 p.m. Donation.

John J. Stokes San Marcos River Park. From TX 80, turn right on River Road for about 1 mile; turn left on County Road to the island where the park is located. Operated by the city of San Marcos, this day-use park is also known as Thompson's Island and is located across the river from the A. E. Wood State Fish Hatchery. The park offers river access but no facilities. Free admission.

Living History Trolley Tour. Tanger Outlet Center Visitor Center, exit 200 from I-35 south of San Marcos; (512) 396-3739. These guided tours are scheduled for 2 p.m. on the first Saturday of each month, departing from the Tanger visitor center. The trolley tours include stops at sites featured in the novels *True Women* and *Hill Country,* as well as along

Courthouse Square, the San Marcos River, Aquarena Center, and historic mansions. Reservations required.

Lyndon Baines Johnson Museum of San Marcos. 131 North Guadalupe St. (across from the courthouse); (512) 353-3300; www.lbjmuseum.com. This museum features LBJ's educational ties to the region, from his years at Texas State University to his teaching days in Cotulla to the signing of the Education Bill. Open Thurs through Sun 10 a.m. to 5 p.m.

Wittliff Collection at the Alkek Library. Texas State University, San Marcos; (512) 245-2313; www.alkek.library.txstate.edu/swwc/wg. Located on the seventh floor of the Albert B. Alkek Library, the gallery traces the history of photography from the nineteenth century through today in both Mexico and the southwestern US Open daily; hours change with university schedule.

Wonder World. 1000 Prospect St.; (512) 392-3760 (for group and tour reservations); www.wonderworldpark.com. Exit at Wonder World Drive on the south side of San Marcos and follow signs for about a mile. A guided tour lasting nearly 1.5 hours covers the entire park, including the 7.5-acre **Texas Wildlife Park,** the state's largest petting zoo. A miniature train chugs through the animal enclosure, stopping to allow riders to pet and feed white-tailed deer, wild turkeys, and many exotic species.

The next stop on the tour is **Wonder Cave,** created during a 3.5-minute earthquake 30 million years ago. The same earthquake produced the Balcones Fault, an 1,800-mile line separating the western Hill Country from the flat eastern farmland. Within the cave is the actual crack in the two land masses, where huge boulders lodged in the fissure. At the end of the cave tour, take the elevator ride to the top of the 110-foot **Tejas Tower,** which offers a spectacular view of the **Balcones Fault** and the contrasting terrain it produced.

The last stop is the **Anti-Gravity House,** a structure employing optical illusions and a slanted floor to create the feeling that you're leaning backward. In this house, water appears to run uphill. Open 8 a.m. to 8 p.m. daily (Summer); in Winter: Mon through Fri 9 a.m. to 5 p.m., Sat and Sun 9 a.m. to 6 p.m.

where to shop

Centerpoint Station. Exit 200 from I-35 south of San Marcos; (512) 392-1103; www.centerpointstation.com. This charming shop, built in the style of an old-fashioned general store, is filled with Texas and country collectibles, T-shirts, gourmet gift foods, cookbooks, and over 3000 advertising signs. Up front, there's counter service for sandwiches, malts, and ice cream.

Prime Outlets San Marcos. Exit 200 from I-35 on the south side of San Marcos; (800) 0628-9465 or (512) 396-220; www.primeoutlets.com. This open-air mall ranks as one of the state's top tourist destinations. Luggage, shoes, leather goods, outdoor gear, china, kitchen goods, and other specialties are offered for sale. Chartered buses from as far as

Dallas and Houston stop here regularly. Recently Prime Outlet San Marcos expanded its offering of luxury brands and brought some of the beauty of Europe to San Marcos. Check out the gondoliers on the mall's Grand Canal as well as reproductions of some of Venice's most notable buildings, including the Doge's Palace and the Campanile. Open daily.

Tanger Factory Outlet Center. Exit 200 from I-35 south of San Marcos; (800) 408-8424; www.tangeroutlet.com. Shops feature name-brand designers and manufacturers in this open-air mall. Housewares, footwear, home furnishings, leather goods, perfumes, and books are available. Open daily.

where to stay

Crystal River Inn. 326 West Hopkins St.; (888) 396-3739 or (512) 396-3739; www.crystal riverinn.com. The Crystal River Inn has elegant Victorian accommodations in rooms named for Texas rivers. Owners Cathy and Mike Dillon provide guests with a selection of special packages, including tubing on the San Marcos River and popular murder mystery weekends where costumed guests work to solve a mystery using clues based on actual events in San Marcos history. $$–$$$.

day trip 05

south

concrete city:
seguin

Many towns boast nicknames, from Austin's "River City" to San Antonio's "Alamo City." Seguin, though, has one of the most unusual: "The Mother of Concrete Cities." A Seguin chemist held several concrete production patents, which accounts for the use of the material in more than ninety area buildings by the end of the nineteenth century.

seguin

You can reach Seguin (pronounced "se-GEEN") by driving south on I-35 from Austin through San Marcos (see South Day Trip 03 for city attractions). It's a 36-mile trip to this town on the Guadalupe River named for Lieutenant Colonel Juan Seguin, a hero of the Texas Revolution. Prior to the Mexican invasion of 1837, Seguin was ordered by his superiors to destroy San Antonio. He refused, thus saving the city. The most beautiful area of Seguin is Starcke Park. It offers picnic tables under huge pecan, oak, and cypress trees, and a winding drive along the Guadalupe River. The tree Seguin is best known for is the pecan. The town even calls itself the home of the "World's Largest Pecan," which is in the form of a statue located on the courthouse lawn at Court Street.

where to go

Chamber of Commerce. 116 North Camp St.; (830) 379-6382; www.seguinchamber .com. Stop here for brochures and maps. Open weekdays.

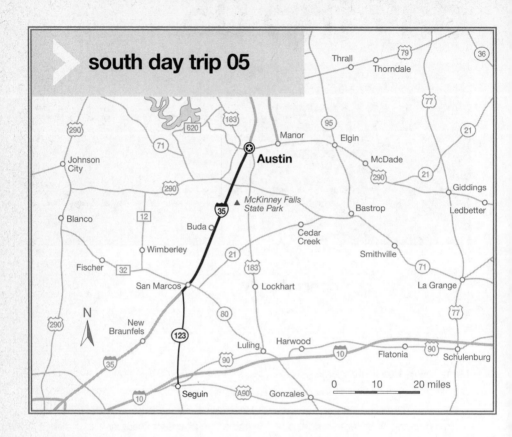

south day trip 05

Thrall
Thorndale
McDade
Manor
Elgin
Austin
McKinney Falls
State Park
Bastrop
Giddings
Ledbetter
Johnson
City
Blanco
Buda
Cedar
Creek
Wimberley
Smithville
Fischer
San Marcos
Lockhart
La Grange
N
New
Braunfels
Luling
Harwood
Flatonia
Schulenburg
Seguin
Gonzales

0   10   20 miles

Heritage Museum. 114 North River St.; (830) 372-0965. This local-history museum is housed in a former grocery store. Exhibits trace the multicultural heritage of this city's early settlers. Open Tues through Fri noon to 5 p.m.

Los Nogales Museum. 415 South River St., just south of the courthouse; (830) 303-7333. Los Nogales, which means "walnuts" in Spanish, houses local artifacts. The small brick adobe building was constructed in 1849. Next door, The Doll House is filled with period children's toys that you can see through the windows. This white miniature home was built between 1908 and 1910 by local cabinetmaker Louis Dietz as a playhouse for his niece. Later he used it to promote his business. Open by appointment though visitors are free to stroll the museum grounds. For tour information, call the Chamber of Commerce.

Sebastopol State Historical Park. 704 Zorn St.; (830) 379-4833; www.tpwd.state.tx.us. This is one of the best examples of the early use of concrete in the Southwest. Sebastopol was once a large home constructed of concrete with a plaster overlay. Today it is open for tours and contains exhibits illustrating the construction of this historic building and its restoration in 1988. Guided tours on Fri through Sun 9 a.m. to 4 p.m.; call the Chamber of Commerce to set up group tours at other times.

Seguin's Lakes. Seguin is surrounded by four lakes on the Guadalupe River that offer bass, crappie, and catfish fishing, including lighted docks for night fishing. RV facilities are available as well. The lakes include **Lake Dunlap** (I-10 to TX 46 exit west of Seguin, then 8 miles on TX 46); **Lake McQueeney** (I-10 to FM 78 exit, then west for 3 miles to FM 725, then turn right and continue for 1 mile); **Lake Placid** (I-10 to FM 464 exit, stay on access road); and **Meadow Lake** (I-10 to TX 123 bypass, then south for 4 miles).

Starcke Park. South side of town, off TX 123; (830) 401-2480. Make time for this pleasant park, where visitors can enjoy golf, tennis, and baseball as well as many riverside picnic spots. Large waterpark is open seasonally. Free admission.

Texas Theatre. 427 North Austin St. This 1931 theater has been used for scenes in two movies: *Raggedy Man* and *The Great Waldo Pepper*. It still sports its original marquee and recalls the old days of small-town Texas theaters. For information, check with the Chamber of Commerce.

True Women Tours. Fans of Janice Woods Wendle's *True Women* can take a guided tour of the sites mentioned in this best-seller and seen in the television miniseries. Led by local docents, the tours take a look at sites that play an important role in the historical novel: the live oak-shaded **King Cemetery,** the old **First Methodist Church** where two *True Women* characters were married, and the river where horses were daringly rescued in the tale.

One of the most memorable stops is the **Bettie Moss King Home,** near the King Cemetery. The home, with its wraparound porch and shady lawn, was where several generations of the King family were raised and was also the childhood home of author Janice Woods

flower power

Is it spring? Grab the car keys in one hand, your camera in the other, and get ready for a bloomin' good time! Starting in late March and extending into early summer, wildflowers line the roadways throughout central and south Texas. The best way to find the top fields is with a quick call to the **Texas Department of Transportation's wildflower hotline** *(800-452-9292). The hotline is active from mid-March until early May, and you can request information by region (Central Texas and Hill Country covers most of this book's scope). Maps showing the best spots for viewing wildflowers are available through the Texas Department of Transportation Web site (www.dot.state.tx.us/travel/flora_conditions.htm).*

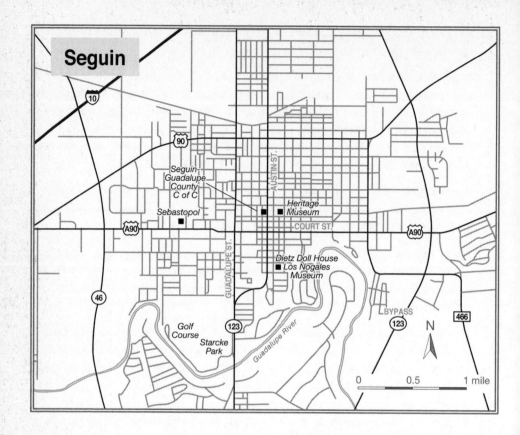

Windle. Today Windle's mother, Virginia Woods, still lives there and often opens her home to tour groups. Woods points out her ancestors' belongings, including the dining-room table that played a part in *True Women,* both in the story and in the writing of the family saga.

Call the **Seguin Chamber of Commerce** for tour times or pick up a map for a self-guided drive (427 North Austin St.). Fee for guided tour.

Wave Pool. Starcke Park East; (830) 401-2482. In this Texas-size pool, youngsters can cool off under the Mushroom Shower or splash in the simulated waves. Nearby, the sprawling Kids Kingdom Playscape makes an excellent stop for energetic young travelers as well. Open seasonally.

where to stay

Weinert House Bed and Breakfast. 1207 North Austin St.; (830) 372-4600; www.weinerthouseseguin.com. Kick back and enjoy small-town life amid 1890s elegance in this historic Victorian home. Four guest quarters are decorated with period antiques. The Senator's Suite includes a fireplace and screened sunporch. $$.

southwest

day trip 01

southwest

the alamo city:
san antonio

Famous humorist Will Rogers once dubbed San Antonio "one of America's four unique cities," and it's easy to agree with the sentiment as you experience the city's gloriously multicultural atmosphere. No recent upstart among Texas cities, San Antonio was an important cultural and commercial crossroads long before the Texans' desperate struggle for independence. The city's history still lives as you walk its winding streets or take a river taxi through quiet canals.

san antonio

San Antonio has the reputation of a fun-loving town. Located 80 miles south of Austin on I-35, the city always has something going on to attract visitors. No matter when you choose to visit, you can bet that somebody, somewhere, is hosting a festival. Perhaps it has something to do with the sunshine or the fresh air, but whatever it is, you can feel it. It sizzles up like fajitas out of the city's Latino heritage, which abounds with colorful traditions and vivid memories.

San Antonio's rich cultural past dates to the early Indians who settled the area. They were followed by the 17th-century Spaniards, who came here in search of wealth. Later a group of Franciscan friars established a chain of missions designed to convert the Indians of the Southwest to Christianity. In 1718 Mission San Antonio de Valero (better known as the Alamo) became the first of five such structures in the city.

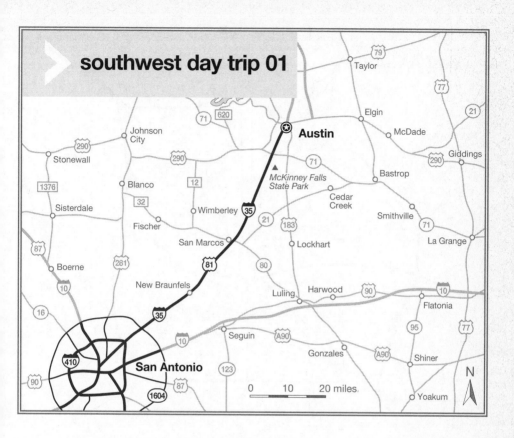

southwest day trip 01

Except for the Alamo, the missions are found in the San Antonio Missions National Historical Park, located within the city limits. The National Park Service has assigned interpretive themes to each of the four—the active parish churches of Mission Concepción, Mission San Juan Capistrano, Mission San Francisco de la Espada, and Mission San José. The latter, established in 1720, hosts a colorful "Mariachi Mass" each Sunday at noon.

San Antonio is also a foodie's paradise. This is the city that heralded the birth of fajitas—strips of marinated charcoal-grilled skirt steak. Here you'll also find to-die-for guacamole, pico de gallo (a Mexican condiment of onions, tomatoes, and chiles), and fresh flour tortillas.

With two excellent theme parks, a world-class zoo, and wonderful museums, San Antonio offers much more to see and do than this book can possibly list. For a complete rundown of possibilities, contact the San Antonio Convention and Visitor Bureau, www.visit sanantonio.com; (800) THE-ALAMO or (210) 207-6700. Stop in the visitor center at Alamo Plaza (across from the Alamo), where you can pick up information on the VIA streetcars that connect major tourist sites. Open daily.

downtown: river walk area

The River Walk stretches for 2.5 miles from South St. Mary's Street to Alamo Street, and along Crockett and Market Streets. The Paseo del Rio, as it's also called, is a European-style river walk that lies below street level. Part of an urban renovation project six decades ago, the River Walk is now a top San Antonio attraction. Its winding sidewalks, which follow an arm of the San Antonio River, are lined with two-story specialty shops, sidewalk cafes, luxury hotels, art galleries, and bars. Like New Orleans's Bourbon Street, this area of San Antonio has an atmosphere all its own. Arched bridges connect the two sides of the walk, so visitors never have to venture up to street level.

One of the busiest sections of the Paseo del Rio extends from the Hyatt Regency Riverwalk at Crockett Street to the Hilton Palacio del Rio Hotel at Market Street. This stretch of walk boasts most of the sidewalk restaurants and shops. From Commerce Street you can head up to the Henry B. Gonzales Convention Center and the Rivercenter Mall.

A great way to get around in this congested area is aboard the VIA downtown trolleys. For just $1.10 you can hop aboard one of four routes for transportation to most major sites. (210) 362-2020; www.viainfo.net.

where to go

The Alamo. 300 Alamo Plaza, between Houston and Crockett Streets; (210) 225-1391; www.thealamo.org. Located in the very heart of San Antonio, the Alamo was once surrounded on all sides by the forces of Mexico's General Santa Anna. Now it's enveloped by high-rise office structures and a central plaza.

This "Cradle of Texas Liberty," situated on the east side of Alamo Plaza, is probably the most famous spot in Texas. Established in 1718 as the Mission San Antonio de Valero, it plunged into history on March 6, 1836, when 188 men died after being attacked by Santa Anna's Mexican forces. Among the most famous defenders were Jim Bowie, William B. Travis, and Davy Crockett.

A symbol of the state's independence and courage, the Alamo draws continuous crowds throughout the year. Visitors entering the main building, the Shrine, can see exhibits such as Bowie's famous knife and Davy Crockett's rifle, "Old Betsy." Those interested also can take a self-guided tour of the museum, the Long Barracks, and the beautiful courtyard. Open daily except Christmas Eve and Christmas Day. Free admission.

Louis Tussaud's Waxworks. 301 Alamo Plaza; (210) 224-9299; http://sanantonio.ripleys .com/wax-works. This attraction has wax figures of movie and TV celebrities as well as a theater of horrors. The "Heroes of the Lone Star" section is interesting, with realistic scenes depicting the fall of the Alamo. Ripley's Believe It or Not! is located in the same building, and you can buy separate or combination tickets to the two attractions. Open daily.

Rio San Antonio Cruises. 205 N. Presa Building B., Suite 201, and with stops along the River Walk; (800) 417-4139 or (210) 244-5700; www.riosanantonio.com. One of the most pleasurable and inexpensive attractions in town, these open barges take passengers on narrated cruises through the heart of San Antonio from morning until late evening. Special dinner cruises afford a romantic look at the city and are arranged by River Walk restaurants. Open daily; hours change seasonally.

San Antonio Children's Museum. 305 East Houston St.; (210) 212-4453; www.sakids .org. This museum specializes in hands-on activities for all ages. A highlight of the museum is its historical San Antonio exhibits. Open Tues through Sun.

San Antonio IMAX Theatre. 849 East Commerce St., Rivercenter Mall; (800) 354-4629 or (210) 247-4629; www.imax-sa.com. This theater features *Alamo . . . The Price of Freedom,* a forty-five-minute movie about the battle of the Alamo. The six-story screen and six-channel sound immerses you in the glory of the struggle, and it's a good thing to see before visiting the historic site. The theater alternates this movie with other IMAX features, so call for showtimes. Open daily.

Steves Homestead. 509 King William St.; (210) 225-5924. This grand home was built in 1876 and is currently the only one in the elegant King William Historic District that is open

king william

Imagine San Antonio without the River Walk. Without the Tower of the Americas. Without the bustling business that fills this modern metropolis.

It is the late 1800s. Texas is still a frontier, gaining statehood after its years as an independent republic and a territory of Mexico. After years of subsistence on a rugged frontier, San Antonio residents are finally ready for comforts, culture, and a community spirit that emphasizes education, music, and the language of their homeland.

With these goals in mind, the **King William district** *was born. Started by the founder of the utopian community Comfort (see Southwest Day Trip 04), this elegant neighborhood on the banks of the San Antonio River soon attained the status of a superior neighborhood. Going back to the mid-1800s, when this district was populated by the Alamo City's most successful businessmen and their families, many of these frontier citizens were German immigrants with names like Guenther, Wulff, and Heusinger. With their wealth gained in merchandising and investing, they set about building the most lavish homes in the city, most in the grand Victorian style.*

For visitors seeking a romantic getaway in San Antonio, a place to enjoy historic elegance in a quiet neighborhood that's within easy walking distance of the River Walk, King William is an ideal destination. Tucked in a quiet neighborhood beneath towering live oak trees, this area is home to numerous bed-and-breakfast establishments. Ranging from country comfort to antebellum elegance, there's a bed-and-breakfast for every taste.

to the public. The Victorian mansion's interior is filled with original furniture, and the grounds include several antique carriages and the gardener's quarters, now a visitor center. Open daily.

Tower of the Americas. 600 HemisFair Plaza Way in HemisFair Park; (210) 223-3101; www.toweroftheamericas.com. San Francisco has its Golden Gate Bridge, St. Louis has the Arch, and since the 1968 World's Fair, San Antonio has had the Tower of the Americas. At 750 feet, the Tower's observation deck and top-floor restaurant offers an unbeatable view of the city. From ground level, its the most recognizable landmark in the San Antonio skyline. Open daily.

University of Texas Institute of Texan Cultures at San Antonio. 801 E. Durango Blvd. at HemisFair Park; (210) 458-2300; www.texancultures.utsa.edu. This fascinating museum features exhibits and a multimedia presentation showcasing the twenty-six different ethnic groups who came here from around the world to settle the new frontier called Texas. Open daily.

where to shop

Rivercenter Mall. 849 East Commerce St.; (210) 225-0000; www.shoprivercenter.com. Bounded by Commerce, Bowie, Crockett, and Alamo Streets. This three-story mall is home to several anchor stores as well as specialty shops and restaurants. On the enclosed bridge over the river, vendors sell crafts and specialty items. The River Walk makes a U-turn in an outdoor dining area. Open daily.

La Villita. Exit through Hilton Hotel, then 1 block right on South Alamo Street; www.lavillita .com. This area on the east bank of the San Antonio River was developed in the mid-to-late 18th century by Mexican settlers who lived, without land title, on the outskirts of the Alamo mission. Today La Villita is San Antonio's finest crafts area, filled with weavers, glassblowers, sculptors, and even boot makers. Within the restored buildings, shops sell everything from woven wall hangings to silver jewelry, and the historic Little Church is often the site of weddings. Most shops open daily. Free admission.

where to eat

Boudro's. 421 East Commerce St.; (210) 224-8484; www.boudros.com. Ask many San Antonians for their favorite River Walk eatery, and you'll hear this name. This steak and seafood restaurant offers the finest in southwestern cuisine, usually with a twist that makes it unique even among San Antonio's plethora of excellent restaurants. Start with a cactus margarita, a frozen concoction with a jolt of red cactus liqueur. Follow that eye-opener with an appetizer of smoked chicken or crab quesadillas, or crab and shrimp tamales. Save room, though, for Boudro's specialties—coconut shrimp, pecan-grilled fish fillet, and the specialty of the house, blackened prime rib. Seating is available on the River Walk or in the dining room. $$.

Little Rhein Steakhouse. 231 South Alamo; (210) 225-2111; www.littlerheinsteakhouse .com. Located on the River Walk near the Arneson River Theater, this restaurant offers an excellent selection of fine steaks served on terraces overlooking the river. On less pleasant days, you may choose to dine inside the historic steak house, built in 1847, which witnessed the development of San Antonio under six different flags. The stone building also survived the battle of the Alamo, only a few blocks away. From the extensive menu, you can choose anything from T-bones to rib eye to porterhouse steak, all served with Texas caviar (a mixture of black-eyed peas and chopped onion). Reservations are recommended. $$–$$$.

Schilo's Delicatessen. 424 East Commerce St.; (210) 223-6692. This deli is located up on street level, not on the River Walk, but what it lacks in atmosphere it definitely makes up for in history. Papa Fritz Schilo, a German immigrant, opened a saloon in 1917, but when Prohibition came along, he converted the operation to a deli. It was a lucky break for diners; mere suds could never match the subs and sandwiches that continue to keep this spot packed with locals. Try a Reuben or a ham and cheese, or for dinner go all out with entrees like Wiener schnitzel or bratwurst. $.

where to stay

Emily Morgan Hotel. 705 East Houston St., next to the Alamo; (210) 225-7227; www .emilymorganhotel.com. General Santa Anna was enamored with a mulatto slave named Emily Morgan, who acted as a spy for the Texas army. Thanks in part to her efforts, Sam Houston's troops defeated Santa Anna's men at San Jacinto on April 21, 1836, winning the Texas Revolution. Emily Morgan came to be known as "the Yellow Rose of Texas" and is the namesake of this 177-room hotel. The rooms overlook the Alamo courtyard or Alamo Plaza, and most have Jacuzzis. $$.

Hyatt Regency San Antonio. 123 Losoya St.; (800) 233-1234 or (210) 222-1234; www .hyatt.com. This beautiful hotel, with its open atrium and glass elevators, is located directly on the River Walk. A stream flows through the hotel outside to the River Walk, where an open-air jazz bar provides nightly entertainment. $$$.

Marriott Plaza San Antonio. 555 South Alamo St.; (210) 229-1000 or (800) 421-1172; www.marriott.com. This elegant establishment has the most beautiful grounds of any downtown hotel: six acres dotted with gardens, Chinese pheasants, and historic buildings. Most of the 252 rooms have private balconies. The hotel received international attention in 1992 as host of the initializing ceremony of the North American Free Trade Agreement on the grounds. $$$.

Omni La Mansión Del Rio. 112 College St.; (210) 518-1000; www.omnihotels.com. This Spanish colonial–style hotel has long been a River Walk favorite with travelers. The structure began as St. Mary's Academy in 1854, later becoming a college, a university, and a law school, until 1966 when it became a hotel. Today the hotel captures the atmosphere of San Antonio in its architecture, courtyards, and restaurants, and bar, El Colegio, which recalls the building's early days as a school. $$$.

Watermark Hotel and Spa. 212 West Crockett St.; (866) 605-1212; www.watermarkhotel .com. Located in a historic building, the Watermark Hotel and Spa is aimed at discerning travelers looking for a quiet retreat from the busy River Walk. With 99 luxury rooms, the hotel is also home to a 17,000-square-foot spa, the fine dining restaurant, Pesca on the River, and a rooftop pool. $$$.

Wyndham St. Anthony Hotel. 300 East Travis St.; (210) 227-4392; www.wyndham.com. This historic hotel a few blocks off the River Walk offers 352 rooms and access to a restaurant, health club, and swimming pool. $$$.

hot tamales

Tamales, both mild and spicy varieties, are found on just about every Tex-Mex menu throughout the state, but they're most popular during the Christmas season. Stores and restaurants sell tamales by the dozen during the holidays when it's popular to bring them to office parties and home get-togethers.

Making tamales at home is a time-consuming job, often tackled by large families as a holiday tradition. Tamales start with the preparation of a hog's head, boiled with garlic, spices, peppers, and cilantro. After cooking, the meat is ground and then simmered with spices.

As the filling is prepared, other family members ready the hojas, or corn husks, used to wrap the tamale. Others prepare the masa, a cornmeal worked with lard and seasonings, spread thinly on the shucks before filling with meat. Finally, the tamales are steamed in huge pots.

downtown: market square

Colorful Market Square, bounded by San Saba, Santa Rosa, West Commerce, and Dolorosa Streets, is a busy shopping and dining area from early morning to late evening. It is also the scene of many San Antonio festivals.

To reach Market Square from the River Walk, follow Commerce Street west across the river to just east of I-10. Or leave your car and take an inexpensive ride on the VIA streetcars, the open-air trolleys that stop at many downtown San Antonio attractions. (For information on VIA routes, stop by the San Antonio Visitor Information Center mentioned earlier.)

The history of Market Square goes back to the early 1800s, when Mexico ruled the settlement of San Antonio de Bejar. Fresh produce and meats filled the farmer's market, and pharmaceutical items were available at Botica Guadalupana, today the oldest continuously operating pharmacy in town (and a very interesting place to browse, even if you're feeling fine).

Chili con carne, the state dish of Texas, was invented here over a century ago. Back then, young girls known as "chili queens" sold the spicy meat-and-bean concoction from kiosks.

Today Market Square includes the renovated Farmers' Market Plaza (rife with Mexican imports and crafts rather than produce), an open-air restaurant and shopping area, and El Mercado, the largest enclosed Mexican-style marketplace in the country. Also located nearby are two historic structures: the Spanish Governor's Palace and Navarro House, home of a Texas patriot.

where to go

Casa Navarro State Historical Park. 228 South Laredo St.; (210) 226-4801; www.visit casanavarro.com. This was formerly the residence of José Antonio Navarro (1795–1871), a signer of the Texas Declaration of Independence. The adobe and limestone structure, located just a short walk from Market Square, includes an office used by Navarro, who was a lawyer and legislator. Open Tues through Sun 9 a.m. to 4 p.m.

El Mercado. 514 West Commerce St.; (210) 207-8600; www.sanantonio.gov/dtops/ marketsquare. Styled after a typical Mexican market, El Mercado's fifty shops sell a profusion of goods, from silver jewelry, Mexican dresses, and piñatas to onyx chess sets, leather goods, and much more. Prices are slightly higher than in the Mexican markets, and you can't bargain with the vendors like you can south of the border. Open daily. Free admission.

Museo Alameda. 101 South Santa Rosa; (210) 299-4300; www.thealameda.org. San Antonio's newest museum is a unique site, the first formal affiliate of The Smithsonian Institution. Opened in April 2007, the museum is the official Texas State Latino Museum; with 20,000 square feet of exhibit space, the museum is the country's largest Latino museum. The facility includes seven galleries as well as a public sculpture garden. Four of the galleries feature rotating exhibits, including The Smithsonian Gallery. The Tobin Sculpture Garden features items from the Hirshhorn Museum and Sculpture Garden in Washington, D.C.

Spanish Governor's Palace. 105 Military Plaza, (210) 224-0601; www.sanantonio.gov/ dtops/SpanGovPal.asp. Part of an old Spanish fort that was built at the site in 1722, this structure was converted to a military commander's residence in 1749. San Antonio was once the capital of the Spanish province of Texas, and the Spanish governors occasionally resided here. The walls are 3 feet thick, and the home is filled with Spanish colonial antiques. Open daily.

where to eat

La Margarita. 120 Produce Row; (210) 227-7140; www.lamargarita.com. This establishment also is owned by Mi Tierra and is best known for its excellent fajitas, which are brought to your table in cast-iron skillets. Open for lunch and dinner. $–$$.

Mi Tierra. 218 Produce Row; (210) 225-1262; www.mitierracafe.com. This is the place to head for an unbeatable Tex-Mex meal that includes homemade tortillas, enchiladas, and chiliquiles, a spicy egg-and-corn tortilla breakfast dish served with refried beans. Decorated year-round with Christmas ornaments, this San Antonio institution is open 24 hours a day, 365 days a year. $–$$.

within the city

Although the downtown area has plenty of attractions, other stops lie on the outskirts of the city, including a zoo, missions, and botanical gardens.

where to go

Buckhorn Saloon and Museums. 318 E. Houston St.; (210) 247-4000; www.buckhorn museum.com. There's nothing more Texan than Lone Star beer, and you can sample the product at the Buckhorn Saloon. This historic bar once was frequented by short-story writer William Sydney Porter (O. Henry), whose home has been relocated to the brewery grounds 2 blocks from the Alamo.

The Buckhorn Saloon building also contains the Buckhorn Hall of Horns and the Buckhorn Hall of Feathers, each containing their respective mounted specimens of animal horns and Texas birds. Separate buildings house the Hall of Texas History Wax Museum, with figures that re-create Texas's early historic events, and the Buckhorn Hall of Fins, which includes specimens from the Gulf of Mexico and Texas rivers. Open daily.

Fort Sam Houston Self-Guided Tour. North New Braunfels Avenue and Stanley Road; (210) 221-1886; www.nps.gov/history/NR/travel/tx/tx39.htm. This National Historic Landmark, an army base dating back to 1870, has nine times as many historic buildings as Colonial Williamsburg. These include the residence where General John J. Pershing lived in 1917; the Chinese Camp, once occupied by Chinese who fled Mexico to escape Pancho Villa; and the home where Lieutenant and Mrs. Dwight Eisenhower lived in 1916. Visitors can stroll past the structures (they are not open to the public). Call for hours. Free admission.

The post also includes two museums. The **Fort Sam Houston Museum** (210-221-1886; www.ameddregiment.amedd.army.mil/fshmuse/fshmusemain.htm) is filled with exhibits about the site's early days. Open Wed through Sun. Free admission. The **U.S. Army Medical Department Museum** (210-221-6358; www.ameddregiment.amedd.army.mil/museum2/index.htm) houses exhibits on military medical practices dating to the Revolutionary War. Open Tues through Sat. Free admission.

Japanese Tea Gardens. 3800 North St. Mary's St., by the zoo; (210) 207-3211. San Antonio's semitropical climate encourages the lush flowers, climbing vines, and tall palms found inside this quiet, serene place. Koi (large goldfish) swim through the ponds complete with beautiful rock bridges and walkways. Open daily. Free admission.

Marion Koogler McNay Art Museum. 6000 North New Braunfels Ave.; (210) 824-5368; www.mcnayart.org. Located in a Spanish Mediterranean mansion that was once the home of art lover Marion Koogler McNay, the museum houses a nationally known collection of modern art as well as medieval and Gothic works. It also holds the largest collection of

European and American graphic art in the Southwest. In the Tobin wing, visitors find one of the country's best theater arts research centers. Open Tues through Sun. $.

San Antonio Botanical Gardens and Halsell Conservatory. 555 Funston Place, near Fort Sam Houston; (210) 207-3250; www.sabot.org. Roses, herbs, a garden for the blind, and native plants are found within the lovely setting of these thirty-three-acre gardens.

The centerpiece here is the $6.9 million Halsell Conservatory. The futuristic-looking, 90,000-square-foot structure is composed of seven tall glass spires. A self-guided tour of these seven areas takes visitors through the plants and flowers found in different environments, from desert to tropics. The conservatory sits partially underground for a cooling effect in the hot Texas summers. Open daily. $.

San Antonio Museum of Art. 200 West Jones Ave.; (210) 978-8100; www.samuseum .org. This extensive art museum is housed in the former Lone Star Brewery. The collection ranges from ancient Egyptian artifacts to 19th-century art. The museum now boasts the Nelson A. Rockefeller Collection of Mexican Folk Art, one of the best in the nation. Open Tues through Sun. $.

San Antonio Missions National Historical Park. This national park stretches for 9 miles along the San Antonio River and is composed of four remaining missions (outside of the Alamo) constructed by the Franciscan friars in the eighteenth century. The missions are active parish churches today, and all are open to the public. For a map of the mission locations, visit the National Park Service Web site at www.nps.gov/saan. Each of the four illustrates a different concept of mission life.

Mission San José. 6701 San José Dr.; (210) 932-1001. The most complete structure in the tour, Mission San José was built in 1720. It has beautiful carvings, eighty-four rooms that once housed Indians, a restored mill with waterwheel, and what may be the only complete mission fort in existence. Make this mission your first stop; it is also home to the Visitors Information Center.

Mission Concepción. 807 Mission Rd.; (210) 534-1540. Built in 1731 this mission holds the title as the oldest unrestored stone church in the country.

Mission San Juan Capistrano. 9102 Graff Rd.; (210) 534-0749. This mission was relocated here from East Texas in 1731 but never completed.

Mission San Francisco de la Espada. 10040 Espada Rd.; (210) 627-2021. Established in 1731, its original chapel was in ruins by 1778 and the building was reconstructed around 1868.

San Antonio Zoological Garden and Aquarium. 3903 North St. Mary's St.; (210) 734-7184; www.sazoo-aq.org. This world-class zoo features barless "habitat cages" for many of its animals. The cliffs of an abandoned quarry are home to more than 3,000 birds, fish, mammals, and other fauna, making the zoo one of the largest animal collections in North America. There's a children's petting area, a reptile house, and an aquarium. Open daily year-round; call for seasonal hours.

Witte Museum of History and Science/H–E–B Science Treehouse. 3801 Broadway; (210) 357-1900; www.wittemuseum.org. This excellent museum focuses on natural history, especially as it relates to the state's Native American, Spanish, and Mexican heritage. Open daily. The museum is also home to the H–E–B Treehouse, a collection of hands-on exhibits illustrating scientific principles.

far northwest

Beyond Loop 410, the city begins to give way to the Hill Country, the rolling, oak-covered land that's still largely rural. This is also the home of San Antonio's two theme parks.

where to go

SeaWorld San Antonio. Ellison Drive and Westover Hills Boulevard, off TX 151; 18 miles northwest of downtown, between Loop 410 and Loop 1604; (800) 700-7786; www.seaworld.com. This 250-acre, Texas-size park is the largest marine-life park in the world. It's the home of Shamu the killer whale, plus dolphins, penguins, sea otters, and more. Visitors can enjoy two fast-moving water rides as well as acres of quiet gardens dotted with statues of famous Texans. Entertainment includes twenty-five shows, featuring a waterskiing extravaganza and breathtaking cycling performances. Interactive programs enable visitors (for an additional fee) to don wet suits for up-close encounters with beluga whales or California sea lions, to dine with killer whales, or to go behind the scenes to watch the care of more than 11,000 animals. The park also offers two roller coasters and plenty of water rides. Other attractions include a beautiful coral reef, a petting pool with people-friendly dolphins, and a Garden of Flags overlooking a map of the United States. Painted on concrete, the map is the size of a parking lot, and children are encouraged to race from "coast to coast." Open Mar through Dec with changing hours. Call for hours.

Six Flags Fiesta Texas. I-10 and Loop 1604, 15 miles northwest of downtown; (800) 473-4378 or (210) 697-5050; www.sixflags.com/fiestaTexas/index.aspx. This $100-million-plus theme park focuses on the history, culture, and music of San Antonio and the Southwest. The main draw of this 200-acre spread is live entertainment. Seven theaters delight visitors with more than sixty performances daily, including the award-winning and always packed "Rockin' at Rockville High" Grease-style musical production. For thrill seekers, there are thirteen rides that range from whitewater rafting to the Rattler, one of the tallest wooden roller coasters in the world and a real white-knuckle ride.

Thrills also abound on the Superman Krypton Coaster, a mile-long thrill ride that takes riders through six inversions and a 114-foot vertical loop at 70 miles per hour.

The park is divided into five "villages," each featuring a different style of music and entertainment: Hispanic (Los Festivales), German (Spassburg), country-western (Crackaxle Canyon), rock 'n' roll (Rockville), and the Boardwalk, a 1950s-themed area complete with a sand "beach," and a 90-foot Ferris wheel that provides an unbeatable view of the park and, just at the edge of the horizon, the city. A new section, Wiggles World, designed for kids two to six years old, is inspired by the pop group The Wiggles. Open seasonally Mar through Oct; call for hours.

where to stay

Hyatt Regency Hill Country Resort. 9800 Hyatt Resort Dr.; (800) 233-1234 or (210) 647-1234; www.hyatt.com. This full-service resort offers the area's most luxurious getaway with 27 holes of golf and a four-acre water park with a cascading waterfall and man-made Ramblin' River for inner-tube floaters. This 500-room resort nestles on 200 acres of a former cattle ranch, rolling land sprinkled with prickly pear cacti, wildflower meadows, and live oaks. With its limestone architecture and western decor, the four-story hotel captures the atmosphere of the Hill Country, from windmills to gingerbread trim featuring the Lone Star (which often decorated homes of the German pioneers who settled the area). For meetings, the resort boasts 41,800 square feet of flexible function space, ranging from boardrooms and ballrooms to indoor and outdoor pavilions. $$$.

especially for winter texans

Admiralty RV Resort Park. 1485 North Ellison Dr., off Loop 1604; (877) 236-4715 or (210) 647-7878; www.admiraltyrvresort.com. This 240-pad RV park is located minutes from SeaWorld and Loop 1604. It includes a heated pool, brick patios at each site, cable TV hookups, and organized get-togethers during the winter (potluck dinners, card games, and dominoes). Winter residents can take advantage of special monthly rates.

day trip 02

southwest

old-world fun:
gruene, new braunfels

Fun abounds along the track of this day trip whether it be splashing in waterparks and scenic Hill Country rivers, boot-scooting at famous Greune Hall, or soaking up German heritage at Wurst Fest in New Braunfels.

gruene

Once a separate community but now part of New Braunfels, Gruene is a popular destination for shoppers and water recreation lovers. Head south on I-35 for 30 miles to San Marcos (see South Day Trip 03 for attractions in that city). Continue south for 17 miles to exit 191. Turn west and continue to the intersection with Hunter Road, then turn left and continue to this historic area.

Once a ghost town, Gruene has been transformed into a very popular shopping destination. A historic inn, river rafting, lots of good food, and Texas's oldest dance hall draw visitors from around the state.

Like Waxahachie and Refugio, the pronunciation of Gruene is one of those things that sets a real Texan apart. To sound like a local, just say "Green."

In the days when cotton was king, Gruene was a roaring town on the banks of the Guadalupe River. Started in the 1870s by H. D. Gruene, the community featured a swinging dance hall and a cotton gin. Prosperity reigned until the boll weevil came to Texas, with the Great Depression right on its heels. Gruene's foreman hanged himself from the water

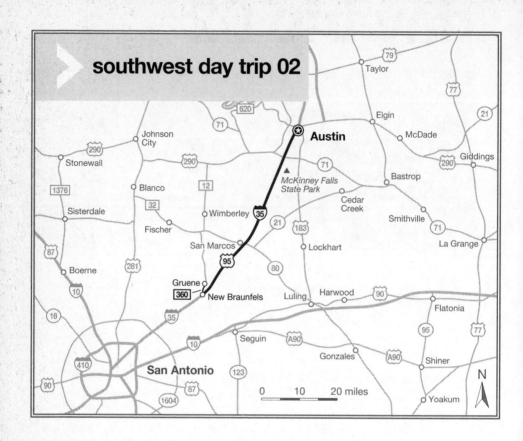

tower, and H. D.'s plans for the town withered like the cotton in the fields. Gruene became a ghost town.

One hundred years after its founding, investors began restoring Gruene's historic buildings and, little by little, businesses began moving into the once-deserted structures. Now Gruene is favored by antiques shoppers, barbecue and country music lovers, and those looking to step back into a simpler time. On weekdays you may find Gruene's streets quiet, but expect crowds every weekend.

There's free parking across from the Gruene Mansion Inn, former home of H. D. Gruene. Today the mansion is a private residence owned by the proprietors of an adjacent bed-and-breakfast.

Gruene is compact, with everything within easy walking distance. If you'd like more information on the community's history, pick up a free copy of "A Pedestrian Guide for Gruene Guests" at local shops.

More than one hundred arts and crafts vendors sell their wares during Market Days. This event is held Feb through Nov on the third Sat and Sun of the month, and a Christmas market takes place on the first weekend in Dec.

where to go

Gruene Hall. 1281 Gruene Rd.; (830) 606-1281; www.gruenehall.com. The oldest dance hall in Texas is as lively today as it was a century ago. Dances and concerts are regularly held here (even though the hall has no air-conditioning), and it is also open to tour. Burlap bags draped from the ceiling dampen the sound, and 1930s advertisements decorate the walls. The hall opens at 11 a.m. most days. On weekdays, there's usually no cover charge for evening performances; weekend cover charges vary with the performer. Call for a schedule of events.

Gospel Brunch with a Texas Twist. 1281 Gruene Rd.; (830) 606-1281; www.gruenehall .com. Gruene Hall hosts this event on the second Sunday of every month. Put your hands together and enjoy the sounds of gospel in this New Orleans–inspired event that includes brunch and, for an extra charge, libations. Seating is limited, so reservations are a must.

where to shop

Buck Pottery. 1296 Gruene Rd.; (830) 629-7975; www.buckpottery.com. Here you can watch potters at work in the back room. This shop sells dinnerware, gift items, and outdoor pots, all made with unleaded glazes. Open daily.

Gruene Antique Company. 1607 Hunter Rd.; (830) 629-7781. Built in 1904, this was once a mercantile store. Today it's divided into several vendor areas and filled with antiques. Open daily.

Gruene General Store. 1610 Hunter Rd.; (830) 629-6021 or (800) 974-8353. This shop brings back memories of small-town life during Gruene's heyday as a cotton center. This was the first mercantile store, built in 1878 to serve the families that worked on the cotton farms. It also served as a stagecoach stop and a post office. Today instead of farm imple- ments and dry goods, this 1990s general store sells cookbooks, fudge, and Texas-style clothing. Belly up for a soda at the old-fashioned fountain, and have a taste of homemade fudge.

Gruene Haus Country Store. 1297 Gruene Rd.; (830) 620-7454. Built in the 1880s, this shop was the former home of H. D. Gruene's suicidal foreman. Linens, lace runners, silk bluebonnets, gifts for cat lovers, and decorative accessories are for sale. Open daily.

Gruene River Company. 1404 Gruene Rd.; (888) 705-2800 or (830) 625-2800; www .gruenerivercompany.com. See the Guadalupe at your own pace—during a leisurely tube ride or on an exciting white-water raft journey—with this outfitter.

Lone Star Texas Eclectic. 1613 Hunter Rd.; (830) 609-1613; www.lonestaringruene .com. Bring the cowboy look to your home with the accessories in this shop. Lamps, din- nerware, and folk art are offered for sale.

Old Gruene Market Days. (830) 832-1721; www.gruenemarketdays.com. Shoppers flock to this community especially during Old Gruene Market Days. The event includes plenty of arts and crafts, a farmers market, and lots of live entertainment. More than 125 vendors give you the chance to make purchases including one-of-a-kind quilts, pottery, jewelry, and more. Held the third full weekend of the month from Feb through Nov and the first weekend of Dec.

Texas Homegrown. 1641 Hunter Rd.; (830) 629-3176; www.texas-homegrown.com/default.aspx. Like the name suggests, the merchandise is Texas-themed and features everything from bluebonnet earrings to coyote T-shirts. Open daily.

where to eat

Gristmill River Restaurant and Bar. 1287 Gruene Rd.; (830) 625-0684; www.gristmill restaurant.com. Housed in the ruins of a 120-year-old cotton gin, this restaurant serves chicken, chicken-fried steak, catfish, burgers, and other Texas favorites. You can eat inside or outside on the deck overlooking the Guadalupe River. Open daily. $$.

where to stay

Gruene Mansion Inn. 1275 Gruene Rd.; (830) 629-2641; www.gruenemansioninn.com. Guests at this inn stay in restored 1870s cottages on a bluff overlooking the Guadalupe River as well as in the historic mansion, a converted corn crib, and a former carriage house. Thirty lovely rooms are decorated with period antiques and each includes a private entrance, private bath, and porch. A two-night rental is required on most weekends. $$$.

new braunfels

Continue south on Gruene Road into New Braunfels. This city has just about everything to offer travelers, including historic buildings, German food, an enormous water theme park, and enough antiques shops to merit the title "The Antique Capital of Texas."

If you're looking for a romantic getaway in a historic inn or a weekend of outdoor fun, New Braunfels is the place. Just a half hour south of Austin on I-35, this town of 36,500 offers something for every interest, from antiques and water sports to German culture.

In the 1840s, a group of German businessmen bought some land in Texas, planning to parcel off the acreage to German immigrants. Led by Prince Carl of Germany's Solms-Braunfels region, the group came to Texas to check on their new purchase. They discovered that it was more than 300 miles from the Texas coast, far from supplies in San Antonio, and located in the midst of Comanche Indian territory. Prince Carl sent a letter warning other settlers not to come, but it was too late—almost 400 already had set sail for Texas. The prince saved the day by buying another parcel of land, this in the central part of the state. Called "The Fountains" by the Native Americans, it offered plentiful springs and agricultural

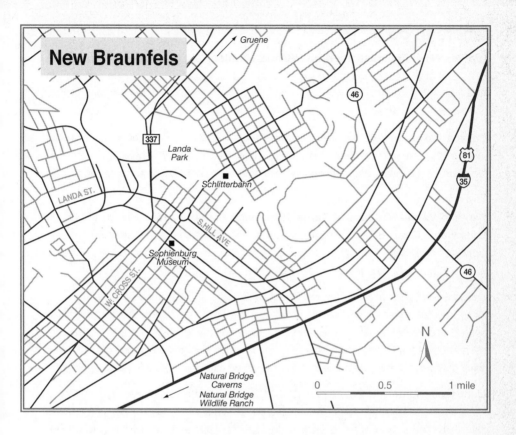

New Braunfels
Gruene
46
337
Landa Park
81
35
Schlitterbahn
LANDA ST.
S. HILL AVE
Sophienburg Museum
46
W. CROSS ST.
N
Natural Bridge Caverns
Natural Bridge Wildlife Ranch
0   0.5   1 mile

opportunities. The Germans soon divided the land into farms, irrigating with spring water. The settlement they founded was named New Braunfels in honor of their homeland.

New Braunfels has never forgotten these ties to the old country. Even today German is spoken in many local homes. Every November the town puts on its lederhosen for Wurstfest, one of the largest German celebrations in the country.

The German settlers were a practical lot, and they saved old items of every description. Everything from handmade cradles to used bottles and jars was kept and passed down through generations.

The early settlers of New Braunfels also were attracted by the Comal and Guadalupe Rivers. Today swimmers, rafters, inner-tubers, and campers are drawn to these shady banks. The 2-mile-long Comal holds the distinction as the world's shortest river. Its crystal-clear waters begin with the springs in downtown Landa Park, eventually merging with the Guadalupe River, home to many local outfitters. Located on the scenic drive called River Road, the outfitters provide equipment and transportation for inner-tubers and rafters of all skill levels who like nothing better on a hot Texas day than to float down the cypress-shaded waters.

where to go

Greater New Braunfels Highway Visitors Center. 390 South Seguin Ave.; (800) 572-2626 or (830) 625-7973; www.nbcham.org. Southbound I-35 Frontage and Seguin Avenues at I-35 exit 187. Drop by for maps, brochures, shopping information, and friendly hometown advice about the area. Open daily.

Canyon Lake. FM 306, northwest of town; (800) 528-2104; www.canyonlakechamber .com. With 80 miles of protected shoreline, Canyon Lake is very popular with campers, bicyclists, scuba divers, and boaters. The lake has seven parks with boat ramps and picnic facilities.

Heritage Village-Museum of Texas Handmade Furniture. 1370 Church Hill Dr., in Conservation Plaza; (830) 629-6504; www.nbheritagevillage.com. This 19th-century home contains cedar, oak, and cypress furniture handcrafted by early German settlers. Open 1 p.m. to 4 p.m. Feb through Nov. Closed Dec and Jan.

Landa Park. Landa and San Antonio Streets; (830) 221-4350. Named for Joseph Landa, New Braunfels's first millionaire, this downtown park includes a miniature train, a glass-bottom boat cruise, a golf course, and a 1.5-acre spring-fed swimming pool. This is the headwaters of the Comal River, where springs produce eight million gallons of pure water every hour. Picnicking is welcome in the park, but no camping. Free admission.

Lindheimer Home. 491 Comal Ave.; (830) 608-1512. Located on the banks of the Comal River, this home belonged to Ferdinand Lindheimer, a botanist who lent his name to more than thirty Texas plant species. Now restored, it contains early memorabilia from Lindheimer's career as both botanist and newspaper publisher. A backyard garden is filled with examples of his native flora discoveries. Open Tues through Fri 10 a.m. to 2:30 p.m., Sat and Sun 2 p.m. to 5 p.m., but hours are seasonal so call before you go.

McKenna Children's Museum. 801 West San Antonio St.; (830) 620-0939; www.nbchil dren.org. Bring the kids to enjoy hands-on fun at this interactive museum that features a television studio. Open daily in summer, Tues through Sat for the remainder of the year.

Natural Bridge Caverns. 26495 Natural Bridge Caverns Rd., on RR 3009, southwest of New Braunfels; (210) 651-6101; www.naturalbridgecaverns.com. Named for the rock arch over the entrance, this cave is one of the most spectacular in the area. The guided tour is well lit; the slope of the trail may be taxing for some. Kids can "pan" for small pieces of amethyst, sapphire, obsidian, topaz, and more at the attraction's Natural Bridge Mining Company. And adventurous travelers can make reservations for the South Cave Tour, rappelling and crawling in spelunking gear to see remote cave regions. Open daily year-round; phone for tour times.

Natural Bridge Wildlife Ranch. 26515 Natural Bridge Caverns Rd., next to the caverns; (830) 438-7400; www.wildliferanchtexas.com. From I-35 south of New Braunfels, take RR 3009 west. From TX 46 west of town, you also can take a left on RR 1863 for a slightly longer but more scenic route.

For more than a century, this property has operated as a family ranch, and since 1984 it has showcased exotic species, today holding the title as the oldest and most-visited safari park in the state. More than fifty native, exotic, and endangered species roam the grounds. The ranch offers a drive past zebras, gazelles, antelope, ostriches, and more. You'll be given animal feed when you arrive, so be prepared for the animals to come right up to the car for a treat. (Watch out or the ostrich will put his head inside the car in search of that food!) A large cat run gives jaguars and cougars plenty of room to stroll, and another area houses three species of primates, as well as scarlet macaws and other exotic birds. A walking area holds some species that require a little more attention, such as reticulated giraffes, Bennett wallabies, and Patagonian cavies. Children love the petting zoo for the chance to get face to face with pint-size, friendly animals. Open daily.

River Road. This winding drive stretches northwest of the city for 18 miles from Loop 337 at the city limits to the Canyon Lake Dam. It's lined with river outfitters and beautiful spots where you can pull over and look at the rapids, which delight rafters, canoeists, and inner-tubers.

Schlitterbahn Waterpark Resort New Braunfels. 381 E. Austin St.; (830) 625-2351; www.schlitterbahn.com. From I-35, take the Boerne exit (Loop 337) to Common Street, then turn left and continue to Liberty Street. This water park ranks first in Texas and is tops in the United States among seasonal water parks. This is the largest water theme park in the state.

Schlitterbahn, which means "slippery road" in German, is also the largest tubing park in the world, with tube chutes, uphill water coasters, water slides, children's playgrounds, and more. The Comal River supplies 24,000 gallons a minute of cool spring water and also provides the only natural river rapids found in a water theme park.

Among the most colorful rides is the Soda Straws, made of huge Plexiglas-enclosed slides that take riders from the top of a 27-foot concrete soda to a pool below. In 1986 the cola glasses were filled with 2,000 gallons of soda and Blue Bell ice cream to create the world's largest Coke float. There's a steep 60-foot Schlittercoaster and the mile-long Raging River tube chute for daredevils, and a 50,000-gallon hot tub with a swim-up bar and the gentle wave pool for the less adventurous.

Two popular attractions here are the Boogie Bahn, a moving mountain of water for surfing, and the Dragon Blaster, the world's first uphill water coaster. The latter shoots inner-tube riders uphill for a roller-coaster-type ride through hills, dips, and curves. Plan to spend a whole day here, and bring a picnic if you like. Open May through Sept.

Sophienburg Museum. 401 West Coll St.; (830) 629-1572; www.sophienburg.com. For a look at the hard-working people who settled this rugged area, spend an hour or two here. Named for the wife of settlement leader Prince Carl, the museum's displays include a reproduction of an early New Braunfels home, a doctor's office (complete with medical tools), a blacksmith's shop, and carriages used by early residents. Open Tues through Sat 10 a.m. to 4 p.m.

where to shop

New Braunfels Marketplace. Exits 187 and 189 off I-35; (830) 620-7475; www.nbmarket place.com. What started out as a single factory store has become a destination for shoppers from Houston and Dallas. Goods from sportswear to books to leather goods are featured in the many shops. Open daily.

where to eat

Naegelin's Bakery. 129 South Seguin Ave.; (830) 625-5722; www.naegelins.com. Naegelin's has operated on the same spot since 1868. The original building is gone, replaced by the current structure in 1942. The store's specialty is apple strudel, a 2-foot-long creation that is certain to make any pastry-lover's mouth water. During the holidays, some of Naegelin's biggest sellers are springerle, a licorice cookie, and lebkucken, a frosted gingerbread cookie. Open Mon through Sat. $.

New Braunfels Smokehouse. 1090 N. Business 35 at TX 46 and US 81; (830) 625-2416; www.nbsmokehouse.com. If you get the chance to attend Wurstfest, you'll undoubtedly sample the product of this smokehouse. For this fall event, New Braunfels Smokehouse produces between 40,000 and 60,000 pounds of sausage. The sausage is the specialty of the house, but the restaurant has a little of everything, including smoked ham and barbecue brisket. A large gift shop up front offers Texas specialty foods and cookbooks. The company's mail-order business ships more than 600,000 catalogs to sausage lovers around the country. Open daily. $–$$.

Oma's Haus. 1248 FM 1101 Suite 200; (830) 625-3280; www.omashaus.com. 1 block east of I-35 on TX 46. This restaurant serves a wide selection of German dishes in a family atmosphere. The menu includes chicken and pork schnitzel, and the specialty of the house is called Oma's Pride, a spinach-filled pastry shell. For the less adventurous, chicken-fried steak and chicken breast are also offered. Open for lunch and dinner daily. $$.

where to stay

New Braunfels has plenty of accommodations for everyone. Check with the Chamber of Commerce (800-572-2626).

Faust Hotel. 240 South Seguin Ave.; (830) 625-7791; www.fausthotel.com. A New Braun-fels tradition, this 1929 four-story, renovated hotel features a bar that's popular with locals and visitors. The lobby is appointed with beautiful antique furnishings. $$.

Prince Solms Inn. 295 East San Antonio St.; (800) 625-9169 or (830) 625-9169; www.princesolmsinn.com. Built in 1900, this quiet bed-and-breakfast has two suites and a guest parlor downstairs; upstairs there are eight guest rooms. All rooms are furnished with period antiques. $$$.

especially for winter texans

Heidelberg Lodges. 1020 North Houston Ave.; (830) 625-9967; www.heidelberglodges.com. Located near the headwaters of the Comal River, this scenic family resort is popular in the summer with swimmers, snorkelers, and scuba divers. During off-season, Winter Texans are welcomed with potluck dinners and get-togethers. Accommodations include A-frame cottages and motel units. Call for long-term winter rates. $$.

day trip 03

southwest

kodak country:
wimberley, devil's backbone scenic
drive, fischer, blanco

Some of the most scenic highways in the Hill Country await you as you meander west through rugged canyons and wooded valleys. Huge cypress trees line sparkling Hill Country streams and hilltop pullovers command spectacular views. Here, small towns attract resident artisans who display their wares in galleries and small shops.

wimberley

From Austin, follow US 290 west to the small community of Dripping Springs. Turn south on RR 12 and continue 15 miles to Wimberley, a favorite shopping destination from Thursday through Monday. Wimberley's also a great summer destination because of its location on the Blanco River and Cypress Creek.

Wimberley's history goes back to the 1850s, when a resourceful Texas Revolution veteran named William Winters opened a mill here. As was tradition at the time, he named the new community Winters' Mill. When Winters died, John Cade bought the mill, and the town became Cade's Mill. Finally in 1870 a wealthy Llano man named Pleasant Wimberley rode into town. Tired of Indian raids on his horses in Llano, he moved in, bought the mill, and changed the town's name one last time.

The small town of Wimberley is one of those "shop 'til you drop" kinds of places. Even with only 3,700 residents, the town boasts dozens of specialty stores, art galleries and studios, and accommodations ranging from river resorts to historic bed-and-breakfasts.

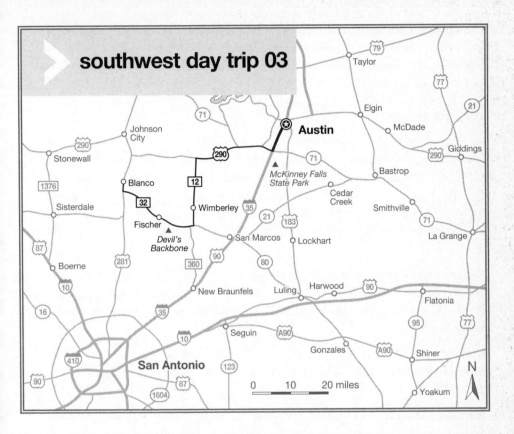

southwest day trip 03

Taylor · Elgin · McDade · Giddings · Bastrop · Smithville · La Grange · Johnson City · Stonewall · Austin · McKinney Falls State Park · Cedar Creek · Blanco · Wimberley · Sisterdale · Fischer · Devil's Backbone · San Marcos · Lockhart · Boerne · New Braunfels · Luling · Harwood · Flatonia · Seguin · Gonzales · Shiner · San Antonio · Yoakum

0 10 20 miles

N

Wimberley is a quiet place except when the shops open their doors on Monday, Thursday, Friday, and on weekends. The busiest time to visit is the first Saturday of the month from April through December. This is Market Day, when more than 400 vendors set up to sell antiques, collectibles, and arts and crafts.

Many visitors come to enjoy the town's two water sources: the Blanco River and clear, chilly Cypress Creek. Both are filled with inner-tubers and swimmers during hot summer months. The waterways provide a temporary home for campers and vacationers who stay in resorts and cabins along the shady water's edge.

where to go

Wimberley Chamber of Commerce. Wimberley North Shopping Center, RR 12 past Cypress Creek; (512) 847-2201; www.wimberley.org. Stop by the Chamber offices on weekdays to load up on brochures, maps, and shopping tips.

Pioneertown. 7-A Ranch Resort, 1 mile west of RR 12 on CR 178, at the intersection with CR 179; (512) 847-2517; www.7aresort.com/pages/town.php. See a medicine show, tour a general store museum, or spend some time at the town jail in this Wild West village. There's also a child-size train ride with a mile of tracks, an old log fort, cowboy shows, and a western cafe. Open weekends year-round for visits and daily during the summer for rides and shops.

where to shop

Like the nearby town of Blanco, Wimberley is home to many artists who've relocated to Texas's serene Hill Country. Specialty shops abound, selling everything from imports to sculpture and antiques. Arts and crafts are especially well represented. Plan to shop Thursday through Monday. Some stores are open all week, but most close midweek, especially during cooler months. A good time to shop is during Market Day, held the first Saturday of every month from March through December at the Wimberley Lions Field, 601 FM 2325.

Rancho Deluxe. On the square, 14010 RR 12; (877) 847-9570 or (512) 847-9570; www .ranchodeluxe.net. Bring the cowboy look to your home with this shop's western merchandise. You'll find everything from spurs and Mexican sideboards, to horns and handcrafted furniture. Open daily.

Wimberley GlassWorks. 6469 RR 12; (800) 929-6686; www.wgw.com. Watch demonstrations on the art of glassblowing and shop for one-of-a-kind creations. Open daily 10 a.m. to 5 p.m.

Wimberley Stained Glass Shop. On the square; (866) 492-7582 or (512) 847-3930, www .wimberleystainedglass.com. Highlighted by handcrafted Tiffany lamp reproductions, this shop also features custom-leaded doors, window panels, and sun catchers. Open daily (afternoons only on Sun).

where to stay

Wimberley is filled with bed-and-breakfast accommodations that range from historic homes in town to ranches in the surrounding Hill Country to camps along Cypress Creek. For information on these many accommodations, give one of the reservations services a call: **Bed and Breakfast of Wimberley,** (800) 827-1913; **All Wimberley Lodging,** (800) 460-3909; **Texas Hill Country Retreats,** (800) 847-8788; www.texashillco.com; **Hill Country Accommodations,** (800) 926-5028. For brochures on Wimberley's other accommodations, call the Chamber of Commerce at (512) 847-2201.

devil's backbone scenic drive

From Wimberley, continue south on RR 12 to RR 32. Turn west and sit back for this slow, scenic drive. There aren't any steep climbs or stomach-churning lookouts; a high ridge of hills provides a gentle drive with excellent views along the way. There's very little traffic, and there's a beautiful picnic spot on the left, just a few miles before Fischer. This stretch of road is often cited as one of the most scenic drives in Texas and is well known for its fall color.

fischer

Continue on RR 32 to the tiny hamlet of Fischer. Retrace your drive south on US 281 for a couple of miles to the intersection with RR 32. Take a left and enjoy a quiet ride through miles of ranch land and rolling hills.

Fischer is on the left side of the road. A short drive on Fischer Store Road takes you right into the community and to the store for which the road is named. Through the years the store has served many purposes, acting as a bank and post office in addition to a mercantile. Today the store is open Wed through Sun and is a nice place to grab a soft drink before continuing on your day trip.

While you're at the store, you'll notice some buildings next door. The red building is home to the Fischer Bowling Club, a nine-pin bowling league. Next door you'll see Fischer Hall, an old-fashioned dance hall that's still popular for wedding and reunion rentals.

blanco

After passing through Devil's Backbone, continue on RR 32 to US 281. Turn right and head north to Blanco, the home of a beautiful state park.

musical chairs with the county seat

Built in 1888, the former **Blanco County Courthouse** has been one of the most used buildings in the county—for everything except as a courthouse, that is. The year after its construction, an election moved the county seat to Johnson City. The courthouse was used for its original purpose for a total of four years, then it went into a long career of different uses. For two different periods, the building served as a schoolhouse; it also became a bank. Later it served the community as a town hall, library, opera house, and even the office of the local newspaper. From 1937 to 1961 the building served as a hospital but later became a Wild West museum and then a barbecue restaurant. Today the building houses the visitor center and is used for community events.

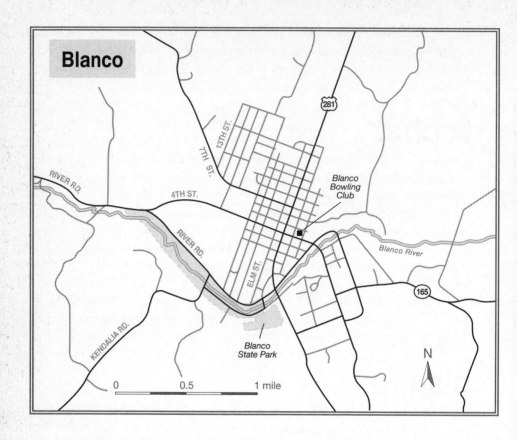

Formerly a "Wild West" kind of town, the community was originally the seat of Blanco County. Although the county seat eventually moved to nearby Johnson City, where it remains today, local residents have restored Blanco's old limestone courthouse as a visitor center, gift shop, and community center. The former courthouse is located at the intersection of US 281 and FM 165. Stop by for brochures and shopping.

Around the courthouse square are several art galleries and antiques shops aimed at weekend visitors, many of whom stop to camp at the Blanco River State Recreation Area south of town.

where to go

Blanco Bowling Club. 310 East Fourth St.; (830) 833-4416. Housed in 1940s buildings, the bowling club and the adjacent cafe have changed little with the passing years. The nine-pin game is still set up by hand. The bowling club opens at 7:30 p.m. Mon through Fri (except during football season, when everyone's at the Friday night high school game). To bowl you must be a league member.

Blanco State Park. South of Blanco on US 281; (830) 833-4333; www.tpwd.state.tx.us/park/blanco. During the Depression, the Civilian Conservation Corps built two stone dams, a group pavilion, stone picnic tables, and an arched bridge in this 104-acre riverside park. Today the park is popular with swimmers, anglers, and campers.

where to eat

Blanco Bowling Club Cafe. 310 East Fourth St.; (830) 833-4416. This is a traditional Texas diner, with linoleum floor and Formica tables, and chairs filled with locals who come here at the same time every day. Chicken-fried steak is the specialty; on Friday nights there's a catfish plate, too. Stop by in the morning for huge glazed twists and doughnuts made from scratch. Open daily for breakfast, lunch, and dinner (no dinner on Sun). $.

day trip 04

southwest

that's history:
comfort, sisterdale, boerne

This is a cultural journey from Austin, a trip through three small towns that share a strong German heritage. It includes some curving farm-to-market roads that are very susceptible to flooding. If it's raining heavily, save this trip for another day!

comfort

From Austin, head west on US 290 to Johnson City and Fredericksburg (see West Day Trip 02 for attractions in this city). In Fredericksburg, turn south on US 87 and continue for 23 miles. This small community is big in history and attractions. The downtown area is a National Historic District, filled with homes and businesses built by early settlers.

Comfort was founded by German pioneers in 1854 who wanted to name the town Gemütlichkeit, meaning peace, serenity, comfort, and happiness. After some deliberation, though, they decided on the easier-to-pronounce "Comfort" instead.

Today Comfort offers tourists numerous historic buildings to explore, filled with antiques shops and restaurants. Visitors also find a historic inn. Weekends are the busiest time to visit, but even then the atmosphere is relaxing, unhurried, and, well, comfortable.

where to go

Bat Roost. FM 473, on private land; (830) 995-3131. As you leave Comfort for Sisterdale, this historic structure sits 1 mile from town on the right side of the road behind private gates.

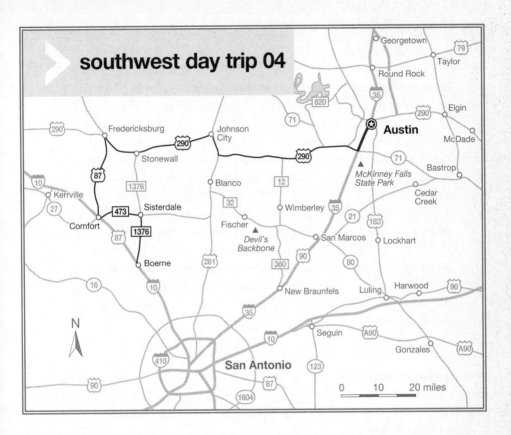

southwest day trip 04

Georgetown
Taylor
79
Round Rock
35
620
Elgin
71
290
McDade
290
Fredericksburg
Johnson City
290
Austin
Stonewall
290
Bastrop
71
87
McKinney Falls State Park
10
1376
Blanco
12
Cedar Creek
Kerrville
27
473
Sisterdale
32
Wimberley
35
21
183
Comfort
Fischer
87
1376
Devil's Backbone
San Marcos
Lockhart
90
Boerne
281
360
80
16
10
Harwood
90
New Braunfels
Luling
35
N
10
Seguin
A90
Gonzales
A90
410
San Antonio
123
90
87
0   10   20 miles
1604

While it's generally known now that bats feed on disease-spreading mosquitoes, the folks here have been aware of the importance of these furry mammals since 1918, when Albert Steves constructed hygieostatic bat roosts in an experimental attempt to control malaria. The roosts were intended to encourage the area's large bat population to remain in the region. Only sixteen such roosts were built in the country, and this is the oldest of three known still to exist. Free, but view only from the road.

Bat Tunnel. 15 miles northeast of Comfort off FM 473 on old TX 9; (830) 995-3131. View the evening flight of 1.2 million Mexican free-tailed bats from this abandoned railroad tunnel now managed by the Texas Parks and Wildlife Department. Closed Oct to May. Free admission.

where to shop

Bygone Days. TX 87; (830) 995-3003. This year-round Christmas store features handmade Santa Claus figures as well as numerous antiques, all in a historic building with original counters and fixtures. Open daily.

treue der union

"Treue der Union" (True to the Union) Monument. *High Street, between Third and Fourth Streets; (830) 995-3131. During the Civil War, German residents of Comfort who did not approve of slavery and openly swore their loyalty to the Union were burned out of their farms. The Confederates responsible also lynched locals who refused to pledge their allegiance to the movement. Several German farmers decided to defect to Mexico but were caught by Confederate soldiers and killed on the banks of the Nueces River, their bodies left unburied.*

Finally retrieved in 1865, the remains were returned to Comfort and buried in a mass grave. A white obelisk, the oldest monument in Texas and the only monument to the Union located south of the Mason-Dixon Line, was dedicated here in 1866. The shrine has received congressional approval to keep the flag at half mast, one of only six such sites in the country. The flag that waves here has thirty-six stars, the same number it had when the marker was dedicated in 1866. Free admission.

The Comfort Common. 818 High St.; (830) 995-3030; www.bbhost.com/comfortcom mon. This combination bed-and-breakfast inn and indoor shopping area is located within the historic Ingenhuett-Faust Hotel. Several buildings behind the hotel display antique primitives and furniture. Open daily.

where to stay

The Comfort Common. 818 High St.; (830) 995-3030; www.comfortcommon.com. This bed-and-breakfast operates within the 1880 Ingenhuett-Faust Hotel. The five suites are decorated in English country, American country, and Victorian decor. All rooms include private baths and period furnishings. The backyard cottage has a fireplace and complete kitchen. All rates include breakfast. As rooms book quickly for weekends, consider a midweek stay. There is a two-night minimum stay on weekends. $$–$$$.

sisterdale

From Comfort, head out on FM 473 to nearby Sisterdale, best known as the home of a small winery. The burg, like nearby Boerne, was settled by a group of intellectuals. Today the population has dwindled to a handful of residents, and you have to look carefully to keep from passing right through town.

where to go

Sister Creek Vineyards. 1142 Sisterdale Rd.; (830) 324-6704; www.sistercreekvineyards
.com. These vineyards thrive in "downtown" Sisterdale, located between the East and West
Sister Creeks. The winery, a restored cotton gin, produces traditional French–style wines.
Open daily for self-guided tours.

Sisterdale General Store. FM 473; (830) 324-6767. This historic general store and adjoining bar have served generations of customers. The bar sells Sister Creek Wine. Closed Mon.

boerne

From Sisterdale, head south on FM 1376 to Boerne (pronounced "Bernie"). Boerne is
located on the banks of Cibolo Creek in the rolling Texas Hill Country. The community was
founded in 1849 by German immigrants, members of the same group who settled nearby
New Braunfels. They named the town for author Ludwig Börne, whose writings inspired
many people to leave Germany for the New World.

During the 1880s, Boerne became known as a health spot, and vacationers came by
railroad to soak in mineral-water spas and enjoy the clean country air. Although no mineral
spas remain today, Boerne still offers a country atmosphere and dozens of antiques shops
in which to browse. Thanks to its proximity to San Antonio and Austin, the town gets pretty
busy on weekends.

Summer also brings seasonal fun to Boerne. A favorite activity on Main Plaza is Abendkonzerte, summer concerts performed by the Boerne Village Band. For nearly 140 years this
German band (the oldest continuously active German band in the country and the oldest in
the world outside of Munich) has entertained residents and visitors with its Old World sound.
Abendkonzerte takes place on select Tuesday nights throughout the summer.

where to go

Chamber of Commerce. 126 Rosewood Ave.; (830) 249-8000. Stop here for brochures
and maps to Boerne attractions and shopping areas. Open Mon through Fri, and Sat
morning.

Agricultural Heritage Center and Museum. TX 46 East, 1 mile from Main Street at
102 City Park Rd.; (210) 508-6853; www.agmuseum.org. This museum features farm and
ranch tools used by pioneers in the late 19th and early 20th centuries, including a working
steam-operated blacksmith shop. Six acres surrounding the museum are covered with
hand-drawn plows, wagons, early tractors, and woodworking tools. Open Sat 10 a.m. to 4
p.m. and by appointment. Closed Dec and Jan.

Cascade Caverns. From I-10 take exit 543 and follow signs on Cascade Caverns Road;
(830) 755-8080; www.cascadecaverns.com. This family-owned cavern, located in a

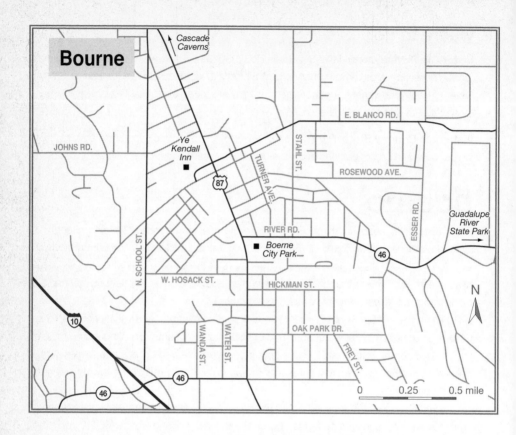

105-acre park, maintains a year-round temperature of 68°F, so this attraction is popular on both cold winter days and sweltering summer days. The cave has a 100-foot waterfall, an unusual underground sight. Guided tours take forty-five minutes. Open daily.

Cave Without a Name. 325 Kreutzberg Rd.; (888) 839-2283 or (830) 537-4212; www.cavewithoutaname.com. Guided tours take groups through six rooms of this family-owned cavern, now designated a National Natural Landmark. A subterranean river and numerous cave formations fill the tour. Open daily.

Cibolo Nature Center. 140 Boerne City Park Rd., TX 46 at Cibolo Creek; (830) 249-4616; www.cibolo.org. Enjoy grassland, marshland, and woodland in this park that offers a slice of the Hill Country. Visitors can also view dinosaur tracks. The wilderness area includes both reclaimed prairie and reclaimed marsh, with walking trails that range from a quarter mile to 1 mile in length. Free admission.

Guadalupe River State Park. 13 miles east of Boerne off TX 46 at 3350 Park Rd. 31; (830) 438-2656; www.tpwd.state.tx.us/spdest/findadest/parks/guadalupe_river. The star of this park is the clear, cold Guadalupe River. Camp, swim, hike, or just picnic on its scenic banks, or on Saturday mornings, take an interpretive tour of the Honey Creek State Natural Area to learn more about the plants and animals of the region.

Honey Creek State Natural Area. Spring Branch, 13 miles east of Boerne off TX 46 on Park Road 31; (830) 438-2656; www.tpwd.state.tx.us/spdest/findadest/parks/honey_ creek. Use of this park is limited to those on guided tours. A two-hour guided look at the park's history and ecology is offered every Saturday morning at 9 a.m.; reservations aren't necessary, but call to confirm that a tour will be offered. Access into the park is through the Guadalupe River State Park.

Kuhlmann-King Historical House and Graham Building and Museum Store. Main Street and Blanco Road; (830) 249-2030. The Kuhlmann-King house was built by a local businessman for his German bride in 1885. Today the two-story stone home is staffed by volunteers. The Graham Building next door is home to the Boerne Area Historical Preservation Society with exhibits on local history. Open Sun afternoon.

where to eat

Limestone Grille. 128 West Blanco St., Main Plaza inside Ye Kendall Inn; (800) 364-2138 or (830) 249-2138; www.yekendallinn.com. In 1859 the owners of this two-story structure began renting rooms to stagecoach travelers, eventually developing the property into an inn. Over the years its famous guests have included Confederate President Jefferson Davis and President Dwight D. Eisenhower. Along with thirteen bed-and-breakfast rooms furnished with period antiques, the inn includes a restaurant with adjoining bar. Open daily for lunch, dinner Tues through Sat. $$$.

Peach Tree Kountry Kitchen. 448 South Main St.; (830) 249-8583. This casual eatery serves up good, old-fashioned family fare such as meatloaf and chicken-fried steak. Open for lunch Tues through Sat. $$.

Po Po Family Restaurant. 829 FM 289 (6 miles north of Boerne, half mile off I-10 at exit 533); (830) 537-4194; www.popofamilyrestaurant.com. Once a stagecoach stop, this site now houses a locally popular restaurant. Along with its home-cooked meals, the restaurant is also known for its plates themselves—over 1,300 of them decorate the walls! Open daily for lunch and dinner. $$.

day trip 05

southwest

cowboy country:
bandera, medina, vanderpool

In the far west reaches of the Texas Hill Country the antelope (well, white-tailed deer) play, cowboys (both real and pretend) ride herd, and brilliant maple trees blaze so brightly in the fall you'll think you're in New England. The ranches are a little bigger here, the towns a little farther apart, and you'll learn the meaning of the longtime Texas slogan "Drive Friendly" as oncoming motorists are quick to greet you with a welcoming wave.

bandera

Take I-35 south from Austin through San Marcos and New Braunfels (see South Day Trip 03 and Southwest Day Trip 02 for information). In New Braunfels, take TX 46 west to Boerne (see Southwest Day Trip 04). Continue on TX 46 for 11 miles until it adjoins TX 16. Continue west for 12 miles to Bandera, "The Cowboy Capital of the World." This town is well known for its plentiful dude ranches, country-western music, rodeos, and horse racing.

Once part of the Wild West, Bandera Pass, located 12 miles north of town on TX 173, was the site of many battles between Spanish conquistadors and both Apache and Comanche Indians. Legend has it that, following a battle with the Apaches in 1732, a flag (or *bandera* in Spanish) was hung at the pass to mark the boundary between the two opposing forces.

Bandera has open rodeos weekly from Memorial Day to Labor Day. Typically rodeos are held Tuesday night at Mansfield Park and Friday night at Twin Elm Guest Ranch. For

144

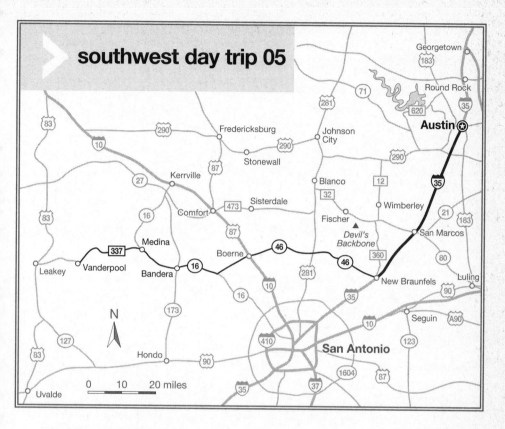

southwest day trip 05

(Map labels: Georgetown 183, Round Rock, Austin, 71, 281, 620, 35, 83, 290, 10, Fredericksburg, Johnson City, 290, 290, 35, Stonewall, 87, Kerrville, 27, Blanco, 12, Wimberley, 21, 183, 32, Sisterdale, 473, Fischer, San Marcos, 16, Comfort, 87, Devil's Backbone, 360, 80, Medina, Boerne, 46, 46, 337, Leakey, Vanderpool, Bandera, 16, 281, New Braunfels, Luling, 90, 83, 16, 10, 35, N, 173, 10, Seguin, A90, 127, 123, 83, Hondo, 410, San Antonio, 0 10 20 miles, 90, 1604, 87, Uvalde, 35, 37)

schedules, call the Bandera Convention and Visitors Bureau at (800) 364-3833 or see www
.banderacowboycapital.com.

Today the wildest action in town occurs in the dance halls every night except Mon and
Tues. Put on your boots, crease your best jeans, and get ready to two-step with locals and
vacationers alike.

where to go

Arkey Blue's Silver Dollar. 308 Main St.; (830) 796-8826. Pick up a longneck, grab a
partner, and start boot-scootin' at this Texas honky-tonk. Owner and singer Arkey Blue
performs country-and-western hits here as crowds fill the sawdust-covered dance floor.

Frontier Times Museum. 510 13th St., 1 block north of the courthouse; (830) 796-3864;
www.frontiertimesmuseum.org. Established in 1927, this museum is a good place to learn
more about Bandera's early days. The stone building is filled with cowboy paraphernalia, Native American arrowheads, and prehistoric artifacts. Its most unusual exhibit is a
shrunken head from Ecuador, part of a private collection donated to the museum. Open
Mon through Sat.

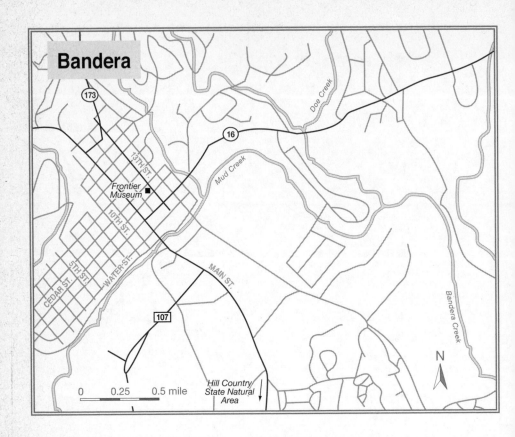

Hill Country State Natural Area. (830) 796-4413; www.tpwd.state.tx.us. South on TX 173 to FM 1077, then right for 12 miles. This rugged park preserves 5,400 acres of Hill Country land. Only primitive camping is available; you must bring your own water and pick up and remove your own trash. This park was originally open primarily for horseback riding, but today it has become popular with hikers and bicyclists. There are 34 miles of quiet trails and camp areas for backpackers and equestrians. Cool off with a dip in West Verde Creek or fish for catfish, perch, and largemouth bass. Horse rentals are available off-site. Open daily Feb through Oct; open Fri through Sun the rest of the year.

Historical Walking Tours. (800) 364-3833. Have a look at the buildings that witnessed Bandera's evolution from a frontier town to a vacation destination with a self-guided tour. Thirty-two sites along the route lead visitors to the county courthouse, the old jail, Bandera's first theater, and many homes that date back to the community's earliest days. Pick up your walking-tour brochure at the Bandera County Visitors Center, 1808 TX 16 South. Free admission.

Medina River. TX 16, east of town. The cypress-lined Medina River is a popular spot during the summer months, when swimmers, canoeists, and inner-tubers enjoy the cool water. The Medina can be hazardous during high water, however, with rocky rapids and submerged trees. There is public access to the river from the TX 16 bridge in town.

Running-R Ranch Trail Rides. Located 11 miles from Bandera off FM 1077; (830) 796-3984; www.rrranch.com. Enjoy one-, two-, or three-hour rides with an experienced wrangler. The ranch also offers all-day rides with a picnic and cowboy cookout. Children six and older are accepted.

where to shop

Love's Antiques Mall. 310 Main St.; (830) 796-3838. Located in the historic Carmichael and Hay Store, this antiques mall features custom-crafted western furniture, wrought iron, sculpture, and collectibles.

where to eat

O.S.T. Restaurant. 305 Main St.; (830) 796-3836. Named for the Old Spanish Trail, this restaurant serves a Texas-size breakfast as well as popular lunches and dinners, featuring Lone Star favorites such as chicken-fried steak, burgers, and fried chicken. Don't miss the bar and its unique barstools—each topped with a saddle. $.

Texaritas Steak House & Mesquite Grill Restaurant. 703 Main St.; www.texassquare .com/texaritas.htm. Part of Old Texas Square, this restaurant offers both indoor and streetside dining featuring Texas favorites, steaks, Tex-Mex, fajitas, and drinks from the adjacent Tequila Rita Cantina. $–$$.

where to stay

The country around Bandera is dotted with dude ranches. Rates usually include three meals daily as well as family-style entertainment and supervised children's programs. Horseback riding is often part of the weeklong package. A minimum stay of two or three days is required at most ranches during peak summer season.

For a complete listing of Bandera's dude ranches, as well as other accommodations and campgrounds, call the Bandera Convention and Visitors Bureau; (800) 364-3833.

Dixie Dude Ranch. (800) 375-YALL; www.dixieduderanch.com. South on TX 173 1.5 miles to FM 1077, then southwest for 9 more miles. Five generations of the Whitley family have welcomed guests to this nineteen-room ranch since 1937.

The Dixie Dude Ranch offers potential cowpokes the opportunity to enjoy a taste of ranch life. Start your morning with a leisurely trail ride followed by a genuine cowboy breakfast, then enjoy a day filled with hiking trails, hunting for Native American arrowheads, taking country-and-western dance lessons, fishing, or tossing horseshoes. The ranch includes nineteen units made up of individual cottages, duplex cabins, and lodge rooms featuring early Texas architecture. Rates include meals and two horseback rides daily. Call for rates.

Flying L Guest Ranch. (800) 292-5134; www.flyingl.com. From TX 16, turn south on TX 173 for 1.5 miles, then left on Wharton Dock Road. This 542-acre ranch has thirty-eight guest houses, each with two rooms, refrigerator, microwave, coffee pot, and TV. You can choose from a variety of packages offering horseback riding, hayrides, and even golf at the ranch's eighteen-hole course. During the summer there's a supervised children's program. Nightly entertainment ranges from western shows to "branding" parties.

LH7 Ranch Resort. FM 3240, 5 miles from Bandera; (830) 796-4314. This 1,200-acre ranch, which raises longhorn cattle, has cottages with kitchenettes, plus RV hookups. There's plenty to keep any cowpoke busy, including angling in a fifty-acre lake, hayrides, trail rides, or nature walks.

Mayan Ranch. TX 16, 2 miles west of Bandera; (830) 796-3312 or (830) 460-3036; www .mayanranch.com. For more than forty years, this sixty-room ranch has entertained vacationers with cowboy breakfasts, cookouts, horseback riding, angling, and hayrides. Summer also brings organized children's programs. Rooms are appointed with western-style furniture. Call for rates.

Old Texas Square Hotel. 703 Main St.; (830) 796-4100; www.texassquare.com. Rooms here are decorated in a Wild West theme, but otherwise it's motel basic with few extras. However, the hotel is the only one on Bandera's Main Street and makes an excellent location from which to enjoy nightlife. The most interesting room here is the John Wayne Room, in which the Duke himself once stayed. $–$$.

Silver Spur Dude Ranch. Located 10 miles south of Bandera on FM 1077; (830) 796-3037; www.ssranch.com. Pull on your boots and grab your Stetson before heading to this 275-acre ranch near the Hill Country State Natural Area. You'll stay busy out of the saddle with nearby angling, tubing, canoeing, golfing, plus swimming in the ranch pool.

Twin Elm Guest Ranch. Just a half mile off FM 470 from TX 16 (4 miles from Bandera); (888) 567-3049 or (830) 796-3628; www.twinelmranch.com. This 200-acre dude ranch is on the Medina River. All the usual cowboy activities are available, from angling to horseback riding to horseshoe pitching. From May through Sept the ranch hosts a weekly rodeo every Fri.

especially for winter texans

Besides the dude ranches, Bandera has excellent RV parks. Many weekly activities are of special interest to the Winter Texans who call Bandera home. Country-and-western dances are held Wed through Sat, and there's bingo on Fri and Sun. For a complete listing, contact the Bandera Convention and Visitors Bureau; (800) 364-3833.

medina

From Bandera, continue west on TX 16 to the tiny community of Medina, best known for its dwarf apple trees that produce full-size fruit in varieties from Crispin to Jonagold.

where to go

Love Creek Orchards. RR 337 west of Medina; (800) 449-0882 or (830) 589-2588; www .lovecreekorchards.com. From May through Oct these beautiful orchards are open to the public by guided tour only; call to set up a tour time. Free admission.

leaf peeping

Are you starting to dream about the feel of a cool autumn breeze? Hearing the crackle of leaves beneath your feet? Smelling the smoke of an evening campfire?

Central Texas may not have the blazing colors of New England, but with a little looking, you will find a brilliant quilt of fall colors.

To find out the status of fall colors, call the Texas Travel Information Center at (800) 452-9292 or the Texas Parks and Wildlife hotline at (800) 792-1112. The brilliant colors require cold night temperatures, an occurrence that can reach the Hill Country valleys long before the warmer city locations.

*The top destination for many leaf peepers is **Lost Maples State Natural Area** in Vanderpool. The maples, located so far from other specimens of the beautiful tree, may seem lost, but there's no doubt that the park itself has been found. This state park is one of the most heavily visited sites in Texas during Oct and Nov when the bigtooth maples provide some of the best color in Texas. Weekend visits during this time can be very crowded and note that the parking here is limited to only 250 cars. The best time to visit is during mid-week when you can enjoy a walk into the park without crowds.*

Fall colors generated by blazing sumacs, sycamores, chinaberries, and cottonwoods can be seen along the scenic drive along RR 1050 from Utopia to US 83. RR 337 from Camp Wood to Leakey is another favorite of ours, as is the Devil's Backbone Scenic Drive, a stretch of RR 32 from Wimberley to Blanco.

taking a shine to medina

If there's any truth to the saying, "An apple a day keeps the doctor away," then the physicians of Medina, Texas, better just close up shop. This Hill Country community is the core of the booming Texas apple industry.

Today Medina is recognized as the capital of the Texas apple industry, a business that took root in 1981 when Baxter Adams and wife Carol moved to Love Creek Ranch outside of Medina. Baxter spent thirty years as an exploration geologist in the oil industry before moving to this region. It's a land of rocky, rugged hills, with fertile valleys irrigated by the cool waters of Love Creek, a spring-fed creek that originates on the ranch.

These valleys gave Adams the idea for an orchard—one that would not require a great deal of land. "I don't have much tillable land," Adams once explained to us, pointing to the steep hills where goats once grazed. "I've got to really make it count. It's a matter of trying to squeeze the most possible dollars out of the smallest possible area."

And that's just what Baxter Adams has done.

This Texas version of Johnny Appleseed specializes in dwarf apple trees, plants which reach a height of only five or six feet. The Lilliputians boast full-size apples, however, up to fifty pounds per tree, in varieties from the common Red Delicious to the more unusual Gala and Crispin.

Baxter and Carol started with just 1,000 trees in 1981, and they were soon in the apple business. Unlike the full-size trees that take seven years to produce a crop, the dwarfs yield fruit in just a year and a half. Another advantage Adams' Apples has over the northern producers is his growing season: Texas apples ripen weeks before their northern cousins.

Every July, the Hill Country celebrates this blooming industry with the International Apple Festival. What began as an orchard party has become a Texas-size festival. The party begins the night before with a street dance and continues the next day with activities for the whole family. Activities include contests for the best apple, best apple pie, and best apple anything. There is also a quilt contest, volleyball championship, and, for the really energetic, a "triapple-on."

where to shop

The Cider Mill and Country Store. Main Street, (TX 16), downtown; (830) 589-2202; www.lovecreekorchards.com. This shop sells Love Creek apples from June through Nov. Butter, sauces, vinegars, jellies, syrups, pies, breads, and even apple ice cream are sold here year-round. If you're ready to start your own orchard but you're short on room, you can buy "the patio apple orchard," a dwarf tree grown on a trellis in a wooden planter. Open daily.

vanderpool

Vanderpool is a quiet getaway in all but the fall months. Tucked into the hills surrounding the Sabinal River, this small town is a center for sheep and goat ranching.

where to go

Lost Maples State Natural Area. 37221 FM 187, (800) 792-1112 or (830) 966-3413; www.tpwd.state.tx.us/spdest/findadest/parks/lost_maples. West on RR 337 to the intersection with RR 187; turn north and continue 5 miles. This state park is one of the most heavily visited sites in Texas during Oct and Nov, when the bigtooth maples provide some of the best color in the state. Weekend visits at this time can be very crowded, so note that parking is limited to 250 cars. The least crowded time to visit is midweek.

There are 10 miles of hiking trails to enjoy all year along the Sabinal River Canyon. In the summer visitors can swim and fish in the river. Camping includes primitive areas on the hiking trails and a thirty-site campground with restrooms and showers as well as a trailer dump station. Open daily.

Scenic Drive. Utopia to US 83. West of Utopia, RR 1050 winds its way through the Hill Country, crossing the Frio River before eventually intersecting with US 83 north of Concan. During late fall, the drive is dotted with blazing sumacs, sycamores, chinaberries, and cottonwoods. Free admission.

Scenic Drive. RR 337. This drive from Camp Wood to Leakey (pronounced LA-key) is often termed the most scenic in Texas and is an excellent spot for fall color. The road climbs to some of the highest elevations in the Hill Country at more than 2,300 feet, and roadside lookouts offer great vistas of reds, greens, and golds. Free admission.

west

day trip 01

west

willie nelson country:
bee cave, spicewood and
south lake travis

Yes, the "red headed stranger" himself, Willie Nelson, one of Austin's most famous residents, owns an 800-acre spread near Spicewood. Willie's place is far more than just a place to kick off his boots, though; the private complex includes a recording studio, golf course, and even a miniature western "town" named Luck that's used for movie shoots. Spicewood and the surrounding communities make an easy getaway from Austin when you're short on time.

bee cave

This small community is quickly growing as Austin expands westward toward the Hill Country.

where to go

Austin Zoo and Animal Sanctuary. 10807 Rawhide Trail, Austin; (512) 288-1490; www .austinzoo.org. The Austin Zoo is a rescue and rehabilitation zoo, home to many animals which have been removed or surrendered by owners because of their inability to care for exotic species. Some have been rescued from circuses, others given up by owners who just didn't realize an exotic animal wasn't the same as a dog or cat. There's nothing fancy about this zoo but look for a wide variety of animals here: lions, tigers, cougars, Galapagos tortoises, monkeys, and more. There's an extensive petting zoo featuring potbellied pigs,

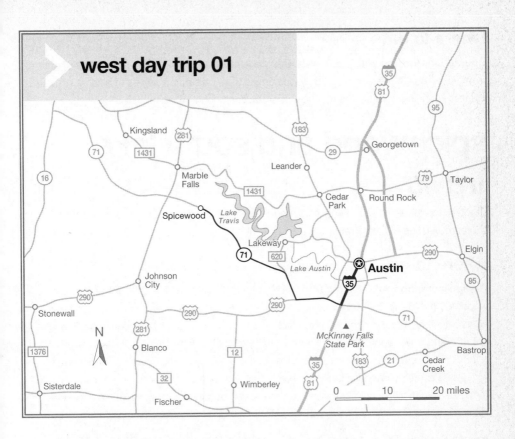

west day trip 01

Barbados sheep, pygmy goats, llama, and deer. A miniature train offers rides through nearby fields, home to Longhorn cattle, a Sicilian donkey, emu, zebra, and others.

Hamilton Pool Preserve. (512) 264-2740; www.co.travis.tx.us. TX 71 west through the town of Bee Cave; turn left onto FM 3238 (Hamilton Pool Road). Travel 13 miles to the preserve entrance, on your right. This beautiful swimming hole is a grotto fed by a 50-foot waterfall. After a dip, enjoy a picnic or hike along the canyon, which is home to several rare plant species. Guided tours are available. Call before a swimming trip to this site as bacteria levels occasionally cause the closing of the pool.

where to stay

Barton Creek Resort and Spa. 8212 Barton Club Dr.; (800) 336-6158 or (512) 329-4000; www.bartoncreek.com. This expansive resort is known for its four golf courses; guests can also sign up for the golf school. The spa features a variety of treatments incorporating local elements such as the Texas mountain laurel body wrap and the Texas margarita salt glow. $$$.

where to eat

County Line on the Hill. 6500 West Bee Caves Rd.; (512) 327-1742; www.countyline
.com. Like its sister restaurant, County Line on the Lake, this eatery serves traditional Texas
barbecue ranging from brisket to ribs. Open daily for lunch and dinner. $$–$$$.

spicewood and south lake travis

This day trip takes anglers, swimmers, and boaters to the numerous parks found on the
southern reaches of Lake Travis.

where to go

Grelle Recreation Area. Upper south side of Lake Travis near the community of Spicewood; (800) 776-5272; www.lcra.org. From Austin, to the southwest, take TX 71 and turn
north onto Spur 191; proceed approximately 1 mile to Spicewood. Take a right onto Burnet
CR 404 and travel approximately 1 mile to the intersection with Burnet CR 412, a gravel
road. Turn left and travel just over a half a mile to the entrance for the Grelle Recreation Area.

Grelle is often visited for its 2-mile hiking trail, which leads visitors along a steep path
to a plateau with views of Lake Travis. The site is also popular for its shoreline. Visitors here
will find only primitive facilities: a composting toilet, metal fire rings, and a small parking area.

Krause Springs. TX 71 to Spur 191, 7 miles after the Pedernales River Bridge; (830) 693-
4181. Turn right on to Spur 191 to a gravel road. Krause Springs is one of Central Texas's
hidden wonders. As its name suggests, the highlight of this private park is the natural
springs. Clear, cool waters and waterfalls draw swimmers and snorkelers during warm-
weather months. Camping also is available.

Muleshoe Recreation Area. Upper south side of Lake Travis near the Ridge Harbor subdivision; (800) 776-5272; www.lcra.org. From Austin, to the southeast, take TX 71. Turn
right onto Burnet CR 404 and proceed about 4.5 miles to Burnet CR 414. Turn right and
travel about 1.5 miles, then turn right before the entrance to Ridge Harbor. The pavement
ends, but continue for about a quarter mile on the gravel road to the entrance. Muleshoe
Bend is appropriately named: A 2-mile looped trail is a favorite with those looking to take
a four-legged ride through undeveloped hill country. Horseback riders and hikers enjoy the
trail located on the upper area of the park. With its 1,000 acres, this is the largest property
in the LCRA system, but it offers only primitive facilities: composting toilets, metal fire rings,
and a parking area.

Narrows Recreation Area. Upper south side of Lake Travis near the community of Spicewood; (800) 776-5272; www.lcra.org. From Austin, to the southeast, take TX 71 and turn

north onto Spur 191; proceed approximately 1 mile to Spicewood. Continue traveling north 1.1 miles on Burnet CR 410 to the intersection with Burnet CR 411, which is a gravel road. Once on CR 411, travel approximately 1.5 miles north to the entrance for the Narrows Resource Area. This free recreation area is used by boaters looking for a launching site onto the upper south side of Lake Travis. The ramp, however, should be used with caution during low water periods. Only minimal facilities (no restrooms or drinking water) are available here, with a few camping sites and metal fire rings. This recreation area should be avoided during heavy rains; the access road traverses a low water crossing that may become impassable. Free admission.

Spicewood Vineyards. (830) 693-5328; www.spicewoodvineyards.com. Off TX 71, turn on to CR 408 south for about a mile then right onto CR 409 for 1.5 miles. This vineyard offers tours and tastings Wed through Sat as well as Sun afternoon.

where to eat

Poodie's Hilltop Bar and Grill. 22308 TX 71 West; (512) 264-0318; www.poodies.info. Willie Nelson is almost an unofficial symbol of Austin, but the musician is all too often on the road again, playing Austin fewer days than he did in his early days. But now there's Poodie's Hilltop Bar and Grill. You might not see Willie during your visit, but keep an eye out for other stars; everyone from Billy Bob Thornton to Merle Haggard has popped in at one time or another. Serving up burgers and Texas food, the roadhouse is really known for its live music, enjoyed almost every night. $–$$.

day trip 02

west

lbj country:
pedernales falls state park, johnson city,
stonewall, luckenbach, fredericksburg,
enchanted rock state natural area

The memory of one of Texas's most famous politicians, President Lyndon Baines Johnson, still looms here over hills and valleys and in local lore. While the larger-than-life Johnson was president in the 1960s, the Hill Country became the focus of attention as world leaders gathered at the Johnson Ranch, dubbed the "Texas White House" for discussion, politicking, and debate.

pedernales falls state park

For the stair-stepped **Pedernales Falls** (830-868-7304), head 32 miles west of Austin on US 290 then north on FM 3232 for 6 miles. A favorite summer getaway, this 4,800-acre state park is highlighted by gently cascading waterfalls. The falls draw swimmers as well as anglers in search of catfish. The falls are spectacular, but visitors should note that this park can experience dangerous flash floods. With even a slight rise in the river, visitors should get to higher ground immediately. Activities such as swimming, angling, hiking, and camping are available. Open daily.

johnson city

From Pedernales Falls State Park, turn southwest on PR 6026 to CR 201 (Pedernales Falls Road) and turn right. Continue to the intersection of RR 2766 (Robinson Road) and head

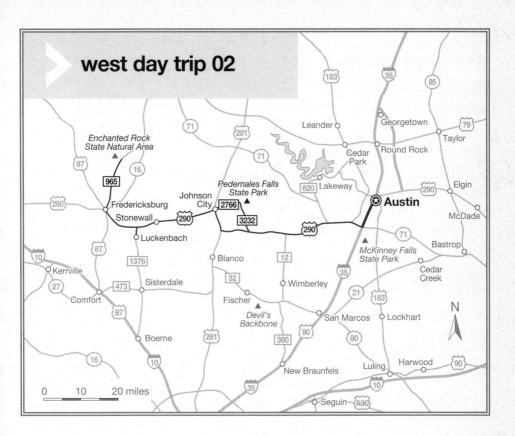

west day trip 02

Enchanted Rock
State Natural Area

[71]
[281]
[183]
[35]
[95]

Leander

Georgetown
[79]
Taylor

[87]
[16]
[965]
[71]

Cedar
Park
Round Rock

Pedernales Falls
State Park
Johnson
City [2766]
[290]
[620] Lakeway
[290] Elgin

[290]
Fredericksburg
Stonewall [290]
[3232]
⊛ **Austin**
McDade

Luckenbach
[290]

[87]
[1376]
Blanco
[12]
[71]
Bastrop

McKinney Falls
State Park
Cedar
Creek

[10]
Kerrville
[473]
Sisterdale
[32]
Wimberley
[35]

[27]
[21]
[183]

Comfort
[87]
Fischer

Devil's
Backbone
San Marcos
Lockhart
N

Boerne
[281]
[90]
[80]

[360]

[16]
[10]
New Braunfels
Luling
Harwood
[90]

0   10   20 miles
[35]
[10]

Seguin [A90]

west for 9 miles to Johnson City and LBJ country. President Johnson's boyhood home is open to visitors, along with the Johnson Settlement where LBJ's grandfather organized cattle drives over a century ago. The Lyndon B. Johnson National Historic Park takes in two areas: Johnson City and the LBJ Ranch, located in Stonewall.

LBJ brought the attention of the world to his hometown, located 14 miles north from Blanco on US 281. The most popular stop here is the LBJ Boyhood Home, managed by the National Park Service. LBJ was five years old in 1913 when his family moved from a country home near the Pedernales River to this simple frame house. The visitor center provides information on this location, nearby Johnson Settlement, and other LBJ attractions. Park admission is free, a stipulation of the late president.

Johnson City hosts Historic Nugent Street Market Days on the third weekend of every month from Apr through Oct, with antiques, crafts, collectibles, and food booths.

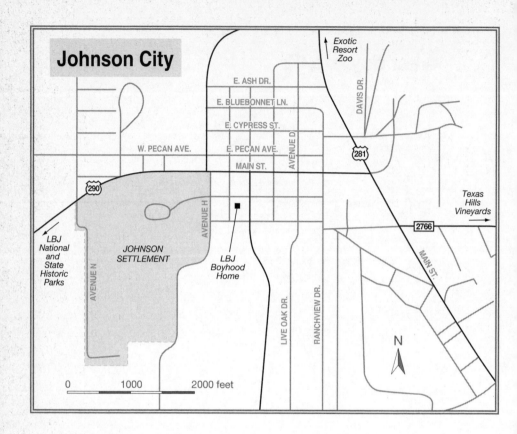

where to go

Captain Perry Texas Ranger Museum. 404 West Main St.; (830) 868-7684; www
.johnsoncity-texas.com. Learn more about the life of a Texas Ranger in the 1830s with a
visit to this one-room cabin. The self-guided look at the furnished cabin, the former home
of Texas Ranger Cicero Rufus Perry, includes a video about the famous law keepers. Open
by appointment. Free admission.

The Exotic Resort Zoo. 4 miles north of Johnson City on US 281; (830) 868-4357; www
.zooexotics.com. Unusual species (including many endangered animals) roam the 137
acres of wooded Hill Country. In this park, leave the driving to someone else and enjoy
a guided ride aboard a safari truck. Professional guides conduct tours of the ranch and
provide visitors with information such as animal behavior as you feed the friendly park
residents. After the tour, you can see some wildlife up close at the petting zoo. Kids enjoy
petting child-size miniature donkeys, baby deer, llama, baby elk, and even a kangaroo at
this special area. Open daily 9 a.m. to 6 p.m.

LBJ National Historic Park. South of US 290 at Ninth Street; www.nps.gov. Park at the visitor center and go inside for brochures and a look at exhibits. From the center you can walk to Johnson Settlement and the LBJ Boyhood Home.

Johnson Settlement. www.nps.gov. The settlement gives visitors a look at the beginnings of the Johnson legacy. These rustic cabins and outbuildings once belonged to LBJ's grandfather, Sam Ealy Johnson, and his brother Tom. The two cattle drivers lived a rugged life in the Hill Country during the 1860s and 1870s. An exhibit center tells their story in pictures and artifacts. You also can tour the brothers' cabins and see costumed docents carrying out nineteenth-century chores. Open daily. Free admission.

LBJ Boyhood Home. Next to the Johnson Settlement. LBJ was a schoolboy when his family moved here in 1913. The home is still furnished with the Johnsons' belongings. Guided tours run every half hour. Open daily. Free admission.

Texas Hills Vineyard. RR 2766, 1 mile east of Johnson City; (830) 868-2321; www.texas hillsvineyard.com. Texas wines produced with an Italian influence are the specialty of this vineyard. Open Mon through Sat 10 a.m. to 5 p.m., and Sun noon to 5 p.m. for tastings.

where to shop

Whittington's Jerky. 604 US 281 South; (877) 868-5501 or (830) 868-5500; www.whit tingtonsjerky.com. This factory produces true Texas jerky; stop by for free samples or to shop for jerky and other food items.

where to stay

The Exotic Zoo Bed and Breakfast. Four miles north of Johnson City on US 281; (830) 868-4357; www.zooexotics.com. The Exotic Zoo, known for its guided safari tours and petting zoo, now operates a four-cabin bed-and-breakfast on the property. Two cabins include kitchenettes; they all include access to two swimming pools, a hot tub, a barbecue area, and a fire pit for evening bonfires. The cabins overlook the animal areas, and guests can fish on a stocked lake, paying only for those fish caught. There is a seven-day cancellation policy on cabin rentals. $$$.

stonewall

Continue west on US 290 to the tiny community of Stonewall, the capital of the Texas peach industry. The road passes through miles of peach orchards, and during early summer, farm-fresh fruit is sold at roadside stands throughout the area. Stonewall is also the home of the LBJ National and State Historic Parks, encompassing the LBJ Ranch. This is a great opportunity to visit a working cattle ranch.

where to go

Grape Creek Vineyards. 4 miles west of Stonewall on US 290; (830) 664-2710; www .grapecreek.com. The fertile land of the Pedernales Valley is a natural for vineyards, and you'll find acres of beautiful grapevines at this winery that produces cabernet sauvignon and chardonnay varieties. The winery is open daily. Call for tour times. Free admission.

LBJ National and State Historic Parks. (830) 644-2252; www.nps.gov or www.tpwd .state.tx.us. Located 14 miles west of Johnson City on US 290, these two combined parks together span approximately 700 acres. The area is composed of three main sections: the visitor center, the LBJ Ranch and tour, and the Sauer-Beckmann Farm. The most scenic route to the LBJ park falls along RR 1, paralleling the wide, shallow Pedernales River. (Exit US 290 a few miles east of Stonewall.)

During Johnson's lifetime, the ranch was closed to all but official visitors. In hopes of catching a glimpse of the president, travelers often stopped along RR 1, located across the river from the Texas White House, the nickname of the Johnsons' home. Today the parks draw visitors from around the world.

Make your first stop the visitor center for a look at displays on LBJ's life, which include mementos of President Johnson's boyhood years. Attached to the visitor center is the Behrens Cabin, a dogtrot-style structure built by a German immigrant in the 1870s. Inside, the home is furnished with household items from more than a century ago.

peach fun

Stonewall is called "The Peach Capital of Texas," and every June Stonewall is ripe with fun and festivities. The third weekend of June is set aside for a celebration of the Hill Country's sweetest product at the annual Peach JAMboree. The festivities are genuine Texas fun, from a rodeo with bareback riding, calf roping, team roping, and bull riding, to a parade and a baking contest at the fire station. Other activities include a fiddlers' contest (open to competitors), a washer pitching tournament, and, of course, the Gillespie County Peach Queen Pageant. The sweetest event is the Peach Show and Auction, with plenty of prize-winning examples of Stonewall's fuzzy treasure.

Gillespie County, including Stonewall and nearby Fredericksburg, is filled with orchards where you can pick your own peaches. These shady groves yield their fruit until late July and offer a dozen varieties. The earliest to ripen are the cling peaches, ones whose fruit clings to the pit. As the summer progresses, varieties such as Red Skin, Loring, and Harvest Gold begin to mature.

While you're in the visitor center, get a free driving permit for a self-guided drive through the LBJ Ranch. You'll drive across the president's spacious ranch, making a stop at the one-room Junction School where Johnson began his education and the small family cemetery along the Pedernales River where LBJ and Lady Bird are buried. Next you'll stop at the president's airstrip. Here you'll park and join a guided tour of the Texas White House, which opened to the public after Lady Bird's death. Presently tours visit LBJ's office in the home; additional rooms will soon be added to the tour.

Other stops on your self-guided drive include LBJ's cattle barns, the reconstructed birthplace home, and the Sauer-Beckmann Living Historical Farm. Here, two 1918 farm homes are furnished in period style. Children can have a great time petting the farm animals. From here, it's just a short walk back to the visitor center. Although the park does not have overnight facilities, there are two picnic areas and hiking trails for day use. Open daily. Free admission.

where to eat

Austin's Restaurant at Rose Hill Manor. 2614 Upper Albert Rd.; (877) ROSEHIL; www .rose-hill.com. The window-lined dining room of this elegant eatery overlooks the scenic countryside. Specialties like New Zealand venison medallions with German potatoes are accompanied by an extensive wine list showcasing Hill Country vintages—the perfect end to a day of wine country touring. Open for dinner Wed through Sun. $$$.

luckenbach

Waylon Jennings's popular country-and-western song made this community a Texas institution. The town consists of a shop or two and a small general store serving as a post office, dance hall, beer joint, and general gathering place.

To reach Luckenbach (888-311-8990; www.luckenbachtexas.com), leave Stonewall on US 290. Turn left on FM 1376 and continue for about 4.25 miles. Don't expect to see signs pointing to the turnoff for Luckenbach Road; they are often stolen as fast as the highway department can get them in the ground. After the turn for Grapetown, take the next right down a narrow country road. Luckenbach is just around the bend.

This town was founded in 1852 by Jacob, William, and August Luckenbach. The brothers opened a post office at the site and called it South Grape Creek. In 1886 a man named August Engel reopened the post office and renamed it Luckenbach in honor of the early founders.

The most happening place in town is the dance hall, an expansive traditional Texas dance hall. Dances are held monthly, usually on Saturday night.

The old post office is still there in the general store, the walls covered with scrawled names penned by Luckenbach fans. The store sells souvenirs of the town. Open daily.

fredericksburg

Retrace your steps from Luckenbach and continue west on US 290 to Fredericksburg, once the edge of the frontier and home to brave German pioneers. These first inhabitants faced many hardships, including hostile Comanche Indians. Now the town is a favorite with antiques shoppers, history buffs, and fans of good German food.

US 290 runs through the heart of the downtown district, becoming Main Street within the city limits. Originally the street was designed to be large enough to allow a wagon and a team of mules to turn around in the center of town. Today, Main Street is filled with shoppers who come to explore the stores and restaurants of downtown Fredericksburg.

Fredericksburg welcomes all visitors—just look at the street signs for proof. Starting at the Adams Street intersection, head east on Main Street and take the first letter of every intersecting street name: they spell "all welcome." Drive west on Main Street starting after the Adams Street intersection. The first letter of the intersecting streets spell "come back."

where to go

Bell Mountain Vineyards. TX 16 North, 14 miles from Fredericksburg; (830) 685-3297; www.bellmountainwine.com. Tour the chateau-style winery that produces chardonnay, Riesling, pinot noir, and several private reserve estate varieties. Guided tours and tastings are offered every Sat from Feb through Dec. Free admission.

Fort Martin Scott Frontier Army Post. 1606 East Main St., 2 miles east of Fredericksburg on US 290; (830) 997-9895; www.fortmartinscott.com. Established in 1848, this was the first frontier military fort in Texas. Today the original stockade, a guardhouse, and visitor center with displays on local Native Americans are open to tour, and monthly historic reenactments keep the history lesson lively. Ongoing archaeological research conducted here offers a glimpse into the fort's past. Open Tues through Sun 10 a.m. to 5 p.m. for self-guided tours. Free admission.

Fredericksburg Convention and Visitors Bureau. 302 East Austin; (830) 997-6523; www.fredericksburg-texas.com. Stop by the visitor center for brochures, maps, and information on a self-guided walking tour of historic downtown buildings, many of which now house shops and restaurants. The staff here also can direct you to bed-and-breakfast facilities in the area. Open daily. Free admission.

Fredericksburg Herb Farm. 407 Whitney St.; (800) 259-HERB or (830) 997-8615; www.fredericksburgherbfarm.com. These gardens produce the herbs for everything from teas to potpourris. Tour the grounds, then visit the shop for a look at the final product. A bed-and-breakfast also is located on-site. Open daily (afternoon only on Sun). Free admission.

National Museum of the Pacific War. 340 East Main St.; (830) 997-4379; www.nimitz-museum.org. This historic park (formerly Admiral Nimitz State Historical Park) is composed of numerous sections: the former Nimitz Steamboat Hotel, the Japanese Garden of Peace, the George Bush Gallery, the Pacific Combat Zone, the Plaza of the Presidents, and the Memorial Wall.

The complex was first named for Admiral Chester Nimitz, World War II Commander in Chief of the Pacific (CinCPac), Fredericksburg's most famous resident. He commanded 2.5 million troops from the time he assumed command eighteen days after the attack on Pearl Harbor until the Japanese surrendered.

The Nimitz name was well known here even years earlier. Having spent time in the merchant marine, Captain Charles H. Nimitz, the admiral's grandfather, decided to build a hotel here, adding a structure much like a ship's bridge to the front of his establishment. Built in 1852, the Nimitz Steamboat Hotel catered to guests who enjoyed a room, a meal, and the use of an outdoor bathhouse.

Today the former hotel houses a three-story museum honoring Admiral Nimitz and Fredericksburg's early residents. Many exhibits are devoted to World War II, including several that illustrate the Pacific campaign. In addition to displays that record the building's past, several early hotel rooms, the hotel kitchen, and the bathhouse have been restored.

Behind the museum lies the Garden of Peace, a gift from the people of Japan. This classic Japanese garden includes a flowing stream, a raked bed of pebbles and stones representing the sea and the Pacific islands, and a replica of the study used by Admiral Togo, Nimitz's counterpart in the Japanese forces.

Follow the signs from the Garden of Peace for one block to the Pacific History Walk. This takes you past a collection of military artifacts, including a "fat man" Nagasaki-type atomic bomb case, a Japanese tank, and a restored barge like the one used by Nimitz. Open daily.

Pioneer Museum Complex. 309 West Main St.; (830) 997-2835. This collection of historic old homes includes an 1849 pioneer log home and store, the old First Methodist Church, and a smokehouse and log cabin. You'll also see a typical 19th-century Sunday house. Built in Fredericksburg, Sunday houses catered to farmers who would travel long distances to do business in town, often staying the weekend. With the advent of the automobile, such accommodations became obsolete. Today the old Sunday houses scattered throughout the town are used as bed-and-breakfasts, shops, and even private residences. They are easy to identify by their small size and the fact that most have half-story outside staircases. Open Mon through Sat 10 a.m. to 5 p.m., Sun noon to 5 p.m.

Torre di Pietra. 10 miles east of Fredericksburg on US 290; (830) 644-2829; www.texas hillcountrywine.com. This family-owned winery carries on a longtime Texas tradition of wine making in a winery that evokes Italy. Along with a selection of semidry, red, and sweet wines as well as ports, the winery produces liquid-filled chocolates containing the Torre di Pietra product. Along with tastings, the winery draws visitors with live music on the shaded patio every Saturday. Open daily.

Vereins Kirche Museum. Market Square on Main Street across from the courthouse; (830) 997-7832 or (830) 997-2835. You can't miss this attraction: It's housed in an exact replica of an octagonal structure erected in 1847. Back then the edifice was used as a church, as well as a school, a fort, a meeting hall, and a storehouse. The museum is sometimes called the Coffee Mill (or Die Kaffe-Muehle) Church because of its unusual shape. Exhibits here display Fredericksburg's German heritage, plus Native American artifacts from archaeological digs. Open daily (afternoon only on Sun). Free admission.

where to shop

Fredericksburg's many specialty shops offer antiques, linens, Texana, art, and collectibles. Most stores are in historic buildings along Main Street.

Charles Beckendorf Gallery. 105 North Adams St.; (800) 369-9004; www.beckendorf .com. This enormous gallery showcases the locally known work of artist Charles Beckendorf and is a good place to pick up a print of regional scenes, from one-room schoolhouses to brilliant fall scenics. Open daily.

Whistle Pik Galleries. 425 East Main St.; (800) 999-0820 or (830) 990-8151; www .whistlepik.com. This fine-arts gallery features bronzes, limited-edition prints, and original artwork. Special events throughout the year showcase artists in a variety of media. Open Mon through Sat 10 a.m. to 5:30 p.m.

where to eat

Altdorf German Biergarten and Restaurant. 301 West Main St.; (830) 997-7865; www .altdorfbiergarten-fbg.com. Take a break from shopping and enjoy some good German food in a pleasant outdoor setting. Sandwiches, steaks, burgers, and Mexican food are served here as well. There's also dining in an adjacent stone building erected by the city's pioneers. The restaurant is open Wed through Mon 11 a.m. to 9 p.m. $–$$.

August E's. 203 E. San Antonio; (830) 997-1585; www.august-es.com. One of Fredericksburg's most sophisticated dining options, August E's features nouveau Texas cuisine in a relaxed setting offering both outdoor deck dining and a main dining room that was formerly a historic train depot. The restaurant is especially known for its dry-aged prime Angus steaks as well as its fresh, never frozen, seafood that is shipped in daily. Open Tues through Fri for dinner only; weekends for lunch and dinner. $$$.

Ausländer Biergarten and Restaurant. 323 East Main St.; (830) 997-7714; www.the auslander.com. This popular German eatery has served up schnitzel, sausage, and suds for over two decades. Opt for indoor or outdoor dining with a selection that includes traditional bratwurst, Wiener schnitzel, Jager schnitzel, and even Texas schnitzel, topped with a spicy ranchero sauce. The beer garden features an extensive selection of beverages accompanied by live music. Open daily 11 a.m. to 9 p.m. $$.

fredericksburg's wine industry

Dawn breaks over a dew-crystallized vineyard. Nearby, the vintner arrives for an early start to the day. In the distance, pickup trucks meander down the ranch-to-market road, greeted by the calls of onlooking cattle and goats.

It's another day in Texas wine country.

Much of the Lone Star State's fast-growing wine industry is centered in the Hill Country near Fredericksburg, founded by German settlers who planted the Vitis vinifera grapes that thrived in the Mediterranean-like climate of their new home. It would be a century before production would begin on a serious scale, but the roots of the Texas wine industry had been planted.

This community remembers its Old World heritage with German-style buildings, shops, and restaurants. Those roots are also evident at the downtown **Fredericksburg Winery** *(247 West Main St.; 830-990-8747; www.fbgwinery.com). Its signature labels like the Texas Chardonnay "Adelsverein" (named for the Society of Noblemen formed by German princes to help emigrants to the newly formed Republic of Texas) feature artwork and a little history.*

Like many local wineries, this is a family-run operation, headed by no-nonsense Cord Switzer (look for the man in the gimme cap), along with his wife Sandy, brothers Jene and Burt, and mother "Oma," charged with labeling each bottle by hand.

14 miles north of Fredericksburg, you'll find **Bell Mountain Vineyards** *(463 Bell Mountain Rd.; 830-685-3297; www.bellmountainwine.com), located in Texas's first designated wine-growing area. Or head east, where "bouquet" describes not only wine but wildflowers.*

Farther east stands Stonewall, home to Lyndon Baines Johnson's "Texas White House," and also home to **Grape Creek Vineyards** *(4 miles west of Stonewall on US 290, 830-644-2710; www.grapecreek.com), where acres of climbing vines yield the prize-winning Cabernet Trois.*

Nearby, **Becker Vineyards** *(10 miles east of Fredericksburg off US 290; 830-644-2681; www.beckervineyards.com), with forty-six acres of French vinifera vines, boasts Texas's largest underground wine cellar. It's filled with specialties such as the 2002 Viognier, an elegant wine with a hint of violets and peach, served at a dinner for Australia's prime minister at President Bush's Prairie Chapel Ranch, and the 2002 Cabernet Sauvignon Reserve, poured at a White House dinner.*

The Cotton Gin Restaurant and Lodging. 2805 South TX 16; (830) 990-5734; www .cottoninlodging.com. Located just a few minutes south of downtown, the Cotton Gin offers elegant dining in a Texas-style environment. The restaurant is surrounded by historic cabins, each available for a bed-and-breakfast stay, as well as a waterfall and pond. Inside, the menu reflects Texas tastes, starting with Shiner Bock–battered onion rings or pecan crusted crab cakes and continuing with entrees including grilled Bandera quail, Gulf shrimp ranchero, and many cuts of steak. Open for lunch and dinner. $$$.

Fredericksburg Brewing Company. 245 East Main St.; (830) 997-1646; www.yourbrew ery.com. This downtown brewery is known for its ales and lagers but is equally notable for its casual restaurant, housed in an 1890 building, which also includes a biergarten. Next door, a "bed-and-brew" offers twelve accommodations. Open Fri and Sat 11:30 a.m. to 10 p.m., Mon and Thurs 11:30 a.m. to 9 p.m., Sun 11:30 a.m. to 7 p.m. $–$$.

Hill Top Cafe. US 87, 10 miles north of Fredericksburg; (830) 997-8922; www.hilltopcafe .com. This local favorite is known not only for its food (especially Sunday brunch), but also for its live music on Fri and Sat nights. Open Wed through Sun for lunch and dinner. $$.

Peach Tree Restaurant. 210 South Adams St.; (830) 997-9527; www.peach-tree.com. Enjoy a lunch of quiche, soup, and salad in this tearoom whose name is synonymous with Fredericksburg. Open Mon through Fri 11 a.m. to 2:30 p.m., Sat 11a.m. to 3 p.m., Sun 11 a.m. to 2 p.m. $.

where to stay

Fredericksburg is the capital city of Texas bed-and-breakfast inns, with accommodations in everything from Sunday houses to local farmhouses to residences just off Main Street. Several reservation services provide information on properties throughout the area.

Gastehaus Schmidt. 231 West Main St.; (830) 997-5612; www.fbglodging.com. This service represents one hundred bed-and-breakfast accommodations, including cottages, log cabins, and a 125-year-old rock barn. All price ranges.

Hangar Hotel. 155 Airport (south of town); (830) 997-9990; www.hangarhotel.com. This stylish hotel is perfect for airplane or history buffs. Built to look like a 1940s aircraft hangar, the hotel is located right at the Fredericksburg airport; you can sit out on the balcony and watch private planes come and go. The stylish touches continue in the rooms, down to chairs covered in bomber-jacket leather. The hotel includes an "officer's club" bar and an adjacent '40s-style diner. $$–$$$.

The Trois Estate at Enchanted Rock. 300 Trois Lane, 16 miles north of Fredericksburg on RR 965; (830) 685-3090; www.troisestate.net. Fredericksburg may be known for its unique lodging options, but the Trois Estate takes it a step further—not only will you not find another property like this in the Hill Country, you'd be hard pressed to spot a similar accommodation anywhere in the world. This sprawling estate, complete with a view of Enchanted Rock, is the home and handiwork of designer (and former '60s musician) Charles Trois. With a style termed "modern Maya," the facility features not only rooms and suites but also a chapel that's popular for weddings (it adjoins an underground swimming pool), an elegant Italian restaurant filled with Trois's collections, and even a toy-gun museum. $$$.

especially for winter texans

If you're traveling by RV or trailer, spend some time at the 113-site **Lady Bird Johnson Municipal Park** (830-997-4202), just southwest of Fredericksburg on TX 16. Campsites have electrical, water, sewer, and cable TV hookups. There's a fourteen-day limit on camping from Apr through Sept. The park includes a self-guided nature trail.

It also sports an eighteen-hole golf course, six tennis courts, badminton and volleyball courts, and a seventeen-acre lake for fishing. Pick up a checklist of birds or insects found in the region.

enchanted rock state natural area

Whether you're a climber or just looking for a good picnic spot, drive out to **Enchanted Rock State Natural Area;** (325) 247-3903; www.tpwd.state.tx.us. Located 18 miles north of Fredericksburg on RR 965, this state park features the largest stone formation in the west. Nationally this 640-acre granite outcropping takes second only to Georgia's Stone Mountain. According to Native American legend, the rock is haunted. Sometimes as the rock cools at night, it makes a creaking sound, which probably accounts for the story.

People of all ages in reasonably good physical condition can enjoy a climb up Enchanted Rock. The walk takes about an hour, and hikers are rewarded with a magnificent view of the Hill Country. In warm weather (from Apr through Oct), start your ascent early in the morning before the relentless sun turns the rock into a griddle.

Experienced climbers can scale the smaller formations adjacent to the main dome. These bare rocks are steep and dotted with boulders and crevices, and ascending them requires special equipment.

Picnic facilities and a sixty-site primitive campground at the base of the rocks round out the offerings. No vehicular camping is permitted. Buy all your supplies in Fredericksburg; there are no concessions. To prevent overcrowding, a limited number of visitors are allowed in the park during peak periods. Arrive early. Open daily.

day trip 03

west

hill country escape:
kerrville, ingram, hunt, y. o. ranch

Whether you're looking for cowboys or for culture, you'll find it in the Kerrville area. Many consider this the capital of the Hill Country. Kerrville offers visitors plenty of fun, with attractions ranging from fine art to outdoor activities to some of the top festivals in the state.

kerrville

To reach Kerrville from Austin, follow US 290 west through Johnson City and Fredericksburg (see West Day Trip 02 for attractions in those cities). Turn south on TX 16 to Kerrville.

Kerrville is popular with retirees, hunters, Winter Texans, and campers. The town of 20,000 residents is home to a 500-acre park and many privately owned camps catering to youth and church groups. Started in the 1840s, the town was named for James Kerr, a supporter of Texas independence. With its unpolluted environment and low humidity, Kerrville later became known as a health center, attracting tuberculosis patients from around the country. The town is still considered one of the most healthful places to live in the nation because of its clean air and moderate climate.

Throughout Kerrville the Schreiner name appears on everything, from Schreiner College to Schreiner's Department Store. Charles Schreiner, who became a Texas Ranger at the tender age of fifteen, came to Kerrville as a young man in the 1850s. Following the Civil War, he began a dry goods store and started acquiring land and raising sheep and goats. The Charles Schreiner Company soon expanded to include banking, ranching, and

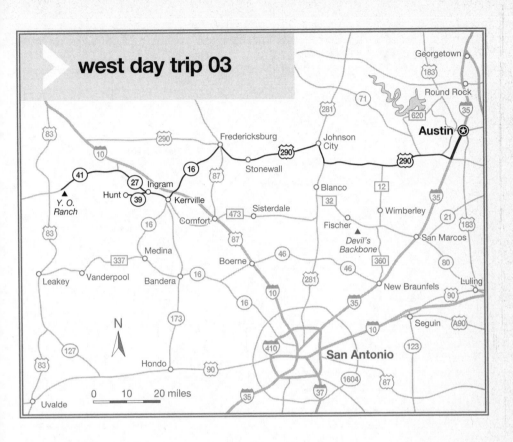

west day trip 03

marketing wool and mohair. This was the first business in America to recognize the value of mohair, the product of Angora goats. Before long, Schreiner made Kerrville the mohair capital of the world.

In 1880 Schreiner acquired the Y. O. Ranch, which grew over the next twenty years to more than 600,000 acres, covering a distance of 80 miles. Today the Schreiner family still owns this well-known ranch, located in nearby Mountain Home.

Start your visit with a look at Kerrville's revitalized downtown, where antiques shops and art galleries offer excellent shopping. Under the Texas Main Street program, the city underwent $9.5 million in renovations. Today travelers can "shop 'til they drop" in one-of-a-kind boutiques and galleries and enjoy the special atmosphere of this revitalized 37-block area.

The high quality of the artwork available in Kerrville attests to the community's status as a magnet for artists from across the Southwest. For a look at more western art, make a visit to the Museum of Western Art. This hilltop museum features western-themed paintings and sculpture.

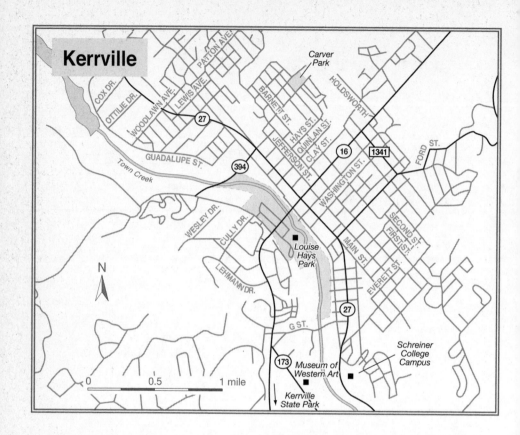

Kerrville

Both fine art and performance art headline Kerrville's well-known festivals. Memorial Day weekend brings artists from around the state to Kerrville to participate in the official Texas State Arts and Crafts Fair, an event that showcases only Texas artists. From late May to mid-June, tap your feet to the tunes of the Kerrville Folk Festival. One of Texas's best-loved music gatherings, this extravaganza of song features more than 150 singer-songwriters. The 18-day festival is held 9 miles south of Kerrville at the Quiet Valley Ranch. On the fourth Saturday of each month, Kerr Market Days (www.kerrmarketdays.org) features the work of over 80 Hill Country vendors selling handcrafted art, furniture, woodwork items, toys, jewelry, native plants and produce.

where to go

The Cailloux Theater. 910 Main St.; (830) 896-9393; www.symphonyofthehills.org. The theater features varied performances including the Kerrville Performing Arts Society, Play-house 2000 (community theater), and the Symphony of the Hills.

The Hill Country Museum. 226 Earl Garrett St.; (830) 896-8633. This local-history museum traces the development of Kerrville. Housed in Charles Schreiner's former mansion built in 1879, the building has granite porch columns, wooden parquet floors, and a bronze fountain imported from France. Open Tues through Sat.

The Kerr Arts & Cultural Center. 228 Earl Garrett St.; (830) 895-2911; www.kacckerr ville.com, Features varying exhibits from several local arts groups. Special events include the Texas Furniture Makers Show, Chocolate Extravaganza Weekend, and the Southwest Gourd Fine Arts Show.

Kerrville-Schreiner Park. 2385 Bandera Hwy. (TX 173), 1 mile southwest on TX 173; (830) 257-5392; www.kerrville.org. This park offers 7 miles of hiking trails, as well as fishing and swimming in the Guadalupe River. During summer months, tubes and canoes are for rent for an afternoon excursion on the river. Mountain bikers will find 6 miles of beginner/ intermediate trails. Campsites include water, electricity, sewage hookups, and screened shelters.

Louise Hays City Park. Off TX 16 at Thompson Dr.; (830) 792-8386. Bring your picnic lunch to this beautiful spot on the Guadalupe River. Ducks and cypress trees abound and kids will enjoy a playscape. Open daily. Free admission.

The Museum of Western Art. 1550 Bandera Hwy. (TX 173); (830) 896-2553; www .museumofwesternart.org. This museum (formerly the Cowboy Artists of America Museum) features work by top western artists. The building is constructed of eighteen boveda brick domes, an old construction method used in Mexico. Western-themed paintings and sculpture fill the museum. The museum also boasts an extensive Western research library. Visitors can take in special programs on the folklore, music, and history of the Old West. Open Tues through Sat 9 a.m. to 5 p.m., Sun 1 p.m. to 5 p.m.

Riverside Nature Center. 150 Francisco Lemos; (830)-25RIVER; www.riversidenature center.org. Features nature trails which focus on native plants of the Hill Country. Facilities include an arboretum, a visitor center and gift shop.

Wolfmueller's Book Store. 229 Earl Garrett St.; (830) 257-7323; www.wolfmuellersbooks .com. This sprawling downtown store draws shoppers from all over. Subjects include Texas history, wildlife, cookbooks, gardening, hunting, nature, and Native Americans.

where to shop

Camp Verde General Store. 285 Camp Verde Rd. East, Camp Verde; (830) 634-7722; www.campverdegeneralstore.com. A working store and post office for over 150 years, this store is adjacent to the site of Camp Verde Army Post, renowned as the location for the army camel experiment in the 1800s. Located 10 miles south of Kerrville on TX 173. Open daily.

James Avery, Craftsman. Located 3.5 miles north of Kerrville on Harper Road; (830) 895-6800; www.jamesavery.com. Since 1954 James Avery has been one of Texas's premier silversmiths. He began crafting silver crosses and religious symbols, but today his work includes gold and silver renditions of many subjects, from prickly pears to dolphins. Shop open Mon through Sat; visitor center open weekdays.

Sunrise Antiques Mall. 820 Water St.; (830) 895-2414. Kerrville's largest antiques shop is housed in a century-old building that once served as a furniture store. Open Mon through Sat.

where to eat

Bill's Barbecue. 1909 Junction Hwy.; (830) 895-5733. This barbecue eatery serves up Texas favorites, such as brisket, sausage, and chicken, with the usual side dishes. Open Tues through Sat 11a.m. to 7 p.m. $$.

Del Norte Restaurant. 710 Junction Hwy.; (830) 257-3337; www.delnorterestaurant.com. This cafe offers Texas favorites including Tex-Mex, barbecue, and chicken-fried steak. Open for breakfast and lunch Mon through Sun. $$.

Francisco's. 201 Earl Garrett St.; (830) 257-2995; www.franciscos-restaurant.com. Located downtown in the historic Weston Building, this restaurant features steak, seafood, and Mexican dishes. Diners can choose to dine indoors or al-fresco at sidewalk tables. Open Mon through Sat 11 a.m. to 3 p.m. and Thurs through Sat 5:30 p.m. to 9 p.m. $$–$$$.

Hill Country Cafe. 806 Main St.; (830) 257-6665. This diner is a favorite with local citizens as well as travelers looking for a small-town atmosphere. The day starts out with traditional American breakfast as well as specialties such as huevos rancheros; for lunch look for burgers as well as chicken-fried steak. Open for breakfast and lunch weekdays; breakfast only Sat. $$.

Joe's Jefferson Street Cafe. 1001 Jefferson St.; (830) 257-2929. This elegant restaurant, housed in a Victorian mansion, serves up Texas and southern favorites, such as shrimp, catfish, and steak. Open for lunch weekdays, dinner Mon through Sat. $$–$$$.

Kathy's on the River. 417 Water St.; (830) 257-7811. This restaurant is an excellent spot for outdoor dining with a view of the river. The menu offers a little bit of everything, from traditional chicken-fried steak to dishes with an Asian flair. Open Wed through Sun. $$–$$$.

River's Edge, a Tuscan Grille. 1011 Guadalupe St.; (830) 895-1169; www.riversedge tuscangrille.com. Scenic views of the Guadalupe River are showcased in this elegant restaurant which features northern Italian dishes. Open Tues through Sat. $$$.

Salada's. 225 Earl Garrett St.; (830) 896-0107. This casual eatery is a hot spot for locals. It features an extensive salad buffet, freshly made soups, potato bar, homemade rolls and

> ## art walk
>
> *Many Hill Country communities offer monthly markets featuring arts and crafts, but Kerrville takes its special event one step further. The "Second Saturday Art Trail" offers visitors not only the chance to shop for art but also to visit the city's growing number of galleries. From 10 a.m. to 6 p.m. on the second Saturday of every month, the city's galleries (now over two dozen strong) open their doors, provide special demonstrations, serve refreshments, and help introduce all the members of the family to various types of artwork. For more information see www.artinthehills.com.*

cornbread, and quiche of the day. Open Mon through Wed 11 a.m. to 3 p.m., Thurs and Fri 11 a.m. to 7 p.m., Sun 11 a.m. to 2 p.m. $–$$.

where to stay

Y. O. Ranch Resort Hotel and Conference Center. 2033 Sidney Baker, at TX 16 and I-10; (830) 257-4440; www.yoresort.com. This 200-room hotel salutes the famous Y. O. Ranch in Mountain Home, located 30 miles from Kerrville. The lobby is filled with reminders of the area's major industries—cattle and hunting. Twelve hotel suites include amenities such as fireplaces, furniture covered in longhorn hide, and wet bars. In keeping with the Wild West spirit, the hotel has a bar called the Elm Water Hole Saloon and a swim-up bar dubbed the Jersey Lilly. $–$$.

especially for winter texans

Kerrville is home to over a dozen RV parks, some of which are designated "adults only." For a listing, contact the **Kerrville Convention and Visitors Center;** (800) 221-7958; www .kerrvilletexascvb.com. The chamber can also provide a listing of condominium and apartment properties with short-term leases. A welcoming committee greets Winter Texans as well as the many retirees who relocate to the area.

ingram

To reach Ingram, leave Kerrville on TX 27 and continue northwest for 7 miles. This small community on the banks of the Guadalupe River was started in 1879 by Reverend J. C. W. Ingram, who built a general store and post office in what is now called Old Ingram.

Old Ingram, located off TX 27 on Old Ingram Loop, is home to many art galleries and antiques shops. Ingram proper lies along TX 27; it features stores and outfitters catering to hunters of white-tailed deer, turkey, and quail. The town is particularly busy during deer season, from Nov to early Jan. Hunting licenses are required and are sold at local sporting-goods stores. For more information call the Texas Parks and Wildlife Department at (512) 389-4800 in Texas or (800) 792-1112 elsewhere, or visit www.tpwd.state.tx.us.

where to go

Hill Country Arts Foundation. Located west of the Ingram Loop at 120 Point Theatre Rd., South Ingram, (TX 39); (800) 459-HCAF or (830) 367-5120; www.hcaf.com. The foundation, located 6 miles west of Kerrville in Ingram, is one of the oldest multidiscipline arts centers in the nation. For more than thirty-five years, this fifteen-acre center on the banks of the Guadalupe River has encouraged students in the fields of art, theater, photography, printmaking, and even quilt making. American musicals and plays are performed during the summer months at the open-air Point Theatre; indoor shows entertain audiences at other times throughout the year. A gallery exhibits the work of many artists and is open daily. The Gazebo Gift Shop is a sales outlet for local artists, open Mon through Fri afternoons. Call for a schedule of play times or special events.

Kerr County Historical Murals. At TX 27 and TX 39. Sixteen murals decorate the T. J. Moore Lumber Company building, the work of local artist Jack Feagan. The scenes portray historical events in Kerr County, starting with the establishment of shingle camps (where wooden roofing shingles were produced in 1846). Other paintings highlight cattle drives, the birth of the mohair industry, and the last Indian raid.

where to shop

Clint Orms Engravers and Silversmiths. 229-B Old Ingram Loop; (830) 367-7949; www .clintorms.com. Mr. Orms' works have been purchased for presidents, top musicians and other well-known personalities. His silver belt buckle sets are of heirloom quality, using the finest materials.

Don Atkinson Custom Boot and Saddle Maker. 229-C Old Ingram Loop; (830) 367-5400; www.donatkinson.com. Mr. Atkinson creates custom-made saddles and boots, each intricate works of art.

Southwestern Elegance. Old Ingram Loop; (830) 367-4749; www.southwesternelegance .com. This unique store specializes in Mexican collectibles and antiques (especially primitives), Mennonite furniture, and Tarahumara Indian collectibles. Open daily; call for hours.

hunt

Continue west on TX 39 for 7 miles to Hunt, a small community best known for its year-round outdoor recreational camps catering to Scouts as well as youth and church groups.

where to go

Kerr Wildlife Management Area. RR 1340, 12 miles northwest of Hunt; (830) 238-4483; www.tpwd.state.tx.us. Enjoy a driving tour over this 6,493-acre research ranch owned by the Texas Fish and Game Commission. Purchased to study the relationship between wildlife and livestock, the ranch is home to white-tailed deer, javelinas, wild turkeys, bobcats, gray foxes, and ringtails. Pick up a booklet at the entrance or write: Kerr Wildlife Management Area, Rte. 1, Box 180, Hunt, TX 78024. Open daily, but call during hunting season when the area may be closed for a hunt. Free admission.

Stonehenge II. FM 1340, just out of Hunt. Located on private land, this replica of England's Stonehenge as well as replicas of two Easter Island moai may be viewed from a roadside parking area. A sign provides information on the original Stonehenge and its smaller Texas cousin. Open daily. Free admission.

y. o. ranch

From Hunt, head west on FM 1340 to TX 41. Turn left and the Y. O. Ranch will soon appear on your right. This ranch dates back to 1880, a part of the 550,000 acres purchased by Captain Charles Schreiner, former Texas Ranger and longhorn-cattle owner.

The Y. O. spans 60 square miles and supports over 1,000 registered longhorns, the largest such herd in the nation. Charlie Schreiner III, the original owner's grandson, brought the breed back from near extinction in the late 1950s, founding the Texas Longhorn Breeders Association. The Y. O. hosts a longhorn trail drive at the ranch each spring.

After the devastating Texas drought in the 1950s, the Schreiners began to diversify the use of their ranch, stocking the land with the largest collection of natural roaming exotics in the country, including many rare and endangered species. More than 10,000 animals range the hills, including zebra, ostrich, giraffe, emu, and ibex.

You may visit the Y. O. Ranch only by reservation. Both day and overnight programs are offered. Day-trippers can enjoy the spread on a lunch tour or photo safari. The ranch also hosts an Outdoor Awareness Program, an environmental education camp that teaches horseback riding, rappelling, gun handling, and wildlife study. Overnight accommodations are available in the 1800s-era cabins; meals are included. For general information, call (800) YO-RANCH or (830) 967-2624; www.yoranch.com.

where to stay

The MO-Ranch. 2229 FM 1340; (800) 460-4401; www.moranch.com. This 500-acre complex of hotel rooms, conference center, summer camp, hiking trails, chapel and more is on the Guadalupe River. The ranch's unique architecture dates back to the 1920s and this facility offers a relaxing atmosphere for family or group retreats. $$$.

northwest

day trip 01

northwest

lakeside luxury:
lake austin, lake travis, lakeway

This is a popular hot weather day trip. Bring your swimsuit from Apr through Oct, along with an old pair of sneakers to navigate the rocky Lake Travis beaches.

lake austin

Within the city limits of Austin you'll find this picturesque manmade "lake." Technically speaking, it's a reservoir and was formed by the construction of the Tom Miller Dam in 1939, which also assists with generating electricity for the city of Austin. Aside from the practicality of Lake Austin and its dam, it offers water-related activities and camping opportunities.

where to go

Loop 360 Boat Ramp. (512) 854-7275. From the intersection of Loop 360 and RR 2222, travel south on Loop 360 across the Loop 360 Bridge over Lake Austin. The entrance to the boat ramp is on the east side of Loop 360, directly below the bridge. As its name suggests, this park is primarily used by boaters as a launch onto Lake Austin. It is located under the south side of Pennybacker Bridge. You'll also find areas for fishing and picnicking. Open daily.

Mary Quinlan Park. (512) 854-7275. From the intersection of RR 620 and RR 2222, take RR 620 south 2.1 miles to Quinlan Park Road. Turn left onto Quinlan Park Road and travel

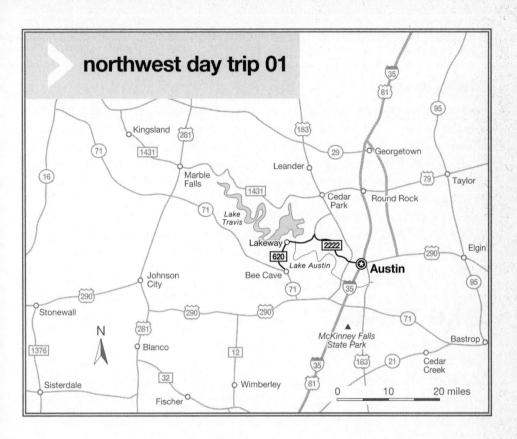

northwest day trip 01

5.5 miles to the park entrance. This quiet park has the only public boat ramp for miles along Lake Austin. It is a beautiful place to enjoy the quiet of one of Lake Austin's narrow passages and to view the bluffs against the water's emerald depths. Open daily.

Mount Bonnell. A beautiful lookout is located within the Austin city limits. Turn left off RR 2222 onto Mount Bonnell Road, which will take you to the highest point in town with a panoramic view of the city and the surrounding hills. Visitors must park and walk up some steep steps to the lookout, but the view is well worth the climb. Free admission.

where to eat

County Line on the Lake. 5204 RR 2222; (512) 346-3664; www.countyline.com. This is one of the few barbecue restaurants in Texas where you could wear a coat and tie and not look like a city slicker. Enjoy full table service at this excellent restaurant on Lake Austin, ordering from a menu that features brisket, sausage, and ribs. Located right on the shores of Lake Austin with an excellent view, this is a popular summer stop. Open for lunch and dinner daily. $$–$$$.

where to stay

Lake Austin Spa Resort. 1705 Quinlan Park Rd.; (800) 847-5637 or (512) 372-7300; www.lakeaustin.com. Located on the shores of Lake Austin, this well-known resort caters to guests, with special menus, dietary consultations, and European spa services. The spa (available to day visitors as well as to guests) and adjoining 40-room resort lie on the shores of Lake Austin, a narrow swath of water that begins at the foot of the Hill Country and flows through the western part of the city. The resort, a longtime favorite in the Lone Star State, became a world-class destination spa in 2004 thanks to the opening of the 25,000-square-foot LakeHouse Spa. The two-story, Texas-sized structure, resembling traditional Hill Country farmhouses with its limestone exterior and screened upstairs porch, houses 30 treatment areas staffed by over 80 therapists. $$$.

lake travis

Continue northwest on RR 2222. This winding road is filled with treacherous curves, so take it slow. At the intersection with RR 620, you have two choices: turn west onto RR 620 and continue to Mansfield Dam and the remainder of this trip, or turn east to some county parks and Austin's best-known outdoor dining spot. This side excursion affords a beautiful drive past some of Austin's most expensive homes.

where to go

Bob Wentz at Windy Point. Comanche Trail, 1 mile past Hippie Hollow; (512) 854-7275; www.lcra.org. Mention Windy Point and Austinites think of windsurfing, sailing, or scuba diving. A top spot on Lake Travis for water sports, this LCRA park offers a hiking and biking trail, sand volleyball courts, and a boat ramp for sailboats. Open daily.

Cypress Creek Park. (800) 776-5272; www.lcra.org. From the intersection of RR 620 and RR 2222, take Bullock Hollow Road west 2 miles. The park entrance is on your left, just before the intersection of Bullock Hollow Road and FM 2769 (Old Anderson Mill Road). A favorite for lake lovers, this day-use LCRA park includes a boat ramp. It is frequented by many campers, boaters, picnickers, and anglers. Open daily and offers unimproved camp sites.

Fritz Hughes Park. (512) 854-7275; www.co.travis.tx.us/tnr/parks/default.asp. From the intersection of RR 620 and RR 2222, take RR 620 south 3.7 miles to Low Water Crossing Road (just before Mansfield Dam). Turn left on Low Water Crossing Road and travel .2 mile to Fritz Hughes Park Road. Turn left to park entrance. Along with Mary Quinlan and Selma

Hughes Parks, this is one of only three access points along the north side of Lake Austin. The small LCRA park is usually frequented by local residents. The park offers picnicking, swimming, and fishing. Open daily. Free admission.

Mansfield Dam Park. (800) 776-5272; www.lcra.org. From the intersection of RR 620 and RR 2222, travel south 4.9 miles. Turn right onto Mansfield Dam Road, just south of Mansfield Dam. The park entrance is on the left. One of the most visited LCRA parks along Lake Travis, Mansfield Dam Park is among the top boat-launching sites on the lake. The park also appeals to campers and picnickers; a primitive area is located nearby. Open daily.

McGregor/Hippie Hollow Park. From RR 620, turn right onto Comanche Trail; (512) 854-7275. This is a clothing-optional park, the only one in the Austin area. On summer weekends, it is packed with nudists, curious onlookers, and swimmers who want to enjoy a beautiful swimming hole. The parking area is located away from the bathing area. (Nudity is not permitted in the parking lot.)

Onlookers outnumber nudists many weekends, but to see the beach (and the swimmers), you must leave your car and walk down the trail to the water's edge. The swimming area is protected from curious boaters by patrolling Parks Department boats. No children allowed. Day use only.

Pace Bend Park. (800) 776-5272; (512) 264-1482; www.lcra.org. From the intersection of RR 620 and TX 71, take TX 71 west 11 miles to RR 2322 (Pace Bend Park Road). Turn right on RR 2322 and travel 4.6 miles to the park entrance. Pace Bend is one of the top parks, not only of the LCRA sites, but also in the entire region. Nine miles of shoreline appeal to swimmers and boaters; horseback riders and hikers also find diversions with a large natural area. Part of the park is managed as a wildlife preserve and can be reached by rugged trails; an excellent destination for wildlife-viewing and bird-watching. Open daily. Offers 20 improved camp sites.

Sandy Creek Park. (800) 776-5272; www.lcra.org. From the intersection of RR 620 and RR 2222, take Bullock Hollow Road west 2.5 miles to FM 2769. Turn left onto FM 2769 and travel 4 miles to Lime Creek Road, through the town of Volente. Entrance is on the left. This quiet park is far less visited than many other north Lake Travis sites and is popular with swimmers and nature lovers. Open daily and offers unimproved camp sites.

Selma Hughes Park. (512) 854-7275; www.co.travis.tx.us/tnr/parks/default.asp. From the intersection of RR 620 and RR 2222, take RR 620 south 2.1 miles to Quinlan Park Road. Turn right on Quinlan Park Road and travel 4.6 miles to Selma Hughes Road. Turn left on Selma Hughes Road and proceed to park entrance. Along with Fritz Hughes and Mary Quinlan Parks, Selma Hughes Park is one of the few public-access sites along this part of

Lake Austin. Here the lake is narrow and quiet, and in the park, visitors are usually local residents. Visitors will find picnicking, swimming, and fishing areas. Free admission.

Tom Hughes Park. (512) 854-7275; www.co.travis.tx.us/tnr/parks/default.asp. From the intersection of RR 620 and RR 2222, take RR 620 south 2.3 miles to Marshall Ford Drive. Turn right onto Marshall Ford Drive and travel .2 mile to Park Drive. Turn right and travel 2.8 miles to park entrance. Scuba divers call this park a favorite. The walk to the water's edge is steep and brushy. Free admission.

Volente Beach Waterpark. 16107 Wharf Cove, FM 2769 in Volente; (512) 258-5109; www.volentebeach.com. This favorite summer hangout offers a pool, giant water slides, a sand beach, motorized water sports, volleyball, and more. There's also a casual restaurant on-site, and visitors may bring coolers with food and drink (no glass containers or alcohol). Hours vary with season.

where to eat

The Oasis. 6550 Comanche Trail; (512) 266-2442; www.oasis-austin.com. Known as "the Sunset Capital of Texas," this restaurant is famous for its open decks overlooking Lake Travis. On weekends this becomes a popular stop after a day of boating or swimming. The lake views and the surrounding hills provide a lovely backdrop for a sunset meal at this unusual restaurant. Open daily for lunch and dinner. $–$$.

lakeway

At the intersection of RR 2222 and RR 620, turn right and continue west on RR 620 across Mansfield Dam to the village of Lakeway and the Lakeway Resort and Conference Center. This 8,000-person resort community boasts recreational facilities and accommodations for golf and tennis buffs. You can't miss it; just look for the water tower shaped and painted like a golf ball.

what to do

Golf. (512) 261-7200; www.clubsoflakeway.com. The Live Oak and the Yaupon eighteen-hole courses are open to the public. Golf packages in conjunction with the Lakeway Inn also are available.

Students of the Academy of Golf Dynamics (800-879-2008) hone their skills on three full-length holes, a driving range, and a putting green. The academy is located in The Hills of Lakeway, a private eighteen-hole course designed by Jack Nicklaus. Call for class information; reservations required. Closed Mon.

World of Tennis. 1 World of Tennis Square; (512) 261-7222 or 261-7257; www.clubsof lakeway.com. The World of Tennis has 16 world-class outdoor courts, including a stadium court as well as two indoor, climate-controlled courts. Tennis packages in conjunction with the Lakeway Inn are available. Open daily.

where to stay

Lakeway Resort and Spa. 101 Lakeway Dr.; (800) LAKEWAY or (512) 261-6600; www .dolce-lakeway-hotel.com. Adjacent to the marina on Lake Travis, this large resort has rooms featuring elegant decor and a lake view. Some accommodations include fireplaces. A lobby bar serves evening cocktails, and the Travis Restaurant offers breakfast, lunch, and dinner. A casual bar features views of the lake. $$$.

day trip 02

northwest

lake love:
jonestown, lago vista, marble falls, kingsland

The Highland Lakes region is made up of a series of seven lakes that form back-to-back "stair steps" along the Colorado River. Built in the 1930s by the LCRA to bring electricity to rural Texas and to control flooding along the river, the lakes now provide 150 miles of water recreation.

To start this day trip and reach the north shores of Lake Travis, head to Cedar Park on US 183 (see Northeast Day Trip 03 for Cedar Park details), then turn west on FM 1431.

jonestown

Head west from Cedar Park, and the road soon begins twisting and turning, dipping into what many describe as the first wave of the Texas Hill Country. Just after Cedar Park gives way to cedar breaks and untamed countryside, you'll pass through a small pocket of homes and a few businesses, the remains of the community of Nameless.

From Nameless, continue west to the community of Jonestown. Named for founders Emmet and Warren Jones, this town was first envisioned as a retirement community on the shores of Lake Travis. Today the town has grown somewhat, though, and serves as a home base for many commuters into Austin.

where to go

Jones Brothers Park. 18100 Park Dr.; (512) 267-3722. This 32-acre public-use park includes a boat ramp, walking paths, picnic areas, children's playscape, and more.

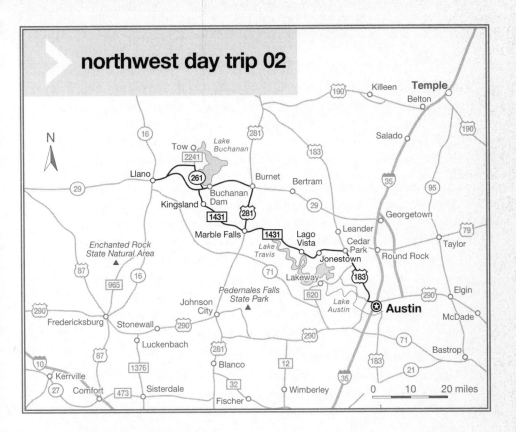

northwest day trip 02

lago vista

With a name that translates as "Lake View," it's no surprise that much of Lago Vista boasts a view of Lake Travis. This sprawling lake offers anglers, boaters, and swimmers innumerable coves and quiet stretches. LCRA operates many public parks in this region. Lago Vista is called the gateway to the Balcones Canyonlands National Wildlife Refuge, a preserve that protects two endangered species. Along with hikes and birding at the refuge, nature buffs also find many opportunities at LCRA parks in the region.

where to go

Balcones Canyonlands National Wildlife Refuge. 5 miles west of Lago Vista on FM 1431; (512) 339-9432; www.fws.gov/southwest/refuges/texas/balcones/index.htm. This preserve protects the juniper habitat of the tiny golden-cheeked warbler and black-capped vireo. The 22-square-mile preserve schedules its public hours around the breeding schedule of the birds, so you may find the park closed at certain periods. The best place to view

lake parks

Arkansas Bend Park. *FM 1431 south to Lohmans Ford Road; (800) 776-5272; www.lcra.org. Turn left on Lohmans Crossing Road and travel 4.5 miles to Sylvester Ford Road. Turn left on Sylvester Ford Road and travel 1.5 miles to the park entrance. This is one of the quieter parks along Lake Travis, thanks to its remote location. The park offers camping, picnicking, fishing, and a boat ramp. Open daily.*

Camp Creek Recreation Area. *(800) 776-5272; www.lcra.org. North side of Lake Travis, about 18 miles west of Lago Vista or 8 miles east of Marble Falls near the Smithwick community. Take FM 1431 to CR 343 and continue about a half mile to the site entrance. Camp Creek Area offers a loop hiking trail and, in early mornings and late evenings, visitors can see local wildlife. The park is shaded by large pecan trees and is especially good for those looking for a quiet, undeveloped site. This area should, however, be avoided during heavy rains. The access to Camp Creek is a steep gravel road with two low-water crossings that are often covered after rainstorms. Open daily. Free admission.*

Gloster Bend Recreation Area. *(800) 776-5272; www.lcra.org. North side of Lake Travis, approximately 6 miles west of Lago Vista near the Travis Peak community. Take FM 1431 to Singleton Road and continue 3.3 miles to the site entrance. This large day-use park, divided into woodlands on the south and grasslands on the north, boasts the highest visitation of all the Lake Travis recreation areas. The site has only minimal facilities, including composting toilets, fire rings, and trash cans. More than 1 mile of shoreline can be easily accessed. Open daily.*

the vireos is at the Shin Oak Observation Deck (it closes when the vireos arrive in the spring). Several hiking trails are open most of the year. The preserve also hosts several special events every year, most notably the Balcones Songbird Festival in the spring. The event includes guided nature walks focusing on birding, wildlife, and butterflies. Free admission.

Flat Creek Estate Vineyard and Winery. (512) 267-6310; www.flatcreekestate.com. Go 6 miles west of Lago Vista on FM 1431, then turn south on Singleton Bend Road. Continue 2.5 miles to Singleton Bend East. Turn left and continue to gate. Tucked in a quiet valley, this winery's twenty acres of vineyards produce Italian, Rhone and port varietal grapes that Flat Creek transforms into wines that have won competitions across Texas and beyond. The winery offers guided tours followed by a tasting. Tours and tastings are offered Tues through Fri noon to 5 p.m., Sat 10 a.m. to 5 p.m. and Sun noon to 5 p.m. Fee for tastings.

Shaffer Bend Recreation Area. *(800) 776-5272; www.lcra.org. 17 miles west of Lago Vista or 9 miles east of Marble Falls near the Smithwick Community. Take FM 1431 to CR 343A and continue about 1 mile. This park is one of the largest on Lake Travis, with 523 acres, and one of the top LCRA parks. Shaffer is a favorite with day-trippers and campers looking for an undeveloped site that offers good lake views, plenty of wildlife, and various kinds of vegetation. The recreation area, located between Marble Falls and Lago Vista on the lake's north shore, is dotted with hills of dense cedar. From these peaks, you can enjoy good lake views at several points along the park road.*

The hills gradually give way to savanna shaded by oaks and pecan trees. Here you can also see the guayacan, a plant not usually seen east of Del Rio. A mile-long swimming area offers a chance to cool off after hiking. Open daily.

Turkey Bend Recreation Area. *(800) 776-5272; www.lcra.org. North side of Lake Travis, approximately 9.5 miles west of Lago Vista. Take FM 1431 to Shaw Drive and continue 1.8 miles to the site entrance. This 400-acre park winds along 2 miles of Lake Travis's northern shoreline. The recreation area is popular with those looking for a real back-to-nature getaway. The site has been left mostly undeveloped, with no restrooms, drinking water, or trash collection. Some primitive campsites are marked with fire rings.*

Horseback riders and hikers frequent the park for its loop trail with good views of the lake. One warning: During hunting season there is hunting on adjacent private land so be wary when approaching fence lines. Open daily.

Lago Vista Airpower Museum and Library. (512) 267-7403. Continue west of Lago Vista on FM 1431, then turn north on Bar-K Ranch Road and follow signs to the airport. The Lago Vista private airport is home to a museum showcasing military aircraft through model plane displays, many photos, and various other displays. Open Sat afternoons from 1 p.m. to 5 p.m. or by appointment. Free admission.

marble falls

Continue west on FM 1431 to Marble Falls. Drive south on US 281 to the overlook at the edge of town for a terrific view of the 780-acre Lake Marble Falls. It's said that this sight inspired local songwriter Oscar J. Fox (who penned "The Cowboy's Lament" and "Get Along Little Dogie") to write his popular tune "Hills of Home." Today a marker commemorates this local hero.

Normally the falls that gave this town its name are beneath the lake, but occasionally the falls are visible when the LCRA does repair work on the dam.

While the town may be named for marble, granite is king here. Granite Mountain at the edge of town is the home of a huge quarry that sells pink granite to places around the country. This quarry supplied the granite used in building the State Capitol and also many of the jetties along the Texas coast. Visitors are not allowed in the quarry but can observe the operation from the rest stop on the side of FM 1431.

where to go

Marble Falls/Lake LBJ Chamber of Commerce. 916 Second St., (830) 693-2815; www .marblefalls.org. Stop by this one-hundred-year-old railroad depot station to get brochures and maps on area shopping, dining, and park recreation. Open Mon through Fri 8 a.m. to 5 p.m.

Granite Beach Recreation Area. Lake LBJ; (800) 776-5272; www.lcra.org. On south side of Lake LBJ next to Wirtz Dam. Access road is off FM 2147, 5 miles west of Marble Falls. FM 2147 can be reached from the east via US 281 or from the west by TX 71. This day-use park is primarily frequented by boaters and offers 17 acres. Open daily. Free admission.

Highland Arts Guild Gallery. 318 Main St.; (830) 693-7324; www.highlandartsguild.org. Have a look here at the work of more than fifty local artists who call the Highland Lakes their home. The gallery sells original arts and crafts, including many bluebonnet paintings. Open Mon through Sat.

Hills of Home Memorial. US 281, south of the Colorado River. The memorial remembers Oscar J. Fox, the composer of "The Cowboy's Lament," "Get Along Little Dogie," and "Hills of Home," said to be inspired by the view from this spot.

where to eat

Blue Bonnet Cafe. 211 US 281 (near the bridge); (830) 693-2344; www.bluebonnetcafe .net. This is an example of a good old-fashioned Texas diner at its best. For more than sixty years, the Blue Bonnet Cafe has served locals and visitors plenty of country cooking, including chicken-fried steak, fried chicken, and burgers. $–$$.

Inman's Ranch House Barbecue and Turkey Sausage. US 281 and Sixth Street; (830) 693-2711. This little restaurant uses Texas's favorite cooking method—barbecue—on turkey to produce a spicy sausage that's mighty tasty and not as greasy as its pork cousin. Beef brisket and sides of coleslaw and beans also appear on the menu. $.

where to stay

Horseshoe Bay Resort Marriott. FM 2147, west of Marble Falls; (866) 799-5384 or (830) 598-8600; www.horseshoebaymarriott.com. Horseshoe Bay, located on Lake LBJ, is one of the premier resorts in Central Texas. Golfers have their choice of three courses, including Robert Trent Jones's Apple Rock. Other features include the Bayside Spa and Fitness Center, Oriental gardens, a yacht club, and tennis courts. $$$.

kingsland

Continue west on FM 1431 from Marble Falls to the fishing community of Kingsland. Once named Granite Shoals, Lake LBJ was renamed for President Lyndon Baines Johnson, who, as a young senator, brought the lakes project to Central Texas. Today the narrow, winding lake is popular with both anglers and water-skiers. Edged by steep hills, its clear and calm waters are protected from the winds that often buffet the larger lakes.

Kingsland is a sleepy community catering to those who come to enjoy a few days of bass fishing. Several lodges lie near the junction of the Llano and Colorado Rivers, where quiet coves afford a catch of black bass, white bass, crappie, catfish, and perch. Be sure to stop at the scenic overlook on FM 1431 just past the edge of town for a grand view of the lake and its shoreline homes.

where to go

Lost Creek Vineyards. 1129 RR 2233, Sunrise Beach; (325) 388-3753; www.lost creekvineyard.com. Seven miles south of Kingsland, near the resort community of Sunrise Beach on Lake LBJ, Lost Creek Vineyards produces a variety of award-winning wines from locally-grown Shiraz and Cabernet Sauvignon grapes. In addition to fields of vines, you'll also find a tasting room, bistro restaurant, sushi bar, and bed and breakfast accommodations on property. It's also a popular spot for weddings and other special events. The winery also hosts a series of outdoor live music events during the warmer months.

Nightengale Archaeological Center. 201 Circle Dr., 9 miles north of Marble Falls on Lake LBJ; (512) 598-5261 or (800) 776-55272; www.lcra.org. From Marble Falls, follow FM 1431 to Burnet CR 126 (at the Twin Isles and Hidden Oaks subdivision), turn left and follow the signs. Discovered in 1988, this archaeological site has yielded artifacts dating from the Paleo-Indian (more than 10,000 years ago) to the late prehistoric periods (700 years ago). A small visitor center and museum house artifacts from the site. Open for tours on Sat afternoons and by appointment. Free admission.

day trip 03

northwest

ranch road rambling:
cedar park, leander, bertram,
burnet, buchanan dam, tow

Leaving bustling US 183 in your rearview mirror, this getaway travels on a winding road that snakes into the northern Hill Country, ending on the shores of massive Lake Buchanan.

cedar park

Cedar Park is north from Austin via US 183. Now primarily a suburb, once this was called "cedar chopper" country. Cedar choppers were independent people who worked the hilly land to the west, cutting juniper trees to provide fence posts for area ranchers. This generations-old trade is still plied by some Hill Country families.

where to go

Austin Steam Train. US 183 and FM 1431; (512) 477-8468; www.austinsteamtrain.org. Take a ride on the Hill Country Flyer, running from Cedar Park to Burnet (where visitors stop to have lunch and shop). Each of the 1930s-era cars is restored to original splendor. Other excursions include the Bertram Flyer for a ride from Cedar Park to Bertram (with a chance to get out and see the old depot), the River City Flyer (which departs from East Austin and travels through Manor and Littig), and the Twilight Flyer, which features evening themed trips such as murder mysteries, holiday lights, and bedtime stories. At press time, a new depot was under construction in Cedar Park on FM 1431 just south of US 183. Reservations required.

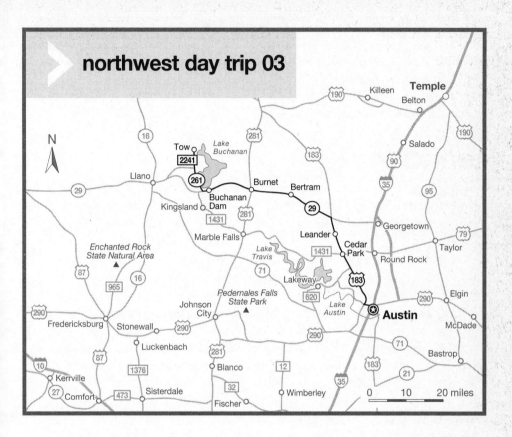

northwest day trip 03

Cedar Park Center. 2100 Ave. of the Stars; (512) 600-5000; www.cedarparkcenter.com. This multi-purpose arena, seating 8,000, is the home ice of the Texas Stars professional hockey team which competes in the American Hockey League as a top-level affiliate of the NHL Dallas Stars. When the Stars aren't in town, the facility hosts other special events. Performances have ranged from country musical artist George Strait to the Cirque du Soleil. Open daily.

where to shop

The Collectible Caboose. US 183 and FM 1431 in The Railyard; (512) 259-9494; www .collectiblecaboose.com. All aboard for this train shop, which features collectibles, train-themed gift items, and, of course, plenty of trains, including all gauges of model railroading.

Lakeline Mall. US 183 and RR 620. Shop this Texas-size mall, with a decor that's complete with a free-standing replica of the State Capitol dome and the Austin skyline. Open daily. (512) 257-7467.

where to eat

J&J BBQ. 300 FM 1431; (512) 918-0314. This former home has been transformed into a casa of 'que with a delightful mix of barbecue and Tex-Mex specialties. Brisket and sausage are tops, but breakfast (including tacos, huevos rancheros and chorizo) is extremely popular, especially on weekends. $.

leander

Continue north on US 183 to neighboring Leander, a town of 25,000 that boasts many historic markers. To the right as you approach town, you'll see a marker for the Blockhouse Creek subdivision, named for a blockhouse used as an interim prison by the Texas Rangers a century ago.

Another historic marker stands just east of US 183 on FM 2243. The Davis Cemetery, as the marker recounts, is the site of a mass grave, a reminder of an Indian attack that ended with the deaths of many pioneers.

Perhaps the most famous Leander historical marker is actually found closer to Cedar Park. This monument recalls the discovery of "Leanderthal Lady" in January 1983. Dating back between 10,000 and 13,000 years, the skeleton and the site are considered one of the country's most important Early Man locations. The historic marker is located east of US 183 on FM 1431, southeast of the intersection with Parmer Lane.

where to go

Dinosaur Tracks. South San Gabriel River, just north of town; (512) 259-1907. Park your car at the bridge and walk upstream for a half mile to see these three-toed dinosaur tracks. Free admission.

where to eat

Selene's Bistro. 1906 S. Bagdad Rd.; (512) 528-9595; www.selenes.com. Fine dining and Leander haven't been synonymous in the past, but Selene's is quickly changing that with its French bistro cuisine at suburban prices. Dinner options range from grilled lamb chops with rosemary jus to roast Cornish game hen to veal marsala. Open for lunch and dinner Tues through Sun. $$.

bertram

From Leander, continue north on US 183 to the intersection with TX 29. Drive west on TX 29 for 12 miles to Bertram. This was once a thriving community, with four cotton gins and a busy railroad constructed to haul granite from Marble Falls to Austin for the construction of the Texas State Capitol. Today, however, this is a sleepy little town most of the year, but on Labor Day weekend the streets throng with travelers from around the state who come for the annual Oatmeal Festival. Visitors attend the celebration to witness an oatmeal cook-off, take part in a fun run, or see a parade. The festival is named for the hamlet of Oatmeal, located 6 miles south of Bertram on RR 243.

where to shop

Jimmy's Antiques. TX 29 east of Bertram; (512) 355-2985. If you're looking for Texas antiques, this is a good place to start. Jimmy's has the usual glassware, china, and jewelry, but it also handles many local treasures, such as Texas Ranger saddlebags, western saddles, Native American artifacts, and arrowheads. Open daily.

burnet

Continue west on TX 29 from Bertram to Burnet. This is the closest town of any size to Lake Buchanan (pronounced "BUCK-an-an"). It's a good place to stop for picnic supplies and sunscreen products during summer visits (there are few facilities once you leave the city limits). Outdoor activities popular throughout the year include spelunking and bird-watching.

where to go

Canyon of the Eagles Lodge and Nature Park. RR 2341; (800) 977-0081; www.canyon oftheeagles.com. This 900-acre park serves as an ecotourism destination for all types of travelers, whether it's strolling on marked nature trails, birding, butterfly watching, fishing, kayaking, or even enjoying the stars at an observatory.

Fort Croghan Grounds and Museum. TX 29 on the western edge of town; (512) 756-8281; www.fortcroghan.org. Fort Croghan was constructed here in the 1840s, one of eight forts built from the Rio Grande to the Trinity Rivers to protect the region from Indian attacks. The museum and the adjacent fort sit on the left side of the road. Exhibits include household items used by residents over one hundred years ago. You can take a walking tour of the fort, the blacksmith shop, the powder house, and a two-room cabin where one family raised ten children. Open Thurs through Sat from Apr through Aug; by appointment and for special events only during winter months. Free admission.

Highland Lakes Squadron of the Commemorative Air Force. At the Burnet Municipal Airport off US 281, 1.5 miles south of Burnet; (512) 756-2226; www.highlandlakessquadron .com. Here you can have a look at World War II airplanes and memorabilia from the men who fought the battles. Operated by the Highland Lakes Squadron of the Commemorative Air Force. Open weekends.

Inks Dam National Fish Hatchery. FM 2342 to intersection with Park Road 4; turn north on Park Road 4 for 1.5 miles; (830) 793-2474. This facility raises fish to be shipped throughout the country. Guided tours can be arranged (call in advance) for a look at the hatching process. Open daily. Free admission.

Inks Lake State Park. From TX 29, turn left onto Park Road 4; (512) 793-2223 for park information; (512) 389-8900 for reservations; www.tpwd.state.tx.us. This 1,200-acre park offers camping, lakeside picnicking, swimming, and even a golf course. White-tailed deer are a common sight during evening hours. Open daily.

Longhorn Cavern State Park. From TX 29, turn left onto Park Road 4; (877) 441-CAVE or (830) 598-CAVE; www.tpwd.state.tx.us or www.longhorncaverns.com. This cavern has few formations but a long and interesting history. In one story, Comanches raided San Antonio, kidnapped a young woman named Mariel King, and brought her back to the cavern, unknowingly followed by three Texas Rangers. A hand-to-hand battle ensued, and Mariel King was rescued. Ending the story with a fairy-tale flourish, Miss King later married one of her rescuers, and the couple lived on in Burnet. The guided tour is easy, with wide, well-lit trails through the huge limestone rooms. Open daily.

Vanishing Texas River Cruise. At Canyon of the Eagles; (800) 4RIVER4 or (512) 756-6986; www.vtrc.com. A few miles past Fort Croghan on TX 29, turn right on FM 2341 and follow the signs 14 miles to the cruise entrance. This excellent bird-watching cruise is popular with travelers who come to see American bald eagles from Nov through Mar. The rest of the year, you might see javelinas, wild goats, and white-tailed deer. The route takes in 50-foot Fall Creek Falls and a narrow, cliff-lined passage on the Colorado River. Cruises also travel past Fall Creek Vineyards on the lake's shore. Some trips include a stop at the Winery for guests age 13 and over. Dinner cruises May through Oct; reservations required. $$.

where to eat

Burnet County BBQ. TX 29; (512) 756-6468. This casual restaurant serves up all the main ingredients of a Texas barbeque: brisket, ribs, and sausage. The atmosphere here is casual and families are welcome. Open Wed through Sun. $.

where to stay

Canyon of the Eagles Lodge and Nature Park. RR 2341; (800) 977-0081; www.canyon oftheeagles.com. Day-trippers who would like to extend their stay at this park find sixty-four lodge rooms, including some located in Hill Country–style cottages with stone accents and metal roofs. All rooms include one or two queen size beds, a coffeemaker, and hair dryer; the cottage rooms offer two queen beds, a mini-refrigerator, and a microwave. The lodge complex includes a pool and restaurant. $$–$$$.

burnet treasure

Longhorn Caverns, outside Burnet, is said to be the home of more than one treasure trove. One tale involves who else but Sam Bass, who allegedly used the cavern as a hideout following nearby robberies. Today the main opening of the cave is called the Sam Bass Entrance. No Bass treasure has been found, but parts of the 11-mile cavern are still being explored.

Another Longhorn Cavern tale involves the search for a treasure supposedly buried on Woods Ranch near Burnet. After years of searching, one of the treasure hunters went to seek the advice of a palmist, whose cryptic recommendation was to dig "under the footprint." There was speculation that this "footprint" might be a foot-shaped impression on the ceiling of one of the Longhorn Cavern rooms. The crew dug below this formation—only to find a container-shaped hole below the surface. Where there had once been a metal container—and possibly a treasure—there was only a rust-lined hole.

The Sam Bass legends are not the only treasure-filled stories flying around the region. One treasure story dates back to an ancient Spanish document regarding an old Spanish mine, located somewhere near Burnet. According to an Austin American newspaper story in the early 1920s, a "pack train of burros carrying forty jackloads of silver was pursued by a band of Comanche Indians and . . . the men in charge of the pack train buried the silver near where the town of Leander is now located."

No one's found the Spanish silver cache, but some treasure seekers in this area have struck gold—or gemstones, as the case may be. In 1925, W. E. Snavely of Taylor, who had hunted treasure for sixty years, found a ruby arrowhead weighing fifteen karats, along with many other gemstones.

buchanan dam

Continue driving west on TX 29 to the village of Buchanan Dam, a fishing and retirement community. Lake Buchanan, the jewel of the Highland Lakes with more than 23,000 surface acres of water, is formed by Buchanan Dam, the largest multiarch dam in the world.

Lake Buchanan's own gem is the freshwater pearl. Created by freshwater mussels in the Colorado River, some pearls found here have been valued at several thousand dollars.

Many anglers are familiar with one of the most popular sites along Lake Buchanan: Black Rock Park. This location now boasts improvements such as new campsites and restrooms. Anglers can try their luck with either bank or boat fishing. Boats can launch without charge from the ramp at neighboring Llano County Park.

Birders also find this park a favorite destination. The northeast side of the lake offers one of the best opportunities to spot the American bald eagle from Nov through Mar. Other species often sighted include great blue herons, kingfishers, double-crested cormorants, roadrunners, ospreys, red-breasted mergansers, common loons, horned grebes, and Bonaparte's gulls.

If you'd like to extend your stay at Black Rock, spend the night at one of the park's thirty campsites, each with a table and grill.

where to go

Buchanan Dam Visitors Center and Museum. TX 29, at the dam; (512) 793-2803. Here you can find brochures on area campgrounds and activities as well as maps of the Highland Lakes. A museum adjacent to the center provides a look at how the mighty Colorado was tamed. Photographs recount the backbreaking labor involved in the massive project. During spring and summer months, tour the dam on Sat and Sun afternoons; call for times. Open Wed through Mon 10 a.m. to 4 p.m. Free admission.

Black Rock Park on Lake Buchanan. (800) 776-5272; www.lcra.org/parks/developed_ parks/black_rock.html. From Burnet, travel west on TX 29 and turn right on TX 261. Drive about 4 miles to the park. This park offers something for everyone. The northeast side of the lake offers some of the area's best birding; the park has also been a longtime favorite with anglers. If you'd like to extend your visit to Black Rock, stay at one of the park's numerous campsites. Sites can fill up on busy weekends, and they are offered on a first-come, first-served basis.

Buchanan Dam Art Gallery. TX 29, 1 mile past the dam; (512) 793-2858. This is the oldest continuously operating artists' cooperative in the country, and it's a great place to buy a bluebonnet painting at a reasonable price. The April arts-and-crafts show is held here, with booths set up outdoors. During the show local artists sell bluebonnets painted on everything from saw blades to mussel shells. Open daily. Free admission.

where to eat

Big John's Bar-B-Q and Steak Barn. TX 29 and FM 1431, 2 miles west of Buchanan Dam; (512) 793-2261. There's nothing fancy about this old-fashioned barbecue joint, serving sliced beef, ribs, steaks, and sausage. Dine indoors or out on big picnic tables. Open Thurs through Sun for lunch and dinner. $$.

tow

If you're interested in wine, take a drive up to the community of Tow (rhymes with "cow") on the edge of Lake Buchanan. From TX 29, head north 8 miles on TX 261, then 6 miles on FM 2241.

where to go

Fall Creek Vineyards. 2.2 miles northeast of the Tow Post Office on FM 2241; (512) 476-4477 (Austin sales office) or (325) 379-5361 (winery); www.fcv.com. Since opening in 1975, Fall Creek has been known as one of the top wineries in Central Texas, winning numerous awards. Located right on the shores of Lake Buchanan, the vineyards here span sixty-five acres. You can take a tour of the entire operation and sample the wine made on the premises. Tours run Mon through Fri 11 a.m. to 4 p.m., Sat, 11 a.m. to 5 p.m., Sun noon to 4 p.m.

day trip 04

northwest

rock hound's delight:
llano, mason

This day trip is filled with winding roads, historic attractions, and natural wonders. Visitors to this Hill Country vicinity must travel over some dirt and gravel roads, especially in rock-hunting areas. Near Mason are numerous low-water crossings, and on some back roads you must drive across dry creek beds. Flash flooding is a very real hazard in the Hill Country, especially during the spring and fall months. Be aware of weather conditions when you make these trips, and never cross swiftly flowing water. To reach Llano, travel US 183 north from Austin through Cedar Park and Leander. Take TX 29 West to Burnet and continue through Buchanan Dam (see Northwest Day Trip 03 for local attractions).

llano

Continuing west on TX 29 from Buchanan Dam, you'll see an increasing number of granite outcroppings—huge boulders protruding from the rugged land. This entire region is called the Llano Uplift, a geological formation caused by igneous rocks from 40 miles below ground being pushed up to the surface.

As a result of the formation, the rich minerals found here turned Llano into a boomtown in the 1880s. Huge deposits of iron ore were found in the area, and some industrialists had dreams of making Llano the "Pittsburgh of the West." Tent cities were erected, mining went full swing, and downtown Llano was spruced up with the money that came pouring into town. All too soon, though, one hard fact came to light: To make steel you have to have

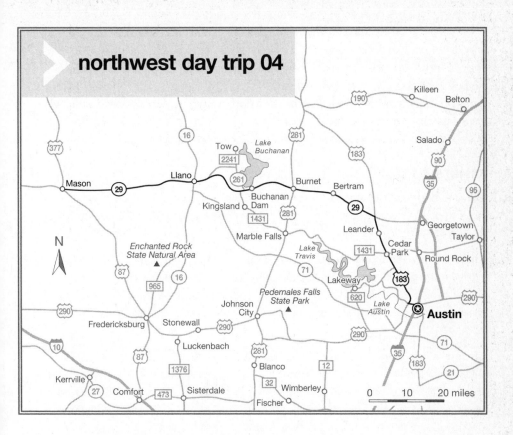

northwest day trip 04

coal as well as iron, and there was no coal in the area. To bring coal in was far too costly. As quickly as it began, the iron ore business came to a halt.

But Llano was by then well known for another mineral: granite. During its heyday, the city boasted ten granite quarries and five finishing plants and shipped several varieties of granite around the country. When rail prices increased, Llano's granite business also came to a stop, although vast quantities of granite still remain.

Granite brought many prominent people to the area. Sculptor Frank Teich, a nationally famous German artist, owned a monument company (as well as the town of Teichville). His World War I monument stands on the courthouse lawn here. Teich came to Llano for its healthy climate when doctors told him that he had only six months to live. Either the doctors were wrong in their diagnosis or Llano's healthy atmosphere really worked, because Teich lived in the town for another thirty-eight years! Even today, Llano is listed by the U.S. Census as one of the healthiest places to live in the country.

Another prominent Llano citizen was Professor N. J. Badu, a mineralogist who came to town to operate a manganese mine and tried to focus the attention of the mineralogy world on Llano's many minerals. Today his home is an elegant restaurant.

The Llano area is still a collector's paradise, with more than 240 different rocks and minerals discovered in the region. The area's granite, feldspar, graphite, and talc have commercial value, while the more precious yields, such as garnet, amethyst, tourmaline, and quartz—even gold and silver—are sought by visiting rock hounds.

Public rock hunting is allowed on the Llano River in town. Stop by the park on the south bank of the river just across from the public library and try your luck. The riverbanks are dotted with rocks of all varieties and offer some pretty picnic spots as well.

where to go

Hill Country Wildlife Museum. 326 Ford St.; (325) 247-2568. This museum is home to the Campbell Collection, considered the world's third-largest taxidermy collection. Open Thurs through Sat.

Llano County Historical Museum. 310 Bessemer Ave., TX 16; (325) 247-3026. This museum, housed in the old Bruhl Drugstore, has displays on the area's early Native American history and Llano's boomtown days. An exhibit contains samples of Llano's many rocks and minerals. Open Wed through Sat 11 a.m. to 5 p.m., and Sun afternoons. Free admission.

Llano Historic Railyard District. 100 Train Station Dr.; (866) 539-5535 or (325) 247-5354; www.llanochamber.org/Parks_Sites.html. The extension of the Austin and Northwestern Railroad to Llano in 1892 was a major event in the city's history. For a time Llano was the last train stop for settlers heading west. The railroad also benefitted the granite mining industry which persists today. Llano also became a shipping out point for cattle. Llano's railroad history is explored in the Railroad Museum and adjacent Visitor's Center.

Robinson City Park. Llano River banks. This park includes RV camping, golf, swimming pool, fishing, picnicking, and it has a playground. Open daily. Free admission.

Walking Tour of Llano. (325) 247-5354. Stop by the Chamber of Commerce at 700 Bessemer Ave. for a brochure outlining twenty-six historic stops in town. Open Mon through Fri. Free admission.

where to shop

Fain's Honey. 3744 S. TX 16 (two miles south of Llano); (325) 247-4867; www.fainshoney .com. Fain's Honey has been a family-owned business since 1926 when it was founded by farmer H. E. Fain. The third generation of Fains now offer natural honey produced in the Llano area as well as molasses, sugar cane syrup and a variety of honey spreads (try the jalapeño honey spread!).

Llano Fine Arts Guild Gallery. 503 Bessemer Ave.; (325) 247-4839. Located across from the Llano County Historical Museum, this art gallery features the works of many local residents. Works range from fine arts to ceramics, photographs, and stained glass. Open Tues through Sun.

where to eat

The Badu House. 601 Bessemer Ave., TX 16; (325) 247-4174; www.baduhouse.com. This two-story stone and brick structure (formerly an inn) was built in 1891 as the home of mineralogist N.J. Badu, who put Llano on the map by discovering the mineral llanite here. The building has been elegantly renovated and is home to a fine restaurant and a special events venue. The restaurant offers everything from filet mignon to oven-roasted quail. $$$.

buried treasure

Following the robber from Round Rock to Burnet and finally to Llano, we're once again on the trail of Sam Bass. Allegedly, the robber hid canvas sacks marked "U.S." and filled with gold in a cave on Packsaddle Mountain. Some say the treasure was found by a Mexican laborer, hired by a local rancher to cut fence posts on Packsaddle Mountain. According to one version of the story, the rancher went to look for the laborer when he failed to return to the ranch. All the rancher found was a cave and a piece of canvas sack with "U.S." imprinted on it. Another version of the story says the gold still lies hidden somewhere in the mountain.

Packsaddle Mountain is also the home of the Blanco Mine, named for a Spaniard who found the location long ago. According to J. Frank Dobie's book Coronado's Children, the mine was rediscovered in the 1800s by a Llano settler named Larimore. While hunting, Larimore discovered the old mine—with its contents of lead and a high percentage of silver.

In 1860 Larimore took a last trip to the mine with a man named Jim Rowland. The two men hauled out several hundred pounds of the metal, shaping it into bullets. Larimore, who was leaving the country, declared that he would hide the mine so well no other person would ever find it. Supposedly he diverted a gully directly into the mine, filling it with silt. Rowland carved his initials on a large stone marking the entrance to the mine, then covered it with earth . . . where it remains today.

Llano County is home to other buried treasure sites, including $60,000 in gold and silver coins buried by Sam Bass near the community of Castell in the western part of the county. Bass buried the loot on a creek bed, marking the spot with a rock in a fork of a tree.

Cooper's Old Time Pit Barbecue and Catering. 506 West Young St. (TX 29 West); (325) 247-5713; www.coopersbbqllano.com. Step up to the smoker and pick out your meat—brisket, sausage, pork ribs, beef ribs, chicken, sirloin steak, pork chops, and even goat. The pit master slices off the amount you want, then you go inside and help yourself to white bread, beans, and sauce in the cinder block dining room. $.

Inman's Kitchen and Catering Service. 809 West Young St. (TX 29 West); (325) 247-5257. Barbecue is king here, including beef brisket, chicken, pork, and the restaurant's specialty: turkey sausage. This spot is more elegant than many barbecue restaurants, with a carpeted, air-conditioned dining area. Lunch and dinner served Mon through Sat; Sun during deer season. $.

Miller's Smokehouse. 705 West Young St.; (866) 570-0315 or (325) 247-4450; www .millerssmokehouse.com. Stop by to take home a fragrant reminder of your Llano visit or to stock up for your day trip picnic. Miller's sells all manner of smoked meats including ribs, hams, beef and pork tenderloin, and a large variety of smoked sausage as well as venison sausage and meat cuts. If you are a hunter, Miller's can process your deer for you. They also sell mail order. $–$$.

where to stay

Dabbs Hotel. 112 East Burnet St., behind the Llano Museum; (325) 247-7905. At the turn of the 20th century, this railroad hotel was the last outpost of civilization for frontiersmen heading west. Today's guests stay in one of twelve quiet rooms with period furnishings, double beds, a breezy screened porch, and a peaceful atmosphere overlooking the Llano River. Saturday night features western cookouts. Dinner reservations required. $.

mason

From Llano, continue west on TX 29 for 34 miles to Mason, once the home of the late Fred Gipson, author of *Old Yeller*. Like neighboring Llano, the land around Mason is rocky and dotted with granite.

Mason was settled by cattle ranchers and German families who came from nearby Fredericksburg. In 1851 Fort Mason was built on a hilltop to afford a better look at oncoming Comanches. (The post's best-known soldier was Lieutenant Colonel Robert E. Lee.) Constructed of sandstone, in 1869 the fort was dismantled and the salvaged stone was used to build local businesses and homes.

Even after the fort was no longer necessary, frontier justice was still a part of Mason. In 1875 the Mason County War, also known as the Hoodoo War, broke out. It all started when the sheriff arrested a group of men who were taking cattle to Llano, allegedly without the owner's permission. The men were set free on bond and ordered to remain in town, an order they promptly forgot. The sheriff re-arrested as many of the rustlers as he could find.

A few nights later, a group freed the prisoners, sparking a round of shootings and lynchings that left a dozen men dead. The feud continued until January 1877, when the Mason County Courthouse was set on fire, destroying any evidence against the cattle rustlers.

Rock hounds come to Mason County today in search of topaz, the Texas state gem, which develops in colors ranging from clear to sky blue. Most local topaz turns up near the small communities of Streeter, Grit, and Katemcy, all north and northeast of Mason. Searchers usually find the stones in streambeds and ravines by using picks and shovels to loosen rocks and a wire screen to sift the debris. More information on Mason is available on the Mason Chamber of Commerce Web site: www.masontxcoc.com.

where to go

Eckert James River Bat Cave. Write or call the Mason Chamber of Commerce (P.O. Box 156, Mason, TX 76856; 325-347-5758; www.masontxcoc.com) for directions and a map to this bat cave, located about 13 miles south of Mason. The cavern is home to about 6 million Mexican free-tail bats. This is a "maternity cave," used during the spring and summer months by female bats to bear and rear their young. You can view the evening flight out of the cave, a sight heralded by high-pitched sounds. Open Thurs through Sun 6 p.m. to 9 p.m., May through Oct. Free admission.

Fort Mason. Follow Post Hill Street south from the courthouse to Post Hill; (325) 347-5758. These reconstructed officers' quarters are furnished with typical 1850s belongings as well as photographs from Mason's early days. The back porch has an unbeatable view of the town below and miles of Hill Country beyond. Open daily. Free admission.

Gene Zesch Woodcarving Display at the Commercial Bank. 100 Moody St., on the square; (325) 347-6324. Gene Zesch is one of Mason's most famous citizens, known for his humorous woodcarvings of modern cowboys. His work was collected by President Johnson and is sold in galleries nationally. This exhibit features woodcarvings and bronzes made by the artist. Open Mon through Fri. Free admission.

Museum Center. 300 Moody St., south of the square; (325) 347-5758; www.mason countymuseum.org. This local-history museum (formerly the Mason County Museum) is housed in a former elementary school built in 1887. The displays include typical items used by area ranchers and housewives a century ago, from toys to needlework to farm equipment. There is also a display of local rocks and minerals. Open Tues through Sat 10 a.m. to noon, and 1 p.m. to 4 p.m. Closed Jan and Feb.

Old Yeller statue. At the Mason County Library at 410 Post Hill St. In 1956 Mason resident Fred Gipson penned a dog story destined to become a beloved American classic: *Old Yeller*. A bronze statue of Old Yeller stands in front of the Mason County Library. Inside the library, you'll find an exhibit on the town's most famous author. Free admission.

Topaz Hunting. Several private areas charge a daily fee of $5 to $15 per person for topaz hunting. Visitors must bring their own equipment (including water during warm summer months) and may keep whatever they find. Ranches offer topaz hunting from mid-Jan through Sept, closing during deer-hunting season.

White-tailed Deer Hunting. For information on hunting licenses, call the Mason Chamber of Commerce (325) 347-5758 well before deer season begins. Mason County claims to have more white-tailed deer per acre than any other county in Texas. Hunters flock here from around the Southwest to stalk deer during the winter months.

where to shop

Country Collectibles. US 87 North; (325) 347-5249. If your search for topaz is futile, stop by this antiques store, which sells topaz and other stones indigenous to the area, along with arrowheads, willow furniture, and collectibles of every description.

where to stay

Mason County is filled with bed-and-breakfast accommodations, RV campsites, and guest ranches located outside of town. For a free copy of their "Bed and Breakfast and RV Sites" brochure, write or call the Mason County Chamber of Commerce, P.O. Box 156, Mason, TX 76856; (325) 347-5758; www.masontxcoc.com.

regional information

north

day trip 01

Greater Pflugerville Chamber of Commerce
101 South Third St.
Pflugerville, TX 78660
(512) 251-7799
www.pfchamber.com

Round Rock Convention and Visitors
Bureau
120 South Brown St.
Round Rock, TX 78664
(512) 218-7023
www.sportscapitaloftexas.com

Georgetown Convention and
Visitors Information Center
101 West Seventh St.
Georgetown, TX 78626
(800) GEO-TOWN or (512) 930-3545
www.visitgeorgetown.com

Salado Chamber of Commerce
881 North Main St.
Salado, TX 76571
(254) 947-5040
www.salado.com

day trip 02

Belton Area Convention and Visitors Bureau
P.O. Box 659
412 East Central
Belton, TX 76513
(254) 939-3551
www.seebelton.com

Killeen Civic and Conference Center
and Visitors Bureau
3601 South W.S. Young Dr.
Killeen, TX 76541
(254) 501-3888
www.visitkilleen.net

Temple Convention and Visitors Bureau
2 North Main St.
Temple, TX 76501
(254) 298-5561
www.ci.temple.tx.us

day trip 03

Lorena City Hall
114 East Center St.
Lorena, TX 76655
(254) 857-4641

Waco Convention and Visitors Bureau
P.O. Box 2570
Waco, TX 76702
(800) WACO-FUN or (254) 750-8696
www.wacocvb.com

northeast

day trip 01

Hutto Chamber of Commerce
122 East St.
P.O. Box 99
Hutto, TX 78634
(512) 759-4400
www.hutto.org

day trip 02

Taylor Chamber of Commerce
P.O. Box 231
1519 North Main St.
Taylor, TX 76574
(512) 352-6364
www.taylorchamber.org
www.ci.taylor.tx.us

day trip 03

Burleson County Chamber of Commerce
301 North Main St.
Caldwell, Texas 77836
(979) 567-0000
www.burlesoncountytx.com

Bryan–College Station Convention
and Visitors Bureau
715 University Dr. East
College Station, TX 77840
(800) 777-8292 or (979) 260-9898
www.bryan-collegestation.org

east

day trip 01

Greater Manor Chamber of Commerce
11250 TX 290 East
Manor, TX 78653
(512) 272-5699
www.manorchamberofcommerce.com

Elgin Chamber of Commerce
114 Central Ave.
Elgin, TX 78621
(512) 285-4515
www.elgintxchamber.org

Giddings Area Chamber of Commerce
171 East Hempstead
Giddings, TX 78942
(979) 542-3455
www.giddingstx.com

day trip 02

Burton Chamber of Commerce
P.O. Box 670
Burton, TX 77835
(979) 289-3402 (City Hall)

Brenham–Washington County Convention
and Visitors Bureau
314 South Austin St.
Brenham, TX 77833
(979) 836-3695
www.brenhamtexas.com

southeast

day trip 01

Bastrop Visitors Center
1016 Main St.
Bastrop, TX 78602
(512) 303-0904
www.bastropchamber.com

Smithville Area Chamber of Commerce
100 Northwest First St.
Smithville, TX 78957
(512) 237-2313
www.smithvilletx.org

La Grange Area Chamber of Commerce
171 South Main St.
La Grange, TX 78945
(800) LAGRANGE or (979) 968-5756
www.lagrangetx.org

day trip 02

Round Top Area Chamber of Commerce
P.O. Box 216
Round Top, TX 78954
(979) 249-4042 or (888) 368-4783
www.roundtop.org

Fayetteville Chamber of Commerce
202 West Main St.
Fayetteville, TX 78940
(979) 378-4021 or (888) 575-4553
www.fayettevilletx.com

south

day trip 01

Lockhart Chamber of Commerce
631 South Colorado St.
Lockhart, TX 78644
(512) 398-2818
www.lockhartchamber.com

Luling Area Chamber of Commerce
P.O. Box 710
421 East Davis St.
Luling, TX 78648
(830) 875-3214
www.lulingcc.org

day trip 02

Flatonia Chamber of Commerce
208 East North Main St.
P.O. Box 610
Flatonia, TX 78941
(361) 865-3920
www.flatoniachamber.com

Schulenburg Chamber of Commerce
618 North Main St.
Schulenburg, TX 78956
(866) 504-5294 or (979) 743-4514
www.schulenburgchamber.org

day trip 03

Gonzales Chamber of Commerce and
Agriculture
P.O. Box 134
Gonzales, TX 78629
(830) 672-6532
www.gonzalestexas.com

Shiner Chamber of Commerce
P.O. Box 221
817 North Ave. E
Shiner, TX 77984
(361) 594-4180
www.shinertx.com

Yoakum Area Chamber of Commerce
P.O. Box 591
105 Huck St.
Yoakum, TX 77995
(361) 293-2309
www.yoakumareachamber.com

day trip 04

San Marcos Convention and Visitors Bureau
202 North C. M. Allen Parkway
P.O. Box 2310
San Marcos, TX 78667
(888) 200-5620 or (512) 393-5900
www.toursanmarcos.com

day trip 05

Seguin Convention and Visitors Bureau
116 North Camp St.
Seguin, TX 78155
(800) 580-7322 or (830) 379-6382
www.visitseguin.com

southwest

day trip 01

San Antonio Convention and Visitors Bureau
Visitors Center
317 Alamo Plaza
San Antonio, TX 78205
(800) 447-3372
www.visitsanantonio.com

day trip 02

Gruene Tourist Information
1601 Hunter Rd.
New Braunfels, TX 78130
(830) 629-5077
www.gruenetexas.com

New Braunfels Convention and
Visitors Bureau
P.O. Box 311417
New Braunfels, TX 78131
(800) 572-2626 or (830) 625-2385
www.nbcham.org

day trip 03

Wimberley Chamber of Commerce and
Visitors Center
P.O. Box 12
Wimberley, TX 78676
(512) 847-2201
www.wimberley.org

Blanco Chamber of Commerce
312 Pecan St.
P.O. Box 626
Blanco, TX 78606
(830) 833-5101
www.blancochamber.com

day trip 04

Comfort Chamber of Commerce
630 TX 27
P.O. Box 777
Comfort, TX 78013
(830) 995-3131
www.comfort-texas.com

Greater Boerne Convention and
Visitors Bureau
1407 South Main St.
Boerne, TX 78006
(888) 842-8080 or (830) 249-7277
www.visitboerne.org

day trip 05

Bandera County Convention and
Visitors Bureau
P.O. Box 171
Bandera, TX 78003
(800) 364-3833 or (830) 796-3045
www.banderacowboycapital.com

west

day trip 01

Lake Travis Chamber of Commerce
1415 RR 620 South, Suite 202
Austin, TX 78734
(512) 263-5833 or (877) 263-0073
www.laketravischamber.com

day trip 02

Johnson City Convention and Visitors
Bureau/ Visitors Center
100 East Main St.
Johnson City, TX 78636
(830) 868-7684
www.johnsoncity-texas.com

Stonewall Chamber of Commerce
250 Pecan St.
Stonewall, TX 78671
(830) 644-2735
www.stonewalltexas.com

Fredericksburg Convention and
Visitors Bureau
302 East Austin St.
Fredericksburg, TX 78624
(888) 997-3600 or (830) 997-6523
www.fredericksburg-texas.com
www.fredericksburg-lodging.com

day trip 03

Kerrville Convention and Visitors Bureau
2108 Sidney Baker
Kerrville, TX 78028
(800) 221-7958 or (830) 792-3535
www.kerrvilletexascvb.com

West Kerr County Chamber of Commerce
P.O. Box 1006
Ingram, TX 78025
(830) 367-4322
www.wkcc.com

northwest

day trip 01

Lake Travis Chamber of Commerce
1415 RR 620 South #202
Austin, TX 78734
(512) 263-5833 or (877) 263-0073
www.laketravischamber.com

Lakeway City Hall
104 Cross Creek Dr.
Lakeway, TX 78734
(512) 261-6090

day trip 02

Jonestown Chamber of Commerce
18700 FM 1431
Jonestown, TX 78645
(512) 267-5577
www.jonestownchamber.org

Lago Vista Area Chamber of Commerce
and Visitors Bureau
8040 Bar-K Ranch Rd.
Lago Vista, TX 78645
(512) 267-7952 and (888) 328-5846
www.lagovista.org

Marble Falls/Lake LBJ Chamber
of Commerce
916 Second St.
Marble Falls, TX 78654
(800) 759-8178 or (830) 693-2815
www.marblefalls.org

Kingsland Chamber of Commerce
P.O. Box 465
Kingsland, TX 78639
(325) 388-6211
www.kingslandchamber.org

day trip 03

Cedar Park Convention and Visitors Bureau
1490 East Whitestone Blvd., Bldg. 2
Suite 180
Cedar Park, TX 78613
(512) 260-7800
www.cedarparkfun.com

Greater Leander Chamber of Commerce
103 North Brushy
P.O. Box 556
Leander, TX 78646
(512) 259-1907
www.leandercc.org

Burnet Chamber of Commerce
229 South Pierce St.
Burnet, TX 78611
(512) 756-4297
www.burnetchamber.org

Lake Buchanan Chamber of Commerce
and Visitors Center
17816 TX 29
Buchanan Dam, TX 78609
(512) 793-2803
www.buchanan-inks.com

day trip 04

Llano Chamber of Commerce
The Railyard Depot
100 Train Station Dr.
Llano, TX 78643
(325) 247-5354 and (866) 539-5535
www.llanochamber.org

Mason County Chamber of Commerce
108 Fort McKavett St.
Mason, TX 76856
(915) 347-5758
www.masontxcoc.com

festivals and celebrations

Texas undoubtedly has more festivals than any other state. Regardless of the weekend, you'll find some town whooping it up with parades, music, and lots of food. There are festivals for every interest, whether yours is pioneer heritage, German food, or watermelon. For a searchable listing of festivals, go to www.traveltex.com.

january

Hill Country Gem & Mineral Show. Fredericksburg. (830) 895-9630. For nearly four decades, this popular rock show has included gems, minerals, fossils, meteorites, and more with plenty of jewelry, gold panning, and exhibits. Held at the Pioneer Pavilion at Lady Bird Johnson Municipal Park.

february

San Antonio Stock Show and Rodeo. San Antonio. (210) 225-5851; www.sarodeo.com. Spanning eighteen days in Feb, this Texas-size event is one of the top five PRCA rodeos in the country and attracts over one million visitors. Along with a rodeo, the event includes a horse show, livestock show, carnival, top country music performances, and more.

Wine Lovers Trail. Fredericksburg. (866) 621-9463; www.texaswinetrail.com. Over a dozen Hill Country wineries participate in this event. Sample the products of these vineyards and enjoy special events.

march

National Rattlesnake Sacking Championship and Roundup. Taylor. (512) 803-5855; www.taylorjaycees.org. This controversial festival is one of the most unusual events in Texas, held on the last weekend of the month. Two-person teams compete in this national event to see who can sack ten rattlers in the shortest amount of time.

Williamson County "Gemboree". Georgetown. (800) GEO-TOWN or (512) 930-3545; www.visitgeorgetown.org. Dealers from around the U.S. showcase and sell the latest gems and minerals on the market. Demonstrations, exhibits, and lectures are given throughout the day.

april

Antiques Week. Round Top. (281) 237-4747; www.roundtopantiquesfair.com. Held the first weekend of April, this show features dealers from across the nation. It has been called the best antiques show in the state.

Balcones Songbird Festival. Lago Vista. (512) 965-2473, www.balconessongbirdfestival .org. This late April event celebrates two local endangered bird species—the golden-cheeked warbler and the black-capped vireo—as well as other songbirds, butterflies, and wildflowers. Guided nature talks, family activities, photo hikes, and more. Held at the Balcones Canyonlands National Preserve.

Cotton Gin Festival. Burton. (979) 289-3378; www.cottonginmuseum.org. Held at the historic Burton Cotton Gin, this family-friendly event includes a parade (complete with tractors), children's bike parade, children's tractor pull, carnival rides, folk demonstrations ranging from quilting to quilling, arts and crafts, live music, and more.

Folkfest. New Braunfels. (800) 572-2626; www.nbheritagevillage.com/folkfest.html. This event, held at the Conservation Plaza and Museum of Texas Handmade Furniture, showcases the work of New Braunfels craftspeople and furniture makers through demonstrations, food, and live entertainment. Guided tours of local historic buildings also available.

Highland Lakes Bluebonnet Trail. Burnet, Buchanan Dam, Llano, and area communities. (512) 756-4297. The fragrant bluebonnet is the state flower of Texas. For two weekends in early April, a self-guided driving tour will take you past the area's prettiest bluebonnet fields. Each town on the trail, from Burnet to Llano, celebrates with art shows and a festival atmosphere.

River Rendezvous. La Grange. (800) LA-GRANGE; www.lagrangetx.org. This event draws canoeists from around the state. Visitors paddle down the Colorado River and enjoy camping, canoeing, fun, food, and old-fashioned storytelling.

Smithville Jamboree. Smithville. (512) 237-3282; www.smithvilletx.org. This longtime event includes parades, a livestock show, softball, volleyball and horseshoe tournaments, nightly dances, an antique car show, carnival, and canoe races.

Texas Ladies' State Chili Cookoff. Seguin. (800) 580-PECAN; www.seguinchamber .com. Women from around the state test their skills at this chili cook-off. Along with taste testings, visitors enjoy live entertainment.

may

Chip Fest. Manor. (512) 272-5699; www.manorchamberofcommerce.com. Held Memorial Day weekend, this family-oriented event that celebrates "chips" of all kinds, from chocolate chips (in a bake-off) to a chips and salsa contest to cow chip bingo. There's even a 5K run where entrants receive a temporary computer chip that monitors progress and performance during this certified race.

Deutchen Pfest. Pflugerville. (512) 251-5082; www.cityofpflugerville.com. Scheduled for the third weekend in May, this annual event celebrates Pflugerville's Old World heritage with a 5K "Pfun" run, a parade through the historic downtown, rides, live music, and food.

Texas Arts and Crafts Fair. Kerrville. (830) 896-5711; www.tacef.com. Every Memorial Day weekend this festival opens on the grounds of the River Star Arts and Event Park. Originally founded by the state of Texas, this enormous show features the paintings, sculptures, jewelry, and other artwork of over 200 Texas artists, all available to answer questions about their work. A special children's area includes crafts instruction. Musical entertainment and food round out the day.

Viva! Cinco de Mayo. San Marcos. (512) 353-VIVA; www.vivacincodemayo.org. This festival is held on the weekend closest to Cinco de Mayo (May 5), the celebration of the Mexican victory over the French. Besides a carnival and musical performances, there's plenty of Mexican food, including menudo (a dish made from tripe, hominy, and spices).

june

Boerne Berges Fest. Boerne. (888) 842-8080; www.bergesfest.com. This festival, scheduled for Father's Day weekend, includes arts and crafts, live music, and a celebration of summer.

Kerrville Folk Festival. Kerrville. (830) 257-3600; www.kerrville-music.com . This is one of the biggest outdoor music festivals in the state. For eighteen days starting on the Friday of Memorial Day weekend, Quiet Valley Ranch is filled with music lovers who come to hear both local and national performers.

Peach Jamboree. Stonewall. (830) 644-2735; www.stonewalltexas.com. The peach capital of Texas shows off its crop on the third Fri and Sat of June. The local peach pit–spitting record is over 28 feet.

Watermelon Thump. Luling. (830) 875-3214; www.lulingcc.org. On the last Thurs, Fri, and Sat of June, you can enjoy seed-spitting and watermelon-eating contests and championship melon judging. There's also an arts and crafts show, carnivals, live entertainment, and street dances. A Guinness World Record was set here in 1989 for spitting a watermelon seed almost 69 feet.

Western Days Festival. Elgin. (512) 285-4515; www.elgintxchamber.com. Held the fourth week of June, this event includes the Tiny Tots Parade, Tennis Court Dance, volleyball, softball, and horseshoe tournaments, a carnival, arts and crafts, and more.

july

4th of July PRCA Rodeo. Belton. (254) 939-3551; www.rodeobelton.com. For over eight decades, this popular rodeo has bulls against riders. Held at the Bell County Expo Center, the event features bronc riding, roping, steer wrestling, and barrel racing.

Fourth of July Celebration. Round Top. (888) 368-4783 or (979) 249-4042; www.round top.org. One of the oldest celebrations in the country of Independence Day winds through Round Top. Round Top Chamber of Commerce, Round Top, TX 78954.

Frontier Days. Round Rock. (512) 255-5805; www.roundrockchamber.org. Come to Round Rock on the Fri and Sat after Fourth of July to watch a reenactment of the infamous shoot-out between outlaw Sam Bass and the Texas Rangers. There's also plenty of food, games, and the atmosphere of a summer festival.

Half Moon Holidays. Shiner. (361) 594-4180; www.shinertx.com. On the first Sun in July, Shiner celebrates summer with a brisket cook-off, barbecue dinner, fireworks, carnival, horseshoe-pitching tournament, dance, and lots of music.

July Fourth Parade. Seguin. (830) 379-6382; www.seguinchamber.com. Get ready for a red, white, and blue party known as the biggest small-town Fourth of July parade in Texas. The annual Freedom Fiesta has been drawing onlookers and participants since the early 1900s. Activities start with a patriotic parade, followed by food booths, arts and crafts, family entertainment, and kiddie rides, for an old-fashioned street fair atmosphere. That evening, a street dance will keep the mood festive, as will the grand fireworks display in Max Starcke Park.

Night in Old Fredericksburg. Fredericksburg. (830) 997-6523; www.fredericksburg-texas .com. This annual event, held in Market Square, showcases a different local culture every night through arts and crafts, food, dances, and more.

august

Gillespie County Fair. Fredericksburg. (830) 997-2359; www.gillespiefair.com. This event holds the record as the longest-running county fair in the state. The festivities include old-fashioned family fun from carnival rides to food booths.

Grape Stomping Harvest Celebration. Tow. (325) 379-5361; www.fcv.com. Jump in a bin of red grapes and start stomping during this late-August festival. Other activities include Cork Toss, Grape Walk, hayrides, and music.

Hill Country Heritage Day. Johnson City. (830) 868-7128; www.johnsoncity-texas.com. Step back to the pioneer days at a chuckwagon camp with music and cowboy poetry. Held at the Johnson Settlement.

International Barbeque Cook-off. Taylor. (512) 352-6364 or (512) 365-8485; www .taylorjaycees.org. Barbeque beef, chicken, and sausage reign supreme at most Texas barbeque joints, but this mid-August cook-off also features seafood, lamb, goat, and even wild game. Over one hundred teams compete in categories ranging from theatrics to most elaborate cooking equipment.

LBJ Birthday Celebration. Johnson City. (830) 868-7684; www.johnsoncity-texas.com. The legacy of this Hill Country president is remembered with a wreath laying at the president's grave and free ranch tours. Held on the anniversary of LBJ's birth: August 27.

Salado Art Fair. Salado. (254) 947-5040; www.salado.com. More than 100 artists set up booths on the shady banks of Salado Creek in Pace Park. This weekend festival in early Aug is one of the most popular art shows in the state.

september

Comal County Fair. New Braunfels. (830) 625-1505; www.comalcountyfair.org. This long-running fair ranks as one of the largest (and one of the oldest) in the state. The event includes everything from a PRCA rodeo to carnival rides to children's play areas.

Kerrville Wine and Music Festival. Kerrville. (830) 237-3600; www.kerrville-music.com. The Hill Country town celebrates fall with performances by Texas musicians and tasting of Texas wines. Held at Quiet Valley Ranch, the site of June's Kerrville Folk Festival.

Oatmeal Festival. Bertram. (512) 355-2197. This Labor Day weekend festival is named for the nearby community of Oatmeal, and all the events, from the street parade to the midway, continue the theme.

Texas Living History Day. Kerrville. (830) 792-1945; www.texasheritagemusic.org; on the campus of Schreiner University. Held every Sept, thousands attend to learn about the heritage, history, music and culture of Texas. Includes a tribute to the father of country music, Jimmie Rodgers.

october

Czhilispiel. Flatonia. (361) 865-3920; www.flatoniachamber.com/czhili. When tiny Flatonia needed a doctor years ago, local citizens decided to send a hometown girl to medical school. To fund her education, they began this chili cook-off (now the second largest in Texas) and festival held in late Oct. There's lots of music, a quilt show, "the world's largest tented biergarten," and a barbecue cook-off as well.

Fort Croghan Day. Burnet. (512) 756-8281; www.fortcroghan.org. Step back to Burnet's frontier days at this special event on the second Sat in Oct. The day includes demonstrations of pioneer chores ranging from blacksmithing to bread making. Admission and parking at the event are free.

Heart o' Texas Fair and Rodeo. Waco. (254) 776-1660; www.hotfair.com. This ten-day fair draws over 200,000 visitors for a look at a championship rodeo, livestock shows, an art show, and nationally known entertainment.

Hogeye Festival. Elgin. (512) 281-5724; www.elgintx.com. Called "a time for warm hearts and hot guts," this family-friendly event celebrates the sausage heritage of Elgin with events like the Hogalicious Dessert Contest, a hog-calling contest, the crowning of King Hog and Queen Sowpreme, and a pork barbecue contest.

Llano Heritage Day. Llano. (325) 247-5354; www.llanochamber.org. This Hill Country town remembers its roots with Wild West shoot-outs, living-history exhibits, wagon rides, and antiques shows on the third Sat in Oct.

Mesquite Art Festival. Fredericksburg. (830) 997-8515; www.texasmesquiteassn.org. Visitors have the opportunity to shop for one-of-a-kind woodwork at this annual show. A gathering of more than fifty artists who work primarily in mesquite showcases collectibles, cabinets, mantels, sculptures, musical instruments, and other artwork made from the often-maligned tree.

Oktoberfest. Fredericksburg. (888) 997-3600; www.fredericksburg-texas.com. On the first weekend in Oct, head to the "Old Country" by visiting this German Hill Country town. You'll find polka dancing and sausage galore, as well as arts and crafts, a street dance, and rides for the kids. Fri through Sun.

Round Top Antiques Week. Round Top. (979) 249-4042; www.roundtop.org. Called by some the best such show in the state, this extravaganza features antiques dealers from across the United States. Held the first weekend of the month, it attracts shoppers from around the country.

november

Fredericksburg Food and Wine Fest. Fredericksburg. (888) 997-6523; www.fbgfoodand winefest.com. In late Oct the Fredericksburg Food and Wine Fest highlights the top wineries of Texas. Along with award-winning vineyards, the event showcases more than forty vendors who offer a taste of Texas through spices, salsas, cheeses, and more. Two stages offer musical entertainment, and the whole family finds plenty of just-for-fun activities such as grape-stomping and cork-tossing.

Gathering of the Scottish Clans. Salado. (254) 947-5040; www.salado.com. Put on your tartans and grab your bagpipes for the oldest Scottish gathering in the Southwest. If there are Gaels and Celts in your ancestry, you can learn more about your family genealogy. Even if you're not a lass or laddie, enjoy traditional folk dances, Highland games, lots of bagpipe music, and Scottish foods like meat pies and scones.

Nature in Lights. Killeen. (254) 287-4916; http://hoodmwr.com/nature_in_lights.htm. Held at the Belton Lake Outdoor Recreation Area, this drive-through lighting event features 5.5 miles of holiday lighting displays as well as a Santa's Village. Begins in early Nov and continues through New Year's.

Wurstfest. New Braunfels. (800) 221-4369; www.wurstfest.com. Early in Nov, pull on your lederhosen, take out your beer stein, and join the fun at this celebration of sausage making. One of the largest German festivals in the country, Wurstfest features oompah bands and great German food.

december

Christmas on the Chisholm Trail. Belton. (254) 933-5860; www.seebelton.com. Held on the first Saturday evening of Dec, this family event begins with the lighting of the tree in the historic downtown. Other events include madrigals in Victorian dress, cowboy Christmas tales from "The Singing Cowboy," arts and crafts vendors, and more.

Christmas Stroll. Georgetown. (512) 930-3545 or (800) 436-8696; www.visitgeorgetown .org. The courthouse square is lighted with thousands of miniature white lights followed by an evening of shopping, storytelling, and visiting a children's village. The town also hosts a holiday homes tour through several historic structures.

Fort Croghan Spirit of Christmas Past. Burnet. (512) 756-8281; www.fortcroghan .org. Held the second Sat in Dec, this festival is a re-creation of a pioneer Christmas. Fort Croghan is lit by glowing lanterns. Visitors on the candlelight tour are met by carolers and costumed volunteers.

Hill Country Regional Christmas Lighting Trail. Johnson City, Llano, Fredericksburg, Burnet, Boerne, Wimberley, and Marble Falls. www.tex-fest.com. The Hill Country joins together for this trail of Christmas lights and festivities. Blanco's historic courthouse square is lit with festive lights, and Marble Falls celebrates with a walkway of lights every evening. Fredericksburg puts on Weihnachten and candlelight tours of homes. Llano features a Santa Land. Johnson City, the boyhood home of LBJ, is aglow with more than a quarter-million lights.

> **Lights Spectacular.** Johnson City. (830) 868-7684; www.tex-fest.com. One of the biggest displays in the state, this dazzling event features more than 600,000 lights illuminating homes, businesses, and churches, transforming this quiet Hill Country community into a glittering wonderland. The largest light display is on the Blanco County Courthouse, a historic building aglow with more than 100,000 tiny white lights.

> Maps are available at the courthouse for a self-guided drive of Johnson City's fantastic home light displays, erected by local citizens who play a big part in spreading the holiday spirit. The community also has "light art displays," illuminated panels with up

to 1,200 lights. Also a large Christmas tree in Memorial Park on US 290 is illuminated with thousands of colored lights.

Main Street Bethlehem. Burnet. (512) 756-4297; www.burnetchamber.org. Held the first two weekends in Dec, this festival depicts a biblical-era village, complete with live animals and Mary, Joseph, and baby Jesus.

A Timeless Christmas in Johnson City. Johnson City. (830) 868-7128; www .johnsoncity-texas.com. Celebrate the season with lamplight visits to the LBJ boyhood home, thousands of holiday lights, and a chuckwagon camp at the Johnson Settlement.

Walkway of Lights. Marble Falls. (830) 693-1620; www.marblefalls.org. This virtual tunnel of lights is made of more than one million lights that reflect off the waters of Lake Marble Falls, one of the most spectacular lighting experiences in the region. Stroll beneath the lights evenings from late Nov through early Jan.

Wassailfest. New Braunfels. (800) 572-2626; www.nbcham.org. Merchants throughout the downtown area prepare the traditional English holiday drink of wassail and serve it to the evening guests who enjoy live music, horse-and-buggy rides, and a visit from Santa. Look for open houses, caroling, and bell choirs on this special evening of holiday fun.

appendix a

especially for winter texans

If you're among the many lucky travelers who've adopted the Lone Star State as their winter home, welcome to Texas. You've chosen a destination where you can enjoy the excitement of the West, the zest of Old Mexico, the tranquility of the Gulf, and the history of a rambunctious republic, all in one place. Some of the best seasons and reasons to see the state include the changing post oak leaves in fall, the glittering Christmas festivals, and the often sunny Texas winter days.

Texas has an excellent network of state parks, most of which provide campsites with hookups. Generally there is a fourteen-consecutive-days limit for camping at each park. The central reservation number for all Texas state parks is (512) 389-8900 on weekdays 9 a.m. to 6 p.m. or see www.tpwd.state.tx.us/business/park_reservations for online, e-mail, and fax reservations.

Winter Texans will also be interested in state park passes. The **Texas Parklands Passport** (which is also called a Bluebonnet Pass) is for those who meet one of these eligibility requirements:

- If you are age 65 and over and a Texas resident, you can receive 50 percent reduced entry. Residents and nonresidents who turned sixty-five before September 1, 1995, are entitled to waived entry fees at state parks.

- Veterans of the U.S. Armed Forces with a 60 percent or more service-connected disability will receive waived entry fees to state parks.

- Travelers who have been medically determined to be permanently disabled as a result of a mental or physical impairment (including blindness) are entitled to a 50 percent discount.

To get this Texas Parklands Passport, apply at any state park or at the headquarters in Austin. If you don't qualify for the Parklands Passport, you can also purchase an annual pass called the Texas State Parks Pass. It's valid for twelve months and is presently priced at $60 for a one-car membership or $75 for two cars.

appendix b

texas state parks

Texas has an excellent system of state parks offering camping, angling, hiking, boating, and tours of historical sites. Facilities range from those with hiking trails, golf courses, and cabins to others that are largely undeveloped and exist as an example of how the region once looked.

Reservations are recommended for overnight facilities. Pets are permitted if they are confined or on a leash shorter than 6 feet. The central reservation number for all Texas state parks is (512) 389-8900, Mon through Fri 8 a.m. to 6 p.m., and Sat 9 a.m. to noon, or see www.tpwd.state.tx.us/business/park_reservations/ for online, mail, and fax reservations. For TDD service, call (512) 389-8915 weekdays. To cancel a reservation call (512) 389-8900.

For travelers 65 years or older (or those with at least a 60 percent VA disability), there is the free or discounted (depending on age) State Parklands Passport. This windshield sticker permits free entry into any park. For information on park passes and discounts, see Appendix A.

For more information on Texas state parks, call the Texas Parks and Wildlife Department at (800) 792-1112 Mon through Fri during working hours, or at (512) 389-8950 in the Austin area. Texas Parks and Wildlife Department also maintains an excellent Web site: www.tpwd.state.tx.us.

appendix c

guide to tex-mex food

You'll find Tex-Mex food everywhere you go in Central and South Texas. It's a staple with all true Texans, who enjoy stuffing themselves at least once a week with baskets of tostadas, the Mexican plate (an enchilada, taco, and rice and beans), and cold cerveza. Unlike true Mexican food, which is not unusually spicy and often features seafood, Tex-Mex is heavy, ranges from hot to *muy caliente,* and can't be beat.

cabrito—young, tender goat, usually cooked over an open flame on a spit. In border towns, you'll see it hanging in many market windows.

cerveza—beer.

chalupa—a fried, flat corn tortilla spread with refried beans and topped with meat, lettuce, tomatoes, and cheese.

chile relleño—stuffed poblano peppers, dipped in batter and deep fried.

enchilada—corn or flour tortillas wrapped around a filling and covered with a hot or mild sauce. The most common types are beef, chicken, and cheese, and sometimes even sour cream and shrimp.

fajita—grilled skirt steak strips, wrapped in flour tortillas. Usually served still sizzling on a metal platter, with condiments (pico de gallo, sour cream, cheese) on the side.

flauta—corn tortillas wrapped around shredded beef, chicken, or pork and fried until crispy; may be an appetizer or an entree.

frijoles refrito—refried beans.

guacamole—avocado dip spiced with chopped onions, peppers, and herbs.

margarita—popular tequila drink, served in a salted glass; may be served over ice or frozen.

menudo—a soup made from tripe, most popular as a hangover remedy.

mole ("MOLE-ay")—an unusual sauce made of nuts, spices, and chocolate that's served over chicken enchiladas.

picante sauce—a Mexican staple found on most tables, this red sauce is made from peppers and onions and can be eaten as a dip for tortilla chips; ranges from mild to very hot.

pico de gallo—hot sauce made of chopped onions, peppers, and cilantro; used to spice up tacos, chalupas, and fajitas.

quesadilla—tortillas covered with cheese and baked; served as a main dish.

sopapilla—fried pastry dessert served with honey.

tamale—corn dough filled with chopped pork, rolled in a corn shuck, steamed and then served with or without chile sauce; a very popular Christmas dish.

tortilla—flat cooked rounds of flour or corn meal used to make many main dishes, and also eaten like bread along with the meal, with or without butter.

verde—green sauce used as a dip or on enchiladas.

appendix d

lcra parks

When it comes to parks, Austinites have only one problem: selecting from a long list of excellent facilities located near the capital city. Many of these parks are the products of the **Lower Colorado River Authority** (LCRA, 800-776-5272; www.lcra.org), a conservation and reclamation district that generates and transmits electricity produced by the powerful Colorado River. The LCRA also manages the waters of the river and assists riverside and lakeside communities with their economic development.

Among travelers, the LCRA is best known for its parks. These sites, which vary from unimproved sites along the riverbanks to full-fledged parks with boat ramps, fishing piers, and camping, are favorite summer destinations. Scattered from the shores of Lake Buchanan, down through the rest of the Highland Lakes, and along the riverbanks of the Colorado River all the way to Matagorda County on the Gulf Coast, these waters offer vacationers a great place to relax.

index

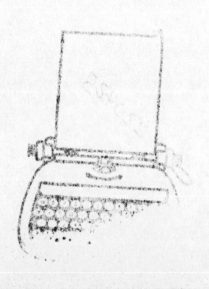

Getaway ideas for the local traveler

Need a day away to relax, refresh, renew?
Just get in your car and go!

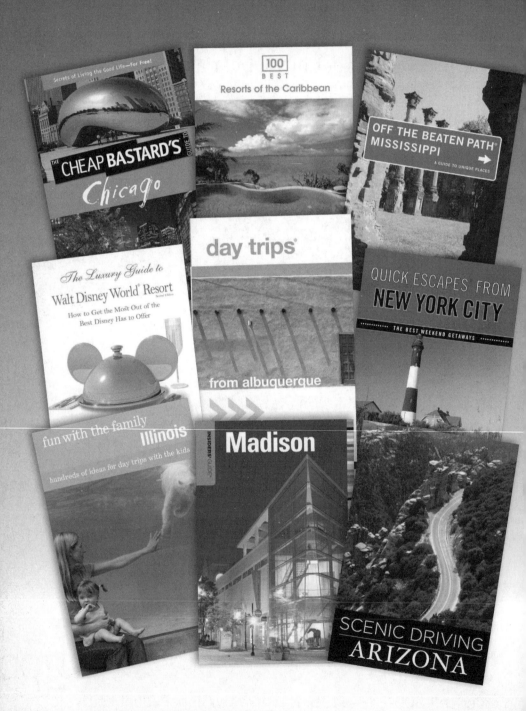